THE TIME OF POLITICS (ZAMANIN SIYASA)

Islam and the Politics of Legitimacy in Northern Nigeria 1950-1966

Jonathan T. Reynolds

International Scholars Publications
San Francisco - London - Bethesda
1999

Library of Congress Cataloging-in-Publication Data

DT
5 (5 . 9
. N 5
R 4 9
1 9 9 9

Reynolds, Jonathan T.
    The time of politics : Islam and the politics of legitimacy in Northern
    Nigeria, 1950- 1966 = Zamanin siyasa / Jonathan T. Reynolds.
        p. cm.
        In English.
        Originally presented as the author's thesis (Ph. D. –University of
        Tennessee, Knoxville, 1995) under the title: Zamanin siyasa.
        Includes bibliographical references and index.
        ISBN 1-57309-272-X (alk. paper)
        1. Nigeria, Northern--Politics and government--20th century. 2. Islam
    and politics--Nigeria, Northern—History--20th century. I. Title.
    DT515.9.N5R49 1998
    320.9669'5'09045--dc21   98-35711
                                                                 CIP

Editorial Inquiries:
International Scholars Publications
7831 Woodmont Avenue, #345
Bethesda, MD 20814
website: www.interscholars.com
To order: (800) 55-PUBLISH

To My Mother

Table of Contents

Acknowledgments

Credit is due to a great number of people in helping me to conceive and complete this book. Dr. Cynthia Fleming and Dr. Rosalind Hackett of the University of Tennessee, Knoxville, both deserve credit for sparking my interest in the study of history and religion in Africa. The entire staff and student body of the African Studies Center at Boston University receives my thanks. Special note is given to Dr. James McCann, Dr. Diana Wylie, and Shaheen Mozaffar for their efforts in reading earlier drafts. The assistance and advice of Dr. Paul Lovejoy and Dr. John Hunwick, both at home and in the field, was greatly appreciated.

A number of individuals offered critical intellectual, financial and pragmatic assistance in Nigeria between 1990 and 1995. The Fulbright Foundation provided resources to support research in 1992-1993. Special thanks are extended to Dr. Abdullahi Mahadi, Dr. M.T. Liman, Dr. Ahmadu Jalingo, Dr. Isa Hashim, Dr. Priscilla Starrat, Dr. Abudallahi Bature, Dr. Phil Shea, Dr. John Lavers, Dr. Andrew Barnes, Mr. Terna Pius Gbasha, Malam Abdulkarim dan Asibe, Ms. Monica Eppinger, and Malam Muktari Shitu. The staffs of the Department of Nigerian Languages at Bayero University, Kano History and Culture Bureau and National Archives Kaduna all deserve note. I am also grateful to all the politicians and religious scholars who so generously gave of their time and knowledge in providing interviews -- *Na Gode.*   Thanks are also extended to the research community at *Sabuwar Kofa,* including Dr. Alaine Hutson, Dr. Douglas Anthony, Dr. Rudy Gaudio, Dr. Jang Tae-Sang, and Matias Krings.

Thanks to my family for all their support, and to Livingstone College for providing me the opportunity to do what I was meant to do... learn, think, write and teach. My apologies to anyone I have failed to recognize.

I alone am responsible for any errors, factual, textual or analytical, found within this work..

Jonathan T. Reynolds
Salisbury, North Carolina

INTRODUCTION:

The period from 1950 to 1966 was one of great political ferment in Nigeria. Indeed, these years are often referred to as zamanin siyasa -- the time of politics.[1] This period saw the advent of electoral and party politics, the transition to self-rule and independence, and the end of the First Republic at the hands of Nigeria's first military coup. In Nigeria's Northern Region, politics during this period were dominated by the conflict between two ideologically antagonistic constituencies, the Northern Peoples Congress (NPC) and the Northern Elements Progressive Union (NEPU). The NPC may best be characterized as a political party made up of those individuals who sought to preserve the position and interests of the Masu Sarauta, the region's traditional ruling class who had held power in the North since Usman dan Fodio's jihad led to the foundation of the Sokoto Caliphate in the early 19th century. In contrast to the conservative NPC, NEPU was a radical party led largely by a young educated cadre who drew upon both Western and Islamic political vocabularies.[2] At its most basic level, the goal of NEPU was to overthrow the rule by the Masu Sarauta and empower the Talakawa, the region's working class through the expansion of voting rights and the replacement of traditional rulers with elected officials.

---

1. Mervyn Hiskett, *The Course of Islam in Africa* (Edinburgh, 1994), pp.120-121.

2. I use the term "conservative" to describe the NPC because a prime goal of this party was to preserve the political and social status quo of the region. Likewise, I refer to NEPU as "radical" because the party sought to bring about extensive changes in the North's political and social organization. It should be noted that the parties referred to themselves in such terms.

The influence of Islam in Northern Nigeria has been growing for several centuries.   Of particular significance to this process was the Sokoto Jihad of 1804, which led to the creation of the Sokoto Caliphate.   Under the leadership of Usman dan Fodio, the (predominantly Fulani) jihadists overthrew the region's Hausa kings (the Habe) on the grounds that they were not upholding the Shari'a and that they were oppressing the Muslim populace.   Being the product of a religious movement, the Caliphate created a political class that drew upon Islam as the key source of its legitimacy.   Further, because Usman dan Fodio carefully defined the reasons for the jihad in terms of Islamic ideology and popularized these justifications in writing and sermons, the jihad also helped create a legacy of Islamic political awareness that would influence generations to come.   Even in the 1950's and 1960's it was essential for both parties to legitimize their political positions and goals in terms of Islamic ideology and in the context of the region's own political history.   Indeed, it is the central goal of this book to show that each party recognized the interrelated nature of religious and political legitimacy in Northern Nigeria and organized their political strategies accordingly.   Of key importance to this goal is the fact that there existed such a wide gulf between the political goals of the two parties.   Thus, while both parties drew upon the same sources to legitimize and facilitate their political stands, including religious texts, historical references, and religious institutions, each party interpreted and utilized these sources in such a way as to support their own, very different, political goals.   Similarly, each party sought to discredit the other by attacking their opponent's dedication to the tenets of Islam.   What was at stake in the conflict between the NPC and NEPU was really no less than a debate over the meaning of the region's Islamic political legacy, and the place and form that legacy would take in the context of a new state moving rapidly towards decolonization and independence.

This argument will be developed through an examination of the various ways in which each party sought to establish its own religious legitimacy. Three basic strategies by which the parties sought to draw upon and promote their own view of the religion of Islam are identified herein. First, each party sought to justify their various political stands in terms of Islamic ideology, particularly by citing such religious sources as the Qur'an and the Hadiths and Sunna of the Prophet, as well as writings by such regional scholars as Usman dan Fodio. Historical reference was another tactic utilized by the parties. As already stressed, the Sokoto Jihad and Caliphate created a strong degree of Islamic and political self-awareness in the region of northern Nigeria. Hence, each party sought to highlight aspects of history, or even construct particular visions of history, that supported their own political goals. Finally, each party sought to utilize religious institutions to facilitate their political goals and bolster their position with the region's Muslim populace. Such a use of institutions for political goals, though, called into question the proper character and duties of an Islamic state in the context of a "modernizing" Northern Nigeria.

It is important here to examine the very question of the relationship between religion and politics in the context of Northern Nigeria during the period from 1950 to 1966. In idealized Islam there is no division between religion and politics, as evidenced in the statement <u>Islam din wa dawla</u> (Islam is religion and state).[3] Such a seamless union of religion and politics is unusual in Islamic history, and certainly did not exist in the context of Northern Nigeria in the 1950's and early 1960's. Rather, in this setting northern political leaders sought to adapt their own political perspectives (themselves largely an outgrowth of the region's own Islamic political history) to a Western-style political system imposed by the departing British administration. This situation was further complicated by the desire of the colonial administrators to try and restrict the more overt blending of religion and politics.

---

3. Charles Butterworth and William Zartman, "Preface," *The Annals of the American Academy of Political and Social Science* (524, November, 1992), p.8.

Such an analysis does not suggest that the politicians in question always were consciously manipulating Islam to meet specific political ends, although this was at times certainly the case. To what degree individual politicians were biased to the political or the religious is almost impossible to determine. What must be realized is that those involved in the struggle for power in the 1950's and 1960's were operating within a political framework which was largely imposed by the colonial rulers. The actual terms of the debate, and the standards by which the candidates would be judged, though, could not be so imposed. These were choices that only the Nigerian politicians and voters could make for themselves. Thus, while the political structure was largely of British origin, the debate was very much northern Nigerian.

In such a setting, it only made sense for the NPC and NEPU to express their conflict in Islamic terms wherever suitable. This is not only because the leadership of these parties were largely devout Muslims. The fact that the great majority of the populace had more experience with Islam than with Western-style party government further reinforced the incentive to place the debate in an Islamic context. The NPC, for its part, stressed themes of tradition and continuity which associated the religion of Islam with a particular ruling class and set of institutions -- the Masu Sarauta and the Native Authorities. Quite to the contrary, NEPU sought to overthrow the rule of the Masu Sarauta and as such presented a vision of Islam that stressed empowerment of the Talakawa -- as evidenced by the NEPU's demands for universal suffrage from the onset of electoral politics. Interestingly, even though the NEPU leaders were far more "nationalist" and anti-colonial than the leaders of the NPC, their own vision of the political system best suited to Nigeria's north was more a blending of Western and Islamic notions of governance.[4]

---

4. In that NEPU tried to harmonize Islamic political philosophy with such Western concepts as humanism and popular sovereignty, the party has a great deal in common with such "Islamic Modernists" as Jamal al-Din Afghani (1838-1897) and Muhammad Abduh (1849-1905). For more information on these individuals, see John L. Esposito, *Islam and Politics* (Syracuse, 1984), pp.46-52.

The Role of the British as the arbiters (though often biased) of the transition to independence complicated the interaction between religion and politics in the North. Founded in 1950 and 1951, respectively, both NEPU and the NPC political parties were required to at least give lip service to a Western-style separation of religion and politics as befitted the parliamentary style of government which the British hoped to establish in Nigeria. Thus, prior to the coming of independence in 1960, the influence of the British served at least to submerge the inherent tendency of the parties to combine religion and politics. It will be shown that such an effort on the part of the British ran contrary to both the desires of the parties and the expectations of the local Muslim populace. Indeed, religious references and justifications are an expected part of politics in Muslim regions. After the withdrawal of colonial rule in 1960, the combination of religion and politics by both parties was to become increasingly overt, blurring the division between the secular and the religious which the British had sought to establish.

In the examination of the role of Islam in the conflict between the NPC and NEPU, several themes are apparent and will run through the various case studies that form the basis of the following chapters. One of the most basic of these themes is that of each party's central strategies in utilizing Islamic sources for political ends.

The most basic approach by the NPC was to utilize its control and influence over religious institutions as a means of consolidating and defending their position in power. Such institutions as the shari'a courts were powerful tools which the NPC could use to limit the political activities of their opponents. Further, as the party which held political power, the NPC commanded resources which allowed it to offer religious services to its supporters. Such services ranged from distributing free religious texts to building Mosques to organizing massive conversion campaigns. All such services helped create an image of the NPC as a devout Muslim party. To make effective use of the institutions of the state, though, the leadership of the NPC had to legitimize themselves as the inheritors of political power in the North, a process which forced them to stress their ties with the region's Islamic political heritage.

In contrast, NEPU lacked the sort of formal authority that would allow it to utilize institutions to any great degree, though the case of education is an exception. Lacking institutional power, the NEPU leaders were left to attack the religious legitimacy upon which the NPC and the Masu Sarauta justified their rule. NEPU maintained that because the ruling class failed to rule according to the tenets of Islam, they were not fit to remain in power. Indeed, the NPC's use of religious institutions, such as the Shari'a courts, for political ends was cited as an example of the party's divergence from the requirements of Islamic governance. Thus, NEPU drew upon its most basic strength, the extensive religious knowledge of its leaders, to launch attacks on the manner in which the NPC and the traditional rulers governed the region. Further, the NEPU leader's claim that the key to Islamic political legitimacy was piety and scholarship was one that supported the party's own political legitimacy -- since most NEPU leaders were themselves scholars of Islam.

Hence, a basic tendency in the conflict between the NPC and NEPU was for the NPC to utilize its control over religious institutions to further its political goals, for the NEPU to attack the legitimacy of this institutional control, and for the NPC to then defend its position in power. Each of these steps required the parties to justify their stands in terms of Islamic ideology and place that interpretation in the context of a particular vision of the North's religious history -- all the more necessary because of the high degree of Islamic self-awareness engendered by the Sokoto Jihad in the region during the early nineteenth century.

To place the general themes outlined above in the context of the period's political conflict, each chapter will examine a case study that will highlight aspects of the role of Islam in the conflict for power between the NPC and NEPU. "The Politics of History" examines what version of the region's political history each party presented and how that image of history supported their own political goals. The NPC presented a positive picture of the Caliphate that stressed its role in unifying the region and purifying the religion of Islam. Since the NPC sought to maintain the political authority of those leaders descended from the founders of the Caliphate, it was important for them to place these leaders in a positive light. Further, throughout the period in question, the NPC stressed the institutional similarities between the Caliphate and the contemporary Native Authority system. NEPU, on the other hand, portrayed the Caliphate as an institution that had quickly perverted the goals of its founders and which failed to adhere to the tenets of Islam. As such, stated NEPU, the NPC continued only to perpetuate a legacy of corrupt political rule built upon a facade of piety.

"The Laws of God and the Nature of the Game" examines how the NPC utilized the region's Islamic courts to limit the activities of its political opponents, particularly NEPU. This chapter focuses on just how the NPC employed the courts as political weapons and how this use was justified in terms of Islamic law. Also examined are the tactics by which NEPU sought to blunt the NPC's control over the courts and how the radical party used the NPC's manipulation of the court system to make a case for the NPC's abuse of the religion of Islam and their position in power. This chapter in particular highlights the NPC's use of religious institutions and NEPU's reliance on religious ideology in the political conflict.

"Politics and the Shari'a" addresses the impact of the conflict in the courts on the region's legal system. The in-court maneuvering of both the NPC and NEPU led to significant changes in the structure of the region's legal system, culminating in the Penal Code of 1959, which supplanted the Shari'a with a secular code (except in the case of Civil Law). Also important to this chapter is an examination of how the Shari'a was interpreted in its application to political cases -- an interpretation that was often influenced by the demands of the British colonial rulers.

"Islam, Politics and Women's Rights" highlights the conflict between the NPC and NEPU over the question of women's suffrage and of women's wider political and social roles. This conflict very much drew into focus the "conservative" and "radical" agendas of the NPC and NEPU, respectively, and how each party drew upon Islamic sources and constructed contrasting images of "tradition" to legitimize their very different political positions. Further, this chapter shows how the line between religious, political, and social agendas was frequently blurred during the period in question.

"Religious Services to the Islamic Community" takes as its subject the various religious services that each party offered to the region's populace as a means of strengthening their credentials as devout Muslims and as parties that could meet the religious needs of the Muslim community within the North. Such activities ranged from Mosque-building and conversion campaigns on the part of the NPC to NEPU's founding of the Islamiyya schools, which combined both Islamic and Western styles of education. This chapter is instrumental in showing just how each party envisioned and constructed the responsibilities of a Muslim government at the time.

"Brotherhoods and Politics" focuses upon the relationship between the political parties and region's dominant Sufi Brotherhoods, the Qadiriyya and Tijaniyya. Most previous studies have either ignored the role of these turuq or have concluded that there existed a clear and natural alliance between the NPC and

Qadariyya and NEPU and the Tijaniyya. My own research does confirm that the Parties and Brotherhoods frequently interacted in the political sphere. But, more importantly, this text maintains that the relationship between the parties and brotherhoods was far more complex than previously suggested, and constantly open to negotiation depending on the political demands of the moment. In particular this chapter will show how seemingly "natural" religio-political alliances could fall prey to political forces.

The conclusion, "Islam, Politics and History in Northern Nigeria" draws together and summarizes the ways in which each party sought to construct an interpretation of Islam and the region's history that supported its own goals. The conclusion also discusses how the interaction of religion and politics during the First Republic influenced Nigerian politics in subsequent years.

This study seeks to fill a void in the literature on Islam and politics in Nigeria, especially when compared to the extensive literature regarding this subject for other Muslim regions. Further, there has been a growing awareness of the relevance of religion to contemporary African Politics. Hayes' *Religion and Politics in Africa* and Sanneh's *The Crown and the Turban* being key cases in point.[5] The current study seeks to add a much-needed historical perspective to the study of religion and politics in Africa. Indeed, while extensive bodies of literature exist for the historical study of both Islam and politics in Nigeria, the literature connecting these two subjects is scanty. This text seeks both to draw upon and draw together these two areas of scholarship.

---

5. Jeff Haynes, *Religion and Politics in Africa* (London, 1996); Lamin Sanneh, *The Crown and the Turban: Muslims and West African Pluralism* (Boulder, 1997). For information on religion and politics in contemporary Nigeria, see Iheanyi M. Enwerem, *A Dangerous Awakening* (Ibadan, 1995) and Williams and Falola, *Religious Impact on the Nation State: the Nigerian Predicament* (Avebury, 1995).

The literature on First Republic politics by political scientists such as Sklar, Whitaker, Post, and Dudley warrants specific comment.[6] These works are particularly valuable in that they are contemporary accounts of politics during the latter 1950's and early 1960's. Because these scholars had direct access to the political players and political events, their resulting works are excellent sources in regards to the actual mechanics of the period's political process. Yet, the contemporary nature of these studies is also their chief weakness. Because these scholars' research was undertaken while NEPU and the NPC were still very much in competition, the interviews and sources upon which they are largely based are very much steeped in a dedication to "idealpolitik" and the various official "party lines." Also, these scholars (excluding Whitaker) were heavily influenced by the belief that "modernization" would inevitably lead to secularization, and that religion would only lose influence in politics in Nigeria in the years to come.

Until recently, scholars of religion in Nigeria have, for their part, avoided the issue of politics.[7] Paden's works present a special case. *Religion and Political Culture in Kano* (1973) deals much more with the competition between the Tijaniyya and Qadiriyya Sufi brotherhoods than it does with partisan politics.[8] *Ahmadu Bello: Sardauna of Sokoto* (1986) includes a significant amount of information regarding the interplay between Islam and politics in the 1950's and 1960's (impossible to avoid when dealing with Ahmadu Bello). Unfortunately, the work is weakened by the strong bias shown towards the person of the Sardauna, a factor which leads many

---

6. B.J. Dudley, *Parties and Politics in Northern Nigeria* (London, 1968); K.W.J. Post, *The Nigerian Federal Election of 1959: Politics and Administration in a Developing Political System* (New York, 1963); Richard L. Sklar, *Nigerian Political Parties: Power in an Emergent African Nation* (Princeton, 1963); and C.S. Whitaker, *The Politics of Tradition: Continuity and Change in Northern Nigeria, 1946-1966* (Princeton, 1970).

7. See, for example, A.I. Doi, *Islam in Nigeria* (Zaria, 1984).

8. John N. Paden, *Religion and Political Culture in Kano* (Los Angeles, 1973).

potentially unpleasant political issues to be overlooked.[9]

With over three decades having passed since the period in question, a reevaluation of the role of Islam in the politics of Nigeria's transition to civilian rule and First Republic is in order. The "realpolitik" of the era has become far more accessible. The politicians of the 1950's and 1960's are often now willing to speak openly of their parties' strategies and agendas. Also, classified government documents from the period are now available, allowing a direct and detailed view into the workings of the British and NPC governments of the time. Access to these documents allows a reinterpretation of the politics of the period – similar to that undertaken by Hargreaves in *Decolonization in Africa*.[10] Thus, new interviews and recently released documents, combined with newspaper articles (often in Hausa) and popular discourse such as political poems and songs, provide a number of voices and perspectives which can be analyzed and compared to piece together a more comprehensive understanding of the era. Interviews with former political activists provide an inside view of the politics of the period, and along with government documents provide very much the "realpolitik" missing from earlier works. Newspapers and poems provide the "idealpolitik" or party-line of political and religious discourse during the period. Finally, earlier observers, in the form of Political Scientists undertaking research, provide an outsider's perspective on the politics of the period. Wherever possible, actual quotes have been used to allow the perspectives and experiences of participants and observers to come through. These voices, taken together with an approach that recognizes the significance of religion in the politics of the developing world and builds upon the benefit of thirty years perspective on the politics of the 1950's and early 1960's, allows a much more

9. John N. Paden, *Ahmadu Bello, Sardauna of Sokoto: Values and Leadership in Nigeria* (Zaria, 1986). See, for example, chapter nine "Religious Issues."

10. John D. Hargreaves, *Decolonization in Africa*, (New York, 1988).

textured and thorough examination of this important period in Nigeria's history.

Finally, this book addresses several more general points. The fact that both parties, one traditional and conservative and the other progressive and radical, were both able to draw upon Islam for their legitimacy helps show to what degree the religion is a flexible and dynamic component in the politics of the developing world. This study also points up that Nigeria's "Muslim north" is not as politically and religiously homogeneous an entity as it is so often characterized. Further, considering that the politics of religion have hardly been limited either to the period in question or only to the northern region, this analysis of previous religious/political junctures should prove useful in understanding the role of religion in more contemporary politics in Nigeria. Thus, it is hoped that this study will not only add to the body of scholarship on Northern Nigeria, but will aid in the understanding of religion and politics on the regional and global scale as well.

THE PHYSICAL, SOCIAL, AND POLITICAL SETTING

The Northern Region of Nigeria, as it existed during the period from 1950 to 1966, comprised an area of almost 300,000 square miles, roughly three-fourths of Nigeria's total land mass.[1] The southern section of the North was frequently referred to as the Middle Belt. This area comprises rolling hills and forests in the west and Nigeria's high central plateau in the east. Farther to the north, the hills give way to open savannah and, eventually, sahel. The region's weather is dominated by a bimodal pattern with the rainy season extending roughly from May to September and the dry season running from October to April.

The political history of Nigeria's north is a long and rich one. Dating back at least to the fifteen century, there existed a number of independent city-states in the region, frequently referred to as the Hausa States. These states drew their wealth not only from the region's fertile agriculture, but also from connections to trans-Saharan trade routes running north and east. Tradition states that it was Yaji dan Tsamiya, a ruler of Kano, who introduced Islam to the region.[2] To varying degrees the Hausa kings drew both on Islam and local religion to legitimize their rule. This combination of religious traditions, though, was to be in part responsible for the

---

1. Whitaker, *Politics of Tradition*, p.15.

2. Hiskett, *Development of Islam*, p.73.

downfall of the Hausa kings. Beginning in 1804, a Fulani scholar and Sufi mystic named Usman dan Fodio waged jihad against the Hausa kings on the grounds that they were not true Muslims. Called the Sokoto Jihad (after the new capital established by dan Fodio's followers), this conflict led to the downfall of the Hausa kings and the creation of the Sokoto Caliphate. Throughout the nineteenth century, the Caliphate administered a region which covered not only much of what was to become Northern Nigeria, but also parts of Benin, Niger and Cameroon. Further, the Caliphate's political, religious, and economic influence stretched throughout West Africa.

The Caliphate's independence was brought to an end in 1903, when the British defeated and killed the Sultan Attihiru and established the system of Colonial Administration known as Indirect Rule. This system maintained the basic structures of the Caliphate's system of administration, but subsumed them under the authority of the British colonial government. The emirates of the Caliphate were renamed Native Authorities and their rulers maintained so long as they swore allegiance to the British crown. The cooperation between the British and the region's traditional rulers was to continue up to independence in 1960.

The Nigerian census of 1952-1953 placed the total Nigerian population at slightly over thirty-one million, of which nearly seventeen million lived in the Northern Region. The major ethno-linguistic groups within the North were reported as the Hausa (5.5 million), the Fulani (3.1 million), and the Kanuri (1.3 million).[3] The northern population was largely rural. In 1966 only some 10% of the population lived in urban centers with populations of more than 20,000. Major towns included Kano, Katsina, Zaria, Maiduguri, Sokoto, and Kaduna. All but the latter two of these

---

3. Sklar, *Nigerian Political Parties*, p.6.

centers had existed as independent city-states for some centuries. Sokoto was established as the new center for religious and political authority following the Sokoto Jihad. Kaduna was founded by Lugard as the seat of colonial power in 1917. Kaduna remained the political capital of the Northern Region after independence in 1960.

The occupational breakdown of the region's populace reflected the rural settlement bias of the time. Some eighty percent of the populace made their living from agriculture. Cash crops, particularly groundnuts and cotton, were the key sources of income for both individuals and the region as a whole. Roughly 10% of the northern population were involved in pastoralism, hunting, fishing or forestry. The remaining segment of the population made their living through skilled and semi-skilled labor in such fields as the governmental service, trading, and manufacturing.[4]

Of the total northern population in 1953, roughly 12 million identified themselves as Muslims. Within this Islamic community, there were distinctions between those Muslims who did and did not belong to the Sufi turuq[5]. While a number of brotherhoods were active in the North at this time, the Qadiriyya and Tijaniyya were by far the most widespread. No real data exists for an accurate estimate of the numbers of northern Muslims affiliated to these brotherhoods.[6] Both turuq probably had membership in the millions in the period of the 1950's and 1960's. After Islam, the largest religious group identified in the 1953 census were Pagans, followed by around one-half million Christians. Both the Pagan and

---

4. Whitaker, *Politics of Tradition*, p.18.

5. Turuq (sing., Tariqa) means "path" or "right way." "Brotherhood" is the common English term used to describe these organizations.

6. British documents from the period speak in general terms such as "many" and "increasing numbers of." Even Paden, in his *Religion and Political Culture in Kano*, which focuses on these brotherhoods more than any other work, avoids any attempt to quantify tariqa membership.

Christian communities were concentrated in the North's southern Middle-Belt region.[7]

As a pre-industrial society, Northern Nigeria's system of class was built around relation to the state, not to any particular economic position. Membership in the dominant class of Masu Sarauta (possessors of rule) was limited to the descendants of those leaders who had supported the jihad of Usman dan Fodio. The great majority of these leaders were Fulani. Those people who did not have such a tie to the state, whatever their ethnicity or economic standing, were deemed Talakawa, which might be roughly translated as "commoners."

In terms of absolute literacy, taking into account Arabic, Hausa, and English, the number of Northerners able to read and write was near 7% in 1953. If only facility in Roman script (Hausa: boko) is taken into account, an important consideration since newspapers and government publications were published almost exclusively in this medium, the region's literacy rate was 2.5%. Further, because literacy in English was far more common in the southern regions of Nigeria (largely due to the restrictions on Christian mission activity in the North), much of the North's English-literate populace was concentrated in the Middle-Belt area.[8] In the upper North, literacy rates in Roman script were markedly lower -- 1.3% in Sokoto and 1.1% in Kano, for example.[9] Because of the limited extent of Western education in the North, access to this schooling was largely restricted to the families and clients

7. Sklar, *Nigerian Political Parties*, p.9. The inaccuracy of the term "Pagan" is recognized and I use the word in part because no truly representative nomer for the great variety of indigenous African religions exists. Pagan is also the term that was most commonly utilized in the documentary record from the period.

8. English literacy in the Western and Eastern Regions was reported as 17.3% and 15.6%, respectively. Sklar, *Nigerian Political Parties*, p.4.

9. Whitaker, *Politics of Tradition*, p.18.

of the <u>Masu Sarauta</u>.[10]

Like the Action Group (AG) in the Western Region and the National Council of Nigeria and the Cameroons (NCNC) in the East, the political parties of the North had their origins in cultural, rather than an expressly political, organizations. Indeed, both the NPC and NEPU grew out of the same cultural organization. This group, named the <u>Jamiyyar Mutanen Arewa</u> (Northern Peoples Congress) was formally inaugurated in Kaduna on 26 June, 1949. While this association was composed almost exclusively of the North's small pool of Western-educated elite, it nonetheless contained members with sharply contrasting political viewpoints. This conflict within the organization was brought to a head in August of 1950, when a small group, largely hailing from Kano, declared themselves as a political party named <u>Jami'yyar Neman Sawaba</u> or Northern Elements Progressive Union (NEPU). NEPU did not seek to separate themselves from the Congress, but instead planned to become the political vanguard which would mobilize the Congress as a vehicle for nationalist agitation.[11] In October of 1950 the newly formed NEPU published a "Declaration of Principles" that called not only for independence from British rule, but also for the end of "the Family Compact rule of the so-called Native Administrations" and the placing of political power "in the hands of the <u>Talakawa</u>."[12]

Such demands on the part of NEPU were clear attacks on the position and rule of the <u>Masu Sarauta</u>. Given that the greater number of the Congress's membership came from or were closely connected to the <u>Masu Sarauta</u>, it is little surprise that the NEPU founders broke from the Congress during the organization's convention (its second) in December of 1950. Having thus been purged of its more

---

10. Sklar, *Nigerian Political Parties*, p.323.

11. Ibid, p.95.

12. AH, RP/153, "Report on Kano Disturbances" 1953.

radical elements, the Congress declared itself a political party -- retaining the name
Northern Peoples' Congress (NPC) -- in October of 1951. The NPC's transition to
political status was in no small part spurred by the early successes of the NEPU
candidates in the first round of popular elections in 1951. Indeed, had it not been for
a convoluted electoral college system that effectively negated the popular vote,
several NEPU members might have been elected to the Northern House of Assembly
in that year. Writing in 1963, Sklar outlined the system as follows:

> In 1951, every Native Authority, typically an Emir, was permitted to
> "nominate" a number of persons equal to 10% of the final electoral
> college who were "injected" into the college. It was understood that
> these nominees included the choices of the Emir, and various
> pressures operated to induce the members of the final colleges to vote
> for them. Thus in Kano Emirate not one of the twenty persons
> elected to the House of Assembly by the final electoral college had
> been elected by the voters at a lower stage; in fact, ten of them had
> been defeated in the earlier balloting. On the other hand, four
> candidates of the radical Northern Elements Progressive Union who
> had been successful at the intermediate stage were defeated in the
> final college by the Native Authority under the 10% rule.[13]

The electoral college system was of British design, and was clearly intended
to maintain the power of the Masu Sarauta in the face of potential democratic
disruption. Indeed, scholars such as Whitaker have correctly noted that the system
of Indirect Rule as established in Nigeria's north was never really designed with
popular political participation in mind.[14] As such, NEPU's call for the replacement
of traditional rulers with elected councils was a direct threat to all the British had
worked to establish in the North during the period of Colonial rule. Only as the NPC
established its power over the course of the 1950's was the electoral college system

13. Sklar, *Nigerian Political Parties*, p.30.

14. See Whitaker, *Politics of Tradition*, pp.28/55-56.

slowly dismantled. Male taxpayer suffrage was introduced in 1956, and it was in this year that NEPU first succeeded in getting a member elected to the regional government. Universal male suffrage was instituted in 1959, just before independence. By this time, as will be seen in the course of this study, the NPC was well enough established that NEPU could little threaten its position in power.

Brief note should be made of the nature of the NPC and NEPU leadership. It is not unjust to characterize the NPC as the party of the Masu Sarauta for the Masu Sarauta. The party called for changes to the system of Native Administrations only when such a move strengthened the position of those bodies. Such a situation is none too surprising when it is taken into account that most (62%) of the NPC members of the NPC's National Executive were employees of the Native Administrations. A similar percentage of the NPC leadership were belonged to the Fulani ethnic group. Wealthy businessmen, most of whom were of Habe (non-Fulani) origin, made up the larger part of the remaining leadership.[15] Further, these business people, whatever their wealth, were still considered Talakawa. This factor would suggest that the political interests of the Masu Sarauta and those of the region's nascent commercial elite were beginning to merge even at this early date.

Many of NEPU's founding members, such as Maitama Sule, had originally been employees of the Native Authorities. When several such individuals came together to found the Northern Elements Progressive Association (NEPA) in 1948, the group, while not expressly political, voiced many reservations regarding the Native Authority system and they were quickly sacked from their positions. The motto of the NEPA foreshadowed the religious overtones that were to become increasingly prevalent in the next two decades: "He who does not fear God fears

---

15. Sklar, *Nigerian Political Parties*, p.323.

everybody, but he who fears God is to be feared by some."[16] Certainly, being fired from the Native Authorities only served to help radicalize these individuals.

While some NEPU founders and leaders, including Aminu Kano and Alhaji Baba dan Agundi, originally had ties to the Native Authorities and Masu Sarauta, many of the party's key members did not. Some, such as Lawan Danbazau, were Islamic Scholars with no Western education at all. Indeed, Malam Danbazau, who was adviser to NEPU on Islamic Law and one of the founders of the Islamiyya schools, consciously avoided learning English.[17] It is worth noting that each of these three individuals was of Fulani ethnicity. A significant number of NEPU leaders, such as Lawan Mai Turari, were petty traders with little formal education, and who certainly had no claim to Sarauta status. The great majority of these petty traders were of Habe (usually Hausa) birth. Hence, the membership of NEPU was made up of a number of different groups who were bound together by their opposition to the rule of the Masu Sarauta and the British.

It should be noted that the lack of formal education on the part of many NEPU members did not mean that these individuals did not play an important role in the battle of ideas between the NPC and NEPU. Many proved themselves to be keen politicians all the same. Lawan mai Turari, who earned his living from selling perfume, was the author of many of NEPU's most powerful political (and religious) poems. Alhaji Tanko Yakasai, whose first occupation was as a tailor, later became editor of the *Daily Comet*. Many NEPU members were taught to read and write by the party's more educated members.[18]

---

16. Whitaker, *Politics of Tradition*, p.358.

17. Lawan Danbazau, 20 January, 1993.

18. Rima Shawalu, *The Story of Gambo Sawaba* (Jos, 1990), p.49.

The relationship of each party to the state apparatus also had significant repercussions in terms of the parties' sources of funding. The relationship of the NPC to the North's traditional rulers meant that the party could draw on the funds commanded by these comparatively wealthy personages. NEPU, on the other hand, had no such wealthy patrons. Indeed, prior to the party's alliance with the NCNC in 1954, NEPU was forced to rely upon public collections for funding -- collections that were subject to the approval of the very Native Authority system which NEPU sought to unseat. Not surprisingly, applications for such collections were frequently refused.[19]

The nature of the wider Nigerian political context needs to be examined as well. One of the most important features of the political organization of Nigeria during the period from 1950 to 1966 was the federal structure of the constitutions which were in force. The Richards constitution of 1946 laid the basis for the three-region system which was to dominate the political landscape until the end of the First Republic in 1966. This situation was reinforced with the Macpherson Constitution in 1951. Important to the Macpherson constitution was the successful demand by the Northern representatives to the constitutional conference that the Northern component of the Nigerian Legislative Council be allocated a minimum of 50% of the seats. This claim was justified on the basis of the North's share of over half of the Nigerian population. Prior to the ratification of the Lyttleton Constitution of 1954, the leaders of the NPC insisted that the individual regions maintain absolute control over the structure and jurisdiction of local government within their borders.[20] Such constitutional conditions guaranteed that the Native Authority system could not be threatened from outside of the North. Further, the 50% allotment of seats to the

---

19. See KSHCB, ACC/832/ Agency Marks Law/30, "Applications for registration of public collection by NEPU, 1947-1961."

20. Whitaker, *Politics of Tradition*, p.30.

North meant that so long as the NPC could maintain control over the politics of the North, it would control the federal government of Nigeria as well. The key means by which the Northern leaders forced these concessions was by threatening to delay the move towards independence, or even refusing to participate in unitary government altogether if their demands were not met.[21]

The Federal system greatly influenced the nature of politics in Nigeria. With a unified North clearly in a position to dominate the nation as a whole, the only hope of the southern parties was to keep the NPC from dominating the North. Hence, the only way to prevent the NPC's control of the country was to deny the NPC seats in its home region. As such, both the AG and the NCNC were active in the Northern Region. Ethnic and regional allegiances proved very difficult to overcome, though, and neither of the southern parties had any significant success in the North. As such, it was really only NEPU, as the main northern opposition, which posed a threat to NPC victory. No doubt this was a key reason for the extensive financial support which the NCNC provided to NEPU from the time of their alliance in 1954.

The NPC was quick to turn the activities of the southern parties, particularly the alliance of the NCNC to NEPU, to its advantage. The party portrayed itself as the defender of the North from the specter of southern domination. In 1954 a *Nigerian Citizen* article read

> [The Sardauna] referred to the NEPU-NCNC alliance
> as a trap and said that every patriot Northerner who
> did not want to be controlled by the South from the
> South should vote for [the NPC].[22]

---

21. Ibid, pp.29-30. For a detailed examination of these constitutions see B.O. Nwabueze, *A Constitutional History of Nigeria* (London, 1981), pp.29-59.

22. *Nigerian Citizen*, 9 December, 1954.

The NPC's "Northernization Campaign," which sought to replace southern Nigerians in the Northern Region government with people of northern birth, was one of many ways the NPC capitalized upon fears of southern domination. Such a plan was clearly an attempt to win over the North's more educated class to the NPC. Some anti-southern propaganda was far more vociferous. In 1959, one British officer reported on an NPC meeting where people were informed that the southerners "were Pagans who did not pray and who eat people."[23] The NPC's portrayal of NEPU as "northern traitors" (as seen above) was continued to the end of the First Republic. In 1965, when Aminu Kano made a trip to Enugu (capital of the Eastern Region) and there suggested that Southerners in the North were not safe, Alhaji Ibrahim Biu (the NPC Minister of Water Resources) stated "This attitude of the NEPU leader is enough to make any patriotic Northerner bury his head in shame."[24]

As the colonial rulers of Nigeria, at least up to 1960, the perspective and goals of the British must not be overlooked. The pro-NPC and anti-NEPU/anti-South bias of the British was an important factor in the politics of Northern Nigeria up to independence. The British had based no small part of the legitimacy of colonial rule on the 'partnership' between the colonial administrators and traditional rulers. Thus, NEPU's attacks on the Masu Sarauta were a threat to the whole legacy of the British presence in the region.

Further, the NEPU leaders' calls for rapid independence and international non-alignment were more threatening to the British than the NPC's calls for "eventual self-government for Nigeria with Dominion Status within the British

23. KSHCB, NCMSIS/C180/s.2/283, June-July, 1959.

24. *Nigerian Citizen,* 17 March, 1965.

Commonwealth."[25] Further, the quasi-Socialist wording of many NEPU statements (particularly the references to the "class conflict" between the Talakawa and the Masu Sarauta) was clearly disturbing to the British in the wider context of the Cold War. Such fears were not necessarily unfounded. Indeed, NEPU did have socialist leanings. Alhaji Tanko Yakasai, editor of the NEPU *Daily Comet* was a member of the Nigerian Communist Party.[26] While such factors help explain the actions of most British administrators in Nigeria at the time, they do not excuse the often blatant disregard for fairness and justice which characterized the final years of colonial rule in the region.

Thus, it is clear that the conflict between the NPC and NEPU was not an evenly matched one. The NPC was larger and better funded. Because of its ties to the Native Authorities, the NPC was effectively the party of government in the North even before the first vote was cast. Despite their officially neutral status, the British colonial administrators had vested interests in the victory of the NPC, and they acted accordingly behind the scenes. All the same, the ability of NEPU to maintain an active opposition to the NPC throughout the 1950's and early 1960's shows that they represented an important political perspective that was not without determined adherents and some degree of popular support. The role of Islam in this struggle between the NPC and NEPU has yet to be properly examined. As such, the following study provides a new perspective on politics in Nigeria's Northern Region prior to the fall of the First Republic.

---

25. AH, RP/A53, Report on the Kano Disturbances, "Aims and Objectives of the Northern People's Congress, 1952."

26. Alhaji Tanko Yakasai, 17 April, 1993.

CHAPTER ONE:

THE POLITICS OF HISTORY

At the time of the advent of party politics in the early 1950's, most of Nigeria's Northern Region was administered under what was known as the Native Authority (NA) system. As the basic units of the British system of Indirect Rule, the Native Authorities were built around the emirate structure which had its foundation in the jihad of Usman dan Fodio, the founder of the Sokoto Caliphate. During this period, though, not all political elements in the North were in agreement as to the future of the Native Authority system. Indeed, the region's two dominant political parties, the conservative Northern Peoples Congress (NPC) and the radical Northern Elements Progressive Union (NEPU), held widely different views regarding the nature and value of the Native Authority system, with the NPC defending their continued political role and NEPU calling for their disbandment. This debate was central to the conflict for power between the two parties for most of the period from 1950 to 1966 and had repercussions that stretched far beyond the contemporary political conflict, since the debate over the value of the Native Authorities was by extension a debate over the legacy of the Native Authorities' point of origin -- the Sokoto Jihad and Caliphate.

Indeed, while both parties claimed to be the legitimate defenders of the ideals of Usman dan Fodio, they held very different views of what those ideals were, and also of the nature of the Caliphate which he founded. Such a situation raises some very important questions to address in this chapter. What image of the Sokoto Jihad did each party seek to present? What aspects of the jihad did they highlight or play down? What image did each party present of the Sokoto Caliphate? What role did they ascribe to the British as the architects of colonialism and the Native Authority system? By what means did the individual parties associate themselves with the images of the jihad and Caliphate which they presented? How did these factors address the parties' immediate political needs?

It will be shown that both parties drew upon symbolic, physical, and ideological connections with the history of the region and of Islam as well, in order to construct an interpretation of the past that helped to legitimize their particular political positions. This process will serve to highlight the lively intellectual debate over the legacy of the Sokoto Jihad and Caliphate that flowed through, and indeed was central to, the contemporary political conflict. Further, this chapter will help to show just to what degree the political debate in the region was inward-looking and self-aware during this period -- rather than being focused on the departing colonial rulers.

BACKGROUND

As previously stated, the Sokoto Jihad led by Shehu Usman dan Fodio and the Caliphate which he subsequently established were among the most important political events in the history of the Northern Nigerian region. Dan Fodio's jihad overthrew the authority of the region's Hausa rulers (the Habe) and replaced them with his own followers, generally drawn from his own Fulani ethnic group. Briefly stated, the Shehu and his followers justified their attack on the existing power structure on the grounds that the Habe rulers, while claiming to be Muslims, were not ruling in accordance with the Shari'a, and that Islam in the region was suffering from impure practices. The jihad succeeded in consolidating an empire which included regions of modern Nigeria, Benin, Niger and Cameroon. In terms of population (estimated at around ten million) the Sokoto Caliphate was the largest empire to date in the West African Soudan. When the Shehu withdrew from politics, the new empire was divided between his son, Muhammad Bello and his brother Abdullahi. It was Bello who established the capital at Sokoto, which stands today as one of the region's major urban centers. Despite various internal conflicts, the basic structure of the Caliphate, a system of local emirates owing ultimate authority to the Sultan of Sokoto, remained intact until 1903, when the Sultan was overthrown by the British under the leadership of Lord Lugard.

Even the advent of colonial rule, though, did not radically change the authority structure of the Caliphate. While the British did indeed replace the Sultan and those Emirs who initially refused to submit, they maintained the existing system of authority and administration, which eventually became the model for the system of Indirect Rule. Under this system, the Emirates were renamed "Native Authorities" (NA) and utilized by the British as the basic units of local and regional administration. The chain of command within the Native Authorities included the Sarki (Emir), his Hakima (district heads), the Dagatai (village heads), the Masu Sarauta (various titled officials), the Ma'aikita (Native Authority employees), the Malamai (religious scholars and leaders), the Alkalai, (judges), and the Yan'doka (police).[1] Such a system spared the British from having to establishing their own low-level administrative network, since such institutions as courts, tax collection systems, police forces, and so on could be left under the jurisdiction of the local

---

1. A.D. Yahaya, *The Native Authority System* (London, 1980), p.5. Among these titled officials, only the Ma'aikita, most of whom were clerks and functionaries, were innovations special to the Native Authority system. All others were traditional posts which could be traced back to the emirate (and in some cases the Habe) political structure.

Emirs.   Further, in local matters and in some regional matters, particularly those involving religious   matters, the Native Authorities retained a high degree of independence from the colonial administration.

THE PARTIES AND THE NATIVE AUTHORITIES

The NPC and NEPU not only held contrasting views regarding the nature of the Native Authority system, but also had very different relationships to the system itself. The NPC, for its part, supported the basic idea of the Native Authorities, and envisioned a continued role for these institutions, and the traditional rulers around whom the system was built, in an independent (northern) Nigeria. The Native Authorities, held the NPC, provided a link to the region's past and provided the populace with a familiar and respected system of government. Such a position on the part of the NPC was hardly surprising, since most of the party's leaders were themselves traditional title holders within the class of Masu Sarauta, and had risen to prominence throughout the Native Authority system. In general, it is safe to characterize the NPC as a political party founded by traditional rulers to maintain their own position of authority in the North. One Nigerian historian characterized the relationship between the NPC and the Native Authorities as follows:

> The NPC, as the Party of Government, was closely identified with the NA at the local level. This relationship was derived from the common social background which the leaders of the two organizations shared. This social background was reinforced by common political values to which the two sets of leaders were committed. The main component of these values could be rendered as a commitment to the preservation of the existing political arrangement in the system. For the NA, this meant that as long as the NPC was in control of the government, the NA could expect to

exercise influence in the political system.[2]

Similarly, an early statement by the NPC regarding traditional leaders reads as follows:

> Jamiyyar [the Congress] does not intend to usurp the authority of our Natural Rulers; on the contrary, it is our ardent desire to enhance such authority whenever and wherever possible.[3]

The association of the NPC with the Native Authority system was of great political benefit. Being closely tied to the apparatuses of local and regional government gave the NPC great potential power for gaining political influence, whether via patronage of allies, coercion of the unaligned, or oppression of opponents. For example, control over the alkali courts gave the NPC great influence over opponents -- particularly NEPU.[4] Access to the resources and institutions of government also provided the NPC with the ability to dispense religious goods and services to supporters -- both current and potential.[5]

Finally, the connection between the NPC and the Native Authorities was a means by which the party gained access to the North's largely rural populace. By being built around the structures of the Native Authorities, the NPC was provided with a party system that stretched to all levels of Northern society -- urban or rural. NEPU had no such ready-made party network, which was one of the key factors that

---

2. A.D. Yahaya, "The Native Authority System in Northern Nigeria, 1950-1960: A Study in Political Relations With Particular Reference to the Zaria Native Authority," PhD (Ahmadu Bello University, Zaria, 1974), p.276.

3. K.W.J. Post, *Nigerian Federal Election of 1959*, p.42.

4. This theme will be examined in detail in chapters two and three.

5. Chapter five deals with this subject in detail.

limited the party's activities to more urban areas.

Under the system of Indirect Rule, the various employees of the Native Authorities were considered by the British colonial officials to be public servants, who were (ideally) to refrain from active political participation. This situation in effect meant that the Native Authorities could not overtly be used as tools to influence politics. Throughout the 1950's, the division between the NPC and the Native Authorities was maintained -- at least on the public and rhetorical level. With the coming of independence in 1960 the functional distinction between the two political organizations was to become increasingly small.

Quite unlike the members of the NPC, the members of NEPU were not drawn from the ranks of traditional leaders, nor did they seek to maintain the authority of these rulers. Indeed, the NEPU leadership identified themselves with a class of religious scholars who had withdrawn from involvement with established political authority during the previous century.[6] As political outsiders, NEPU's leaders accused the Native Authorities of being corrupt oppressors of the Talakawa -- the common people. As one contemporary commentator has stated:

> To [Aminu Kano] the Native Authority system represented gross distortions of the objectives of the jihadist founding fathers of the Sokoto Caliphate because of the neglect of Koranic democratic precepts, women's rights, equality and freedom.[7]

NEPU leadership called for the disbanding of the Native Authorities, and their replacement by democratically elected local councils. Traditional leaders such as the

---

6. Dr. Ahmadu Jalingo, 15 August, 1991.

7. Professor Omo Omoruyi, "Mallam Aminu Kano and the Legacy of Grassroots Politics in Nigeria," Speech given at the First Annual Centre for Democratic Studies Aminu Kano Memorial Lecture, Kano, 17 April, 1992.

Emirs were, if NEPU had its way, to be relegated to purely ceremonial duties.

THE PARTIES, THE SOKOTO JIHAD AND THE CALIPHATE

Each party presented its own version of the nature and significance of the Sokoto Jihad and Caliphate. Three key themes come out in the NPC's presentation of the Sokoto Jihad: Islamic purification and expansion, unification, and Fulani leadership. NEPU, on the other hand, presented the jihad first and foremost as a movement of political reform, but also cast some doubt on the unified nature of the jihad. By focusing on these aspects of the jihad, both political parties sought to construct an image of the region's history that suited their own political strengths and objectives.

More than any other factor, the NPC presented the jihad as a religious movement that purged the region of anti-Islamic practices. NPC references tended to highlight the way in which the jihad cleansed the region of the corrupt Islam that had come to be practiced and replaced it with a pure form of the religion. Further, the NPC stressed that the jihad helped expand the number of adherents to Islam by way of conversions of non-believers. As Sir Ahmadu Bello, the Sardauna of Sokoto and head of the NPC, stated in his 1962 autobiography:

> The religion [Islam] had become very corrupt and many pagan practices had crept in and had taken a firm hold even in the highest quarters. The Shehu Usman declared a Holy War against the polluters of the faith. To cleanse the religion, the Shehu organized revolts in all the great Hausa states[8]

Such an image of the jihad was well suited to the NPC. First, it highlighted the Muslim nature of the North, a factor which the NPC stressed as a means of

---

8. Ahmadu Bello, *My Life* (Cambridge, 1962), p.10.

distinguishing the North from the more Christian and Pagan southern regions. The specter of southern political domination, and the repercussions this domination would have on the religion of Islam was a common theme played upon by NPC politicians. Further, the NPC frequently characterized itself as the 'true Muslim party' which therefore could best represent the region's Muslim majority. Thus, the NPC could claim that it, just like the Shehu and his followers, was seeking to protect and expand the religion of Islam. Further, by highlighting the religious motivations of the jihad, the NPC sought to draw attention away from the political factors, which tended to be highlighted by NEPU (this will be addressed shortly). NPC discussions of the jihad, though, tended to be on a general level, such as that seen in the above quote. Detailed enumerations of the religious justifications for jihad expressed by Shehu dan Fodio are generally not to be found in the NPC literature. As will be seen, NEPU discussions of such issues tended to be much more detailed.

A second key theme presented by the NPC in its references to the Sokoto Jihad was that of unification. The jihad, stated the NPC, helped to bring together the divided states of the region into a single political whole, under the leadership of the Shehu and the Sultans who succeeded him. When speaking at political rallies and ceremonies in the various parts of the Northern Region, it was common for the NPC leaders to stress the role of the local people in supporting the jihad. The following quote is taken from a speech by the Sardauna of Sokoto given in Bauchi province in 1959.

> The Bauchi People have a reputation of being champions of Northern Unity, since the beginnings of Fulani rule in the Region. The Sultan Bello of Sokoto had a great lieutenant in his endeavor to maintain peace and justice in the first Fulani Emir of Bauchi. The people of Bauchi are still holding that favorable position.[9]

---

9. *Nigerian Citizen*, 11 November, 1959.

The Sardauna made a similar comment in Kano that same year, where he stated: "In ancient times, my forefathers considered the people of Kano to be their warriors, and I still regard them so."[10]

The unity theme was of particular importance to the NPC, as was stressed in their party slogan "One North, One People." As Paden has stated, the NPC sought to unify the North because a united northern front provided valuable political muscle on the national level.[11] By stressing the unifying nature of the Sokoto Jihad, the NPC could state that the North had a legacy of political unification and cooperation which dated back a century and a half. As such, they could claim that they were not forcing political unity on the various groups of the North, but were only maintaining a level of cooperation long since established. The various regions and groups of the North were encouraged to support the NPC just as their ancestors had, they maintained, supported the jihad. Similarly, calls for breakaway regions such as the Middle-Belt region proposed by the United Middle Belt Congress (UMBC) were dismissed as opportunistic modern movements which threatened the historical unity of the North.

The political motivations behind the third theme of reference to the Sokoto Jihad by the NPC, that of Fulani leadership, are not so readily apparent. It is certainly true that the great bulk of the leaders of the jihad were indeed Fulani, and this factor was frequently stressed by NPC leaders such as the Sardauna, who frequently referred to the jihad as the "Fulani Jihad" and the caliphate as the "Fulani Empire."[12] Further, most traditional leaders during the period in question considered themselves

---

10. *Daily Times*, 2 December, 1959.

11. John Paden, *Ahmadu Bello*, p.172.

12. See for example, Steven A. Amune, *Work and Worship: Selected Speeches of Ahmadu Bello, Sardauna of Sokoto* (Zaria, 1986), p. 215, and Ahmadu Bello, *My Life*, pp.10-11.

to be Fulani -- descendants of the original participants of the jihad.[13] With the Fulani making up a small percentage of the total populace in the Northern Region, and yet still holding a near monopoly on indigenous political power, it is at first somewhat surprising that the NPC would stress this aspect of the jihad. This is particularly true in light of the fact that opposition parties, such as NEPU, frequently made allegations that the NPC was the party of the "Fulani aristocracy" which did not truly represent the populace of the North. It could well be that the NPC sought to address the issue of Fulani dominance in the jihad and in more contemporary rule head on, since denial of this fact would have been almost impossible. Rather, by stressing the role of the Fulani in the jihad, and stressing that the jihad overthrew the corrupt Islam of the Habe (non-Fulani) Kings, the NPC sought to equate Fulani rule with proper Islamic government. There were certainly times, though, when this approach had to be tempered . In addressing the Minorities Commission in 1958, the Sardauna made the following statement:

> For generations my ancestors have played a large part in the affairs of
> state in this country. I am a Fulani of the Toronkawa Clan. But it is
> not as the Premier of a Fulani Empire that I address you today. It is
> as the Premier of a region, diverse but united, and as head of the only
> party that can claim a large measure of support in every province, in
> every division and virtually in every district.[14]

Thus, while the NPC generally sought to make the best of the issue of Fulani political dominance, they were also aware of the dangers of an apparent ethnic political monopoly.

In contrast to the NPC, NEPU took a very different tack in approaching the

---

13. Post, *Nigerian Federal Election*, p.53.

14. Ahmadu Bello, "Address to the Minorities Commission," 5 February, 1956. From Amune, *Work and Worship*, p.135.

issue of the jihad of Usman dan Fodio. While NEPU did not ignore the issue of the jihad as a movement that sought to purify and expand the practice of Islam in the region, they rather chose to highlight the jihad as a movement of political reform -- a movement that sought the overthrow of corrupt and oppressive rulers. The <u>Habe</u> rulers could be legitimately overthrown because they were not ruling justly, as would proper Muslim leaders. Rather, the <u>Habe</u> were not ruling in consultation (<u>Shura</u>) with their subjects, they lived in excessive grandeur and pomp, they failed to uphold the Shari'a, and they oppressed their people with violence (such as enslavement) and improper taxation (the <u>Jangali</u> or "cattle tax" being a case in point). Because of such corrupt practices, these leaders could be legitimately overthrown as false Muslim leaders.[15] In the eyes of NEPU, the Shehu and his followers sought to purify Islam as a means of bringing justice and freedom to the populace of the region. As one NEPU song stated "I can't forget you Shehu; you worked hard; you worked hard to see that we are free; with Allah's help."[16]

Perhaps one of the most interesting aspects of NEPU's presentation of the history of the Sokoto Jihad, though, was the fact that they were willing to suggest that, while the person and intentions of the Shehu were beyond reproach, the same could not be said for all of his followers. Rather, claimed NEPU, some of dan Fodio's supporters did not seek to overthrow the <u>Habe</u> simply because the these rulers were corrupt, but rather they did so only so they themselves could take power or garner the spoils of war -- particularly slaves.[17] Such a claim ran counter the

---

15. Interview with Alhaji Tanko Yakasai, 21 January, 1993. The religious illegitimacy of the <u>Habe</u> kings is outlined in Usman dan Fodio's *Kitab al-farq*. The parallels between dan Fodio's attack on the <u>Habe</u> and the NEPU's attack on the NPC and Native Authority leaders are clearly intentional. For information on dan Fodio's works, see Murray Last, *The Sokoto Caliphate* (London, 1967), pp.xxv-lxxx.

16. Interview with Dr. Akilu Aliyu, 24 April, 1993.

17. Alhaji Tanko Yakasai, 21 January, 1993.

standard practice of holding all those who took part in the jihad as pious individuals. This stand, though, was central to the NEPU strategy, because it helped lay the basis for their attack on the character of the Sokoto Caliphate itself -- a strategy that will be discussed in more detail shortly.

While both parties present generally positive, if not somewhat divergent, views of the Sokoto Jihad, they offer much less uniform perspectives on the Caliphate that succeeded the jihads. The NPC characterized the Caliphate as the legitimate inheritor of the ideals of Usman dan Fodio. Under the leadership of the Sultan, who was, beginning with Muhammad Bello, a descendant of the Shehu, the Caliphate was the structure that maintained the unity of the empire carved out by the jihad and protected the practice of Islam within the borders of that empire. Indeed, the NPC was careful to stress the fact that the leaders of the Caliphate, both the Sultan and the Emirs, were descendants of those who took part in the jihad. The legacy of descent was a major means by which the NPC sought to legitimize the Caliphate and, by extension, their own leadership. The theme of Fulani leadership, as mentioned previously, was stressed by the frequent reference to the Caliphate as the "Fulani Empire."

The NPC constructed an image of the Caliphate that was generally pious and peaceful and generally avoided mention of or sought to avoid mention of internal conflicts, such as in the case of the Kano civil war of the 1880's. The goals of such a strategy are readily apparent. The Caliphate was legitimate because its leaders were descendants of the jihad's leaders, just as were the leaders of the NPC and the Native Authorities. Similarly, the leaders of the NPC promised to bring peace and unity to the North just as their predecessors ostensibly had done.

While the NPC stressed the continuity between the jihad and the Sokoto

Caliphate, NEPU presented a picture of the Caliphate that stressed its discontinuity with the jihad. This image of the Caliphate was hinted at by the NEPU's suggestion that not all followers of the Shehu sought to support and implement his ideals. Rather, claimed NEPU, the Caliphate was a backslider, and soon after its foundation the leaders slipped back into the ways of those Habe rulers whom they had displaced. Examples of such unIslamic practices included the grandeur and gross display of wealth and the abuse of the Shari'a perpetrated by the Habe rulers. As one NEPU supporter and writer stated: "The public display of wealth and power replaced the moral austerity for which the Fulani leaders of the jihad were renowned."[18]

NEPU also attacked the way in which the leaders of the Caliphate ruled. Editorials and speeches by NEPU members accused the Caliphate's leaders of such evils as confiscation of subjects' property, abuse of the legal system, improper taxation, and territorial wars and slave-raids against neighboring Muslim states (Borno in particular). In closing an article entitled "Islam Faces the Evil Machinations of the NPC" Lawan Danbazau, the Legal Adviser to and one of the founders of NEPU listed the above-mentioned vices of the Caliphate and stated "This was the situation during the times of the Habe and also during the time of the Fulani rulers."[19]

The basis of succession within the Caliphate was also attacked by NEPU, who insisted that under Islam, hereditary succession was not a legitimate basis for leadership.[20] This theme runs through many NEPU arguments against the Caliphate

---

18. Ahmadu Jalingo, "Islam and Political Legitimacy in Northern Nigeria," *Kano Studies* (1982/1985), p. 75.

19. Lawan Danbazau, *Daily Comet*, 14 June, 1960.

20. Jalingo, "Islam and Legitimacy," p.75.

and its successors.[21] Examples of Islamic sources cited to this effect by the NEPU include many Hadiths of the Prophet such as the following.

> God has put an end to the pride in noble ancestry, you are all descended from Adam and Adam from dust, the noblest among you is the man who is the most pious.

and

> Truly, the most worthy of honour in the sight of God is he who fears Him most, not the individual whose lineage is the most famous or the most powerful.[22]

In stressing the continuity between the jihad of Usman dan Fodio, the Sokoto Caliphate, and the Native Authority system, though, the Northern Peoples' Congress was faced with a serious obstacle -- that of the advent and impact of British colonial rule. To legitimize the Native Authority system was to legitimize the British, who had invaded the Caliphate, killed Sultan Attihiru, and subsumed the Emirs into the system of colonial rule via the Native Authority system. One of the most common tactics utilized by the NPC in addressing this dilemma was simply to play down the impact of British colonial rule and to suggest that, in reality, very little changed with the introduction of Colonial rule. To this effect, the Sardauna stated in 1951:

> When the British came to this country they found that we had our chiefs, schools, judges and all that was necessary for civilization. They made some slight changes that were accepted by all the people.[23]

---

21. Interview with M.T.A. Liman, 15 August, 1991.

22. Jalingo, "Islam and Legitimacy," p.75.

23. Ahmadu Bello, 1951. From Usman Abba, *Sir Ahmadu Bello, A Legacy* (Jos, 1992), p.18

One could hardly expect a more generous characterization of colonization.[24]

Indeed, because of the close association between the traditional rulers and the British colonial government (through the medium of Indirect Rule) it was in the interest of the NPC to place colonial rule in as positive a light as possible. On frequent occasions the leaders of the NPC gave glowing reviews of the works of the British in regard to such issues as their role in developing the region and 'helping to bring the North into the modern world.'[25] Many NPC leaders and traditional rulers, including the Sardauna and Emirs such as the Sarkin Kano, Sanusi, held British titles such as "Knight of the British Empire," which they proudly displayed.

The effort to improve the image of the British was so great, in fact, that the leaders of the NPC were willing to present the Sokoto Caliphate in a less favorable light than was commonly the practice, in order to suggest that the British had actually improved the political situation by way of imposing their rule. Speaking at a ceremony in Sokoto to celebrate the granting of self-government to the North in 1959, the Sardauna made the following remarks regarding the period since the coming of the British to power in the region:

> What a splendid journey it has been and what a swift one. Who would have thought on that desperate day on the battle field at Sokoto that, well within a man's lifetime the stumbling collection of squabbling states would be united in dignity and power to form one of the great free countries of the world? Who would have thought on that day of disaster for the Royal House of Sokoto that just over two generations later one of its members would hold the reins of power

---

24. Examples of less-than-slight changes on the part of the British include the outlawing of the slave trade and the (gradual) outlawing of the practice of slavery itself. See Paul Lovejoy and Jan Hogendorn, *Slow Death For Slavery: The Course of Abolition in Northern Nigeria*, 1897-1936, (Cambridge, 1993).

25. Ahmadu Bello in Amune, *Work and Worship*, pp.135-136.

over a modern state covering an area of Africa far greater than Usman
dan Fodio's domains.[26]

Such a quote suggests that the coming of the British actually allowed the "Royal
House of Sokoto" (in the person of the Sardauna) to lead a state far greater even than
that of the Shehu. The characterization of the Sokoto Caliphate as a "stumbling
collection of squabbling states" was a fairly radical departure from the much more
positive appraisal that had been common fare in NPC discussion of the Caliphate.
Such an image of the Caliphate was not to be found elsewhere. Only discussions
involving the impact of the British were to include less favorable pictures of the pre-
colonial state. Such a tendency shows just to what degree the NPC leadership
carefully crafted their perspectives on history to fit the needs and expectations of the
audience at the time.

NEPU also downplayed the impact of the British on the structure and
workings of the Sokoto Caliphate, but only from the perspective that the structure
and workings of the Caliphate were considered by the radical party to have been
corruptions of the intentions of the Shehu and the requirements of Islam even before
the advent of colonial rule. According to NEPU, the main role of the British was to
shore up the faltering collection of Emirates "just as the people were beginning to
throw off the tyrannical yoke of Fulani rule."[27] It is a basic theme of NEPU editorials
and speeches that the Emirs and British formed a partnership for the exploitation of
the region and its populace. In general, stated the NEPU leaders, the British found
the system of "Fulani rule" to be very well suited to the demands of colonialism. For
example, a series of editorials by NEPU legal council Lawan Danbazau stated that

---

26. *Nigerian Citizen*, 18 March, 1959.

27. Alan Feinstein, *African Revolutionary: The Life and Times of Nigeria's Aminu Kano* (Enugu,
1987), p.90.

the British approved of the restriction of education for the masses in the North, because "Lugard understood that it was ignorance that allowed the successive rulers to continue to lord over the inhabitants in the name of religion."[28] The theme of education (both Islamic and Western) as a liberating force is common in NEPU material.[29]

As already stated, NEPU downplayed the overall impact of the British aside from bolstering the rule of the Emirs. As one NEPU editorial stated: "Lugard advised the home office that the existing traditional rulers in the North should be left untouched. They should be left to continue to rule in the same brutal method as before."[30] Changes made by the British were clearly in their own interest, not in that of the region's people.

> Thus, the Europeans left everything untouched in the North except those things that would interfere with their economic objectives. Things such as slave raiding, inter-tribal wars, forceful confiscation of property, slavery etc., were disallowed, but other evils continued.[31]

By associating the Native Authority system and the NPC with British rule, NEPU gained valuable political ammunition. NEPU could claim that the Masu Sarauta had sold out the region's history of independence for the security that came with British backing.

It is worth noting that NEPU did not attack the alliance between the Masu

---

28. *Daily Comet*, 16 June, 1960.

29. See Chapter Five "Religious Services to the Islamic Community."

30. *Daily Comet*, 16 June, 1960.

31. Ibid.

Sarauta and the British on the grounds that the British were not Muslims. NEPU avoided this potentially effective accusation for two reasons. First, the British colonial administrators had been careful not to interfere openly in religious matters and could only be accused, as seen above, of maintaining the status quo. Secondly, NEPU itself was in alliance with the Eastern-based National Council of Nigeria and the Cameroons (NCNC), a party that was generally backed and lead by Ibo Christians. As such, NEPU would only draw the connection between the NPC and their non-Muslim British supporters when the party itself was accused of dealing with non-Muslims -- thus the matter served as a defensive rather than offensive political issue.

IDEOLOGY AND INSTITUTIONS: THE PARTIES AND LINKAGES TO THE JIHAD AND CALIPHATE

From the above discussion, it is clear that both parties had particular perspectives on the nature of the Sokoto Jihad and Caliphate, and that these visions of the region's history were closely tied to their contemporary political goals. It was not sufficient, though, for the parties simply to present a particular version of the region's history. For these images to be politically effective, they had to be tied to the present. Accordingly, each party carefully sought to draw linkages between itself and the vision of the past which it had constructed. To achieve this end, each party drew upon symbolic, physical, and ideological connections to the past.

A common symbol for each party was the flag. Each party's flag incorporated elements of the flag flown by the Shehu during the jihad. Both parties, for example, utilized the same green background for their flag as had been used by Usman Dan Fodio.[32] The NPC, though, took a step beyond simply flying a similar flag, and

---

32. Edward John Rowell-Jackson, "The History of Islam in Hausaland," MA Thesis (Dubuque, Iowa, 1971), p.120.

actually made use of the Shehu's original standard.[33] This flag was moved from Sokoto and was kept at the regional capital of Kaduna. Such an action was clearly an attempt by the NPC to associate their own political leadership with the legacy of the Shehu. To maximize the impact of the flag's presence, the NPC insured that the move was given media attention, and groups of schoolchildren were brought to view the flag.[34] Some NPC backers thought that the flag could be used even more effectively by being flown during political campaigns. As one writer stated:

> I suggest that the Flags of the Shehus of Sokoto and Borno be carried along by the Sardauna's team during his campaign tour and surely all Muslims must follow and vote for the God-fearing Party, the NPC.[35]

NEPU, possibly feeling somewhat upstaged by the whole affair, launched an attack on the NPC's use of the Flag for political ends. An article in the NEPU *Daily Comet* stressed that the flag should remain in Sokoto.

> Are you not aware that the Shehu Usman lived in Sokoto and not in Kaduna? Even the 56 Emirs under the Shehu paid allegiance to him in Sokoto, not Kaduna, and it was there that he gave them flags and enjoined them to do justice. Why is the Northern Nigerian Flag kept at Kaduna and not Sokoto? Do the NPC leaders mean that Kaduna is the cradle of Islam? This is shameful.[36]

---

33. This flag, which had been captured from Sultan Attihiru in 1903, was returned to N. Nigeria on the occasion of the granting of self-rule in 1959. Such an act suggests that the British were well aware of the symbolic connection the NPC hoped to draw between their party and the rulers of the Sokoto Caliphate.

34. *Gaskiya*, 7 June, 1957.

35. NAK, "Political Affairs, 1958-1965," PRE/3, ACC/122, Agency Mark ASI/919, 29 August, 1959. The pre-colonial state of Borno existed in much of the region of north-eastern Nigeria, near lake Chad. The Shehu of Borno held a position similar to that of the Sultan of Sokoto. Within the system of Indirect Rule, the Shehu of Bornu was head of the Bornu province Native Authority and a member of the NPC.

36. Sharif Zango, "Return the Shehu's Flag to Sokoto," *Daily Comet*, 1 September, 1960.

Clearly, by insisting on the separation of the flag from the halls of contemporary political power, NEPU was trying to stress the discontinuity between the current (NPC-led) northern government and that of the Shehu. Further, NEPU stated that the willingness of the NPC to utilize the holy flag of the Shehu in such a way showed that "it is a misconception that the NPC party is a religious party."[37]

The use of the flag of Usman dan Fodio was not the only symbol that the NPC utilized to associate itself with the Caliphate. The Sardauna and other NPC leaders made frequent visits to Usman dan Fodio's tomb in Rabah, in order to show their respect.[38] The very name of the Shehu was utilized by the NPC. One example of this practice were the "Usmaniyya" awards given out by the NPC government (always to its own party members) in recognition for 'outstanding service to the region.' Witness the following newspaper article summarizing the comments of the Sardauna as he presented an Usmaniyya medal to Abubakar Tafawa Balewa, the NPC Prime Minister.

> In presenting the Medal to Sir Abubakar, the Sardauna expressed the hope that he would accept the Medal not because of its value but because of his (Sir Abubakar's) loyalty, and belief in the duties performed by Shehu Usman Dan Fodio **for this country** [emphasis added], and what they were doing in following Dan Fodio's footsteps.[39]

The above quote, in addition to shedding light upon how the NPC used the Usmaniyya medals to link themselves to the past, also reveals the very strong theme of continuity between the Caliphate and the NPC government that was frequently

---

37. Ibid.

38. NAK, "Premier's Touring Notes, 1958-1965," PRE/2, ACC/178-191, Agency Mark PRE/99.

39. *Nigerian Citizen*, 16 June, 1965.

expressed by the party. It is no accident that the deeds of the Shehu are referred to as "the duties performed... for this country." Such a quote suggests that there was no real break between the rule of the Shehu and that of the NPC. The name and person of Usman Dan Fodio were utilized by the NPC on a variety of levels. One recipient of an Usmaniyya medal, Alhaji Ibrahim Imam, used the occasion to suggest that Nigeria should have been renamed "Usmaniyya" with the coming of independence. At least, he said, the Northern Region should still be named as such.[40]

There was even an attempt by the Sardauna to form a Sufi brotherhood with the person of the Shehu as the founding Shaykh. Had this move been successful, it would have further centralized the religious authority based in Sokoto, since most of the Region's Sufis belonged to the Qadiriyya sect, which had its spiritual headquarters in Iraq, where it was founded. Thus, the external focus of the Qadiriyya was seen as a potential threat to the religious legitimacy of the NPC, and the creation of a new brotherhood focused on Usman dan Fodio would have potentially created a local focus of Sufi authority.[41]

The NPC also stressed its relationship to the Caliphate by virtue of its ties to the city of Sokoto. Indeed, it is no accident that the NPC used Sokoto as its de facto base of operations and ceremony. Such activities only helped bolster the links the party sought to draw between itself and the Caliphate. Lavish NPC ceremonies were held at the Sokoto durbar grounds on the occasions of regional self government and Nigerian independence. By holding such celebrations in Sokoto, the NPC was stressing the symbolic return of political power to the capital of the Caliphate.[42]

---

40. *Nigerian Citizen*, 6 March, 1965.

41. See Chapter Six "Brotherhoods and Politics" for more information on this subject.

42. *Nigerian Citizen*, 18 March, 1959. See also *Daily Mail*, 17 June, 1961.

The imagery of the NPC rallies also recalled the region's history. NPC leaders forsook modern Western dress, and always appeared in traditional garb for public Party functions. Party leaders such as the Sardauna and Tafawa Balewa frequently received charging salutes from local horsemen, just as would Emirs.[43] Such activities not only stressed the NPC's ties to the past, but also helped blur the lines between high-ranking traditional rulers and the leaders of the NPC.

While the NPC made the most of such symbolic associations to the Sokoto Caliphate, the two most important connections that the NPC stressed to emphasize its relationship with the Caliphate were its institutional ties to the Caliphate and the descent of its members from the leaders of the jihad and Caliphate. As mentioned, briefly, before, these two factors were the keystones of legitimacy both for the institution of the Native Authorities and the traditional leaders who made up the leadership of the Native Authorities and the NPC.

As already noted, the Native Authorities consisted of the Emirates of the Sokoto Caliphate that were utilized by the British colonial government as the basic units of administration under the system of Indirect Rule. For the purposes of the NPC, it was necessary for the party to play down the impact of the British and stress the continuity between the Native Authorities and the old Caliphate. As the Sardauna described the process in his autobiography:

> [The Native Authorities] are all of them based on historic grounds and their areas have historic boundaries. Lugard saw the administrative genius of the Fulani Rulers and their staffs: he utilized it as the mainspring of the NA system, that he called 'Indirect Rule,' and it has worked well since then.[44]

---

43. Alhaji Tanko Yakasai, 14 May, 1994.

44. Ahmadu Bello, *My Life*, pp.97-98.

In a speech made to the House of Chiefs in 1962, the Sardauna
made the following comments:

> I would like to remind the Honorable members that one hundred and
> fifty years ago this country was ruled by a certain people who now
> form part of the Native [Authority] system. They were succeeded by
> the British some fifty-nine years ago... History has now repeated itself
> and the indigenous sons have succeeded the British.[45]

The two preceding quotes highlight the basic themes upon which the Native
Authorities and NPC based their legitimacy -- institutional continuity of
administrative structures and blood ties between the historic and contemporary
leaders. To further strengthen the ties between the contemporary government and the
Caliphate, the NPC raised the position of the Sultan of Sokoto to that of Minister
without Portfolio in the Northern Region government.[46] Such a move sent a clear
signal that the NPC considered the position of the Sultan to be a serious political post
even in the modern day. Also significant is the fact that the Sardauna made clear that
he would himself be pleased to take the post of Sultan if the position became open.[47]
Paden has even suggested that "If the Sardauna had become Sultan... he might have
tried to set up the Sultan of Sokoto as head of State of Nigeria."[48] While this scenario
would have been unlikely (to say the least) in the context of Nigerian national
politics, it may well be that the Sardauna hoped to reintegrate political and religious
authority in the North with himself as the Sultan.

---

45. Ministerial speech to the House of Chiefs, 14 April, 1962. From Amune, *Work and Worship*,
pp.168-169.

46. Paden, *Ahmadu Bello*, p.215.

47. *Drum*, July, 1965, taken from Abba, *Legacy*, p.76.

48. Paden, *Ahmadu Bello*, p.215.

In no case was the legacy of descent from the leaders of the jihad and Caliphate made more strongly than in that of Ahmadu Bello, the Sardauna of Sokoto. The Sardauna, the head of the NPC and the Premier or the Northern Region, was also the great-great-grandson of Usman dan Fodio and the great-grandson of Muhammad Bello, the founder of Sokoto city. Ahmadu Bello's distinguished lineage was no secret. Indeed, he stresses his descent from dan Fodio and Muhammad Bello in the very first paragraph of his autobiography.[49] References to the Sardauna's heritage were common fare in newspaper articles and party rallies. Such sources frequently attributed his success to his family background. As one article stated:

> [The Sardauna] is never known to have fought a losing battle, because
> he has the blood of the great Usman dan Fodio, the most outstanding
> man of this time, flowing through his veins.[50]

In the course of a debate in the house of assembly, one NPC representative, Alhaji Ladan Baki, referred to the Sardauna as "Our divine leader who is in a way a reincarnation of Uthman dan Fodio."[51] Indeed, it was a common NPC strategy to not only stress the blood linkage between the Sardauna and Usman dan Fodio, but also to compare their exploits. The Sardauna's conversion campaigns in the early 1960's, for example, were frequently compared to dan Fodio's jihad.[52] The Sardauna also at times drew comparisons between himself and his great-great-grandfather.

> I have never sought the political limelight or a leading position in my
> country, but I could not avoid the obligation of my birth and destiny.

---

49. Ahmadu Bello, *My Life*, p.1.

50. *Nigerian Citizen*, 16 January, 1965.

51. Billy Dudley, *Parties and Politics*, p.134.

52. These campaigns are discussed in detail in Chapter Five, "Services to the Islamic Community."

My great-grandfather built an empire in the western Sudan. It has fallen to my lot to play a not inconsiderable part in building a new nation. My ancestor was chosen to lead the holy-war which set up his empire. I have been chosen by a free electorate to help build a modern state.[53]

Interestingly, despite the political capital which the NPC was collecting by stressing the ties between the Sardauna and the founder of the Sokoto Caliphate, it was common for the Sardauna and the party leaders to deny that he was selected to head the party on the basis of his lineage. Rather, it was frequently stated that the Sardauna was selected on the basis of his personal qualifications alone, and his lineage was only a matter of coincidence, albeit one that helped to bolster his legitimacy.[54]

Still, it is unlikely that the members of the NPC were unaware of the political potential of the Sardauna's family background. Indeed, some NPC leaders dispute the suggestion that the Sardauna was selected solely on the basis of his character and ability and state that he was chosen first and foremost because of his heritage. In particular, the issue of lineage was why Ahmadu Bello was named party leader over his chief competitor, Sanda na Alhaji.[55] Paden suggests that the Sardauna was chosen not only because of the popular appeal of his lineage, but also because the Sardauna's family ties to Sokoto insured that he would have the respect of the Emirs, who otherwise might have proven difficult for the party to control.[56] This theory is corroborated by Alhaji Tanko Yakasai, one of the founding members of NEPU.[57]

---

53. Speech in Kaduna, 9 August, 1961, from Abba, *Legacy*, p.85.

54. Interview with Sule Gaya, 21 January, 1993.

55. Interview with Alhaji Baba Daradara, 7 June, 1993.

56. Paden, *Ahmadu Bello*, pp.172-173.

57. Alhaji Tanko Yakasai, 21 January, 1993.

Thus, while it is evident that the NPC found the relation of its leader to the founder of the Caliphate to be of popular advantage, it is interesting that this relationship proved valuable for the internal politics of the party as well.[58]

As previously mentioned, a key NEPU strategy in attacking the legitimacy of the NPC and the Native Authorities was to attack the very concept of inherited rule. As Paden states:

> The challenge [to the Native Authority system] will come from Kano, where Aminu Kano begins to provide the intellectual roots for a radical reinterpretation of the jihadic legacy. While the Sokoto poets may sing of the Sardauna as a "king" (Sarki), Aminu Kano argues that there are no "kings" in the jihad legacy and that the entire authority structure of the emirate provinces is a corruption.[59]

NEPU often publicized that one of the reasons for the overthrow of the Umayyad Caliphate (750 AD) was because the Umayyad Caliphs practiced hereditary rule, which is forbidden by Islam.[60] Since the Umayyads have long been portrayed as perverters of Islam, the comparison of the NPC to the Umayyads was not a favorable one. According to NEPU, "Islam recognizes only one criterion of superiority: more righteous conduct."[61]

The political utility of such an argument is clear. First, this position attacked

---

58. This point is relevant to the question of whether the Sardauna should be considered a reformer or as a reactionary. Did he use his position as a member of the Royal house of Sokoto to reform the traditional rule system of the Native Authorities, or was he a reactionary who simply sought to maintain as much of the system as possible in a time of great political change? Certainly, NEPU considered him to be the latter.

59. Paden, *Ahmadu Bello*, p.378.

60. Ahmadu Jalingo, 15 August, 1991.

61. Ahmadu Jalingo, "Islam and Legitimacy" p.75.

the Caliphate which followed the jihad. Secondly, it attacked the heads of the Native Authorities and the NPC who in large part based their legitimacy on their descent from the leaders of the jihad. Further, this argument had the potential of legitimizing the NEPU's leadership, because while very few NEPU members were descendants of the jihadists, they could lay claim to greater religious legitimacy on the grounds of greater Islamic learning and, they argued, piety. Thus, stated the party's leaders, NEPU's dedication to the ideals of the Shehu in word and deed gave them greater claim to leadership than did mere descent from his person and that of his followers.

> We [NEPU] were the legitimate successors of Usman dan Fodio. Was Dan Fodio corrupt? He was always on the right side of justice. Emirs are the grandchildren of the Shehu -- that's what they were saying. We didn't care about the Emirs being the grandchildren of the Shehu, we cared about what was practiced. They are his grandchildren but do not follow his leadership. So you see, we that were trying to copy Shehu are the real successors, not his so-called grandchildren. If they do not do as the Shehu, just forget about them![62]

Another common theme in NEPU's attack on the current traditional leaders who made up the backbone of the Native Authority system and the NPC was to state that if Shehu Usman dan Fodio were to return, he would be displeased with the contemporary state of affairs.

> If Shehu Uthman dan Fodio were to return today, he would find out that the religion he suffered to reform, the Emirs he appointed and the just system of Law he established were completely debased. Shehu Usman dan Fodio would certainly fight another jihad to remove the Emirs, and destroy the oppressive and anti-Islamic courts.[63]

---

62. Interview with Alhaji Baba dan Agundi, 4 April, 1993.

63. Lawan Danbazau, "Islam Confronts the Evil Machinations of the NPC," *Daily Comet*, 29 January, 1960.

The implications of such a statement are clear. Not only were the current rulers unjust, but a new jihad was needed to remove them. In many ways, NEPU sought to present its political campaign against the Native Authorities and NPC to be a modern jihad to restore the ideals of the Shehu.

It is worth noting that NEPU was not alone in trying to paint a picture of the NPC as a corruption of Islam. Even the Western Region-based Action Group (AG) used similar arguments in its northern campaigns. In an article entitled "If Dan Fodio were Alive today He would Condemn the NPC," the AG stated that it was the party that truly upheld the revolutionary mission of the Shehu.[64] The arguments of the AG, were likely drawn from those of NEPU (whom the Action Group frequently courted as an ally). Further, the party was hobbled by the fact that it was viewed largely as a southern and Christian-led party that had little in common with either the Shehu or most Northerners.

NEPU, for its part, was not faced with the same challenge of legitimacy as was the AG. The NEPU leaders and supporters were clearly Northerners (although their alliance with the Eastern NCNC somewhat weakened this image) and clearly Muslims. Indeed, it was their claim to be more knowledgeable and more pious Muslims on which they based much of their legitimacy. The NEPU leaders could neither claim linkage to the Shehu by way of heredity nor did they desire to. Rather, the NEPU's leadership claimed intellectual descent from scholars who they claimed had opposed the increasingly corrupt leaders of the Caliphate. These scholars, states Ahmadu Jalingo, a member of the NEPU youth wing and later the personal secretary to Aminu Kano, were those who rigidly adhered to the true meaning of Islam. The less puritan scholars, or "establishment malams" took on a role of interpreting the

---

64. *Northern Star*, 9 December, 1959.

Qur'an and the Hadith to support the new political system.[65]

It was from these "radical _malams_" and their legacy of resistance to those in authority that NEPU claimed descent. These _malams_, stated NEPU advocates, had always remained outside of the circles of official power, but had always maintained a high degree of influence and respect among the common people because of their roles as _gardawa_ (teachers) and as practitioners of _tafsir_ (Qur'anic translation and interpretation). Indeed, there is ample evidence to support the existence of "radical" _malams_. These _malams_ frequently sided with NEPU -- a fact recognized by both the British and independent NPC governments. Witness the following security report from 1961 (under the heading "subversive organizations").

> Itenerate Koranic Mallams played an unusually active part in politics during the elections. They were on the side of the opposition parties and campaigned against the chiefs.[66]

Paden has noted that many of the prominent members of NEPU were "_tafsir_ _malams_," including such individuals as Aminu Kano, Sa'ad Zungur, and Isa Wali.[67] Further, Paden was struck by the comparison between Aminu Kano and Abdullahi dan Fodio, the brother of Usman dan Fodio.

> The parallel between Abdullahi dan Fodio and Aminu Kano is noticeable in several respects: both were less involved in brotherhood activities than their counterparts (Usman dan Fodio, Muhammad Bello, Muhammad Sanusi, Ibrahim Niass); both wrote from a position slightly apart from the central power structure (although they later assumed power); both were concerned with the

---

65. Jalingo, "Islam and Legitimacy," p.73.

66. KSHCB, NDMSIS, R.52/325, April/May, 1961.

67. John Paden, _Religion and Political Culture_, p.298.

nature of proper government; and both were <u>tafsir malams</u>.[68]

Indeed, NEPU leaders placed a great store in their role as scholars, and the parallels between the NEPU leadership and the leaders of the jihad was probably not lost on the more historically aware members of the local populace. The radical scholars of NEPU were never hesitant to draw their conservative counterparts into highly complex discussions regarding the Islamic elements of contemporary political debates. A prime example of this tendency was the editorial battle over "The Position of Women in Islam" instigated by Isa Wali, a NEPU member.[69]

Evidence would suggest that the NPC was aware of the threat posed by the NEPU's claim to the intellectual high ground, and sought to take steps to remedy this situation. One of the more ambitious undertakings by the NPC was the funding of the translation (from Arabic to Hausa) and publication of various writings of Usman dan Fodio, such as his *Diya al-Hukkum* ("The Light of Government"). These works were translated "at the Premier's expense" and distributed to <u>malams</u> throughout the region.[70] In 1964 an anthology of the works of the Shehu was released by the Premier's office in a move, says Paden, "to unify the <u>malam</u> class around the memory of the Shehu."[71] This move met with limited success within the community of <u>malams</u>, whether among radical <u>malams</u> or the Tijaniyya and Qadariyya brotherhoods. Still, the Sardauna gave heavy play to this effort in his public appearances, which probably helped improve his wider image as an intellectual and as a devotee of the Shehu.

---

68. Ibid, p.299.

69. See Chapter Four "Islam, Politics and Women's Rights" for a discussion of this incident.

70. NAK, "Requests for Religious Books, 1961-1962," PRE/2, ACC/404, Agency Mark PRE/222, p.17-18.

71. Paden, *Religion and Political Culture*, p.182.

POLITICS AND ETHNICITY

The legacy of the Sokoto caliphate included both ethnic and regional overtones. As already noted, the great majority of the northern population was not Fulani, but rather was made up of the Hausa and other, smaller, ethnic groups. Despite the efforts of the NPC to legitimize the existence of a Fulani ruling class, there was a distinct undercurrent of Hausa resentment to Fulani rule. No doubt NEPU was aware of this factor in their attacks on the "Fulani aristocracy" -- even though many NEPU leaders, such as Aminu Kano, were themselves Fulani. Nowhere was the tendency of anti-Fulani tension more evident than in Kano. Under the Habe rulers, Kano had long been the dominant commercial and political power in the region, but was forced into a subservient position, at least politically and religiously, by the jihad of Usman dan Fodio. Under such a situation, there existed a distinct potential for a "Kano/Hausa" nationalist movement.

During most of the 1950's, there seemed little likelihood that such a situation would come to pass, though. There existed a very close relationship between the Sardauna and Emir Sanusi of Kano, who many considered to be the second most powerful member of the NPC. Sanusi's oldest son had even wedded the Sardauna's daughter.[72] During the early 1960's though, a power struggle erupted between the Sardauna and Sanusi, which resulted in Sanusi's being forced to resign his emirship. This situation provided the impetus for a Kano/Hausa reaction against the powers in Sokoto and against the NPC. NEPU, quick to see a chance to drive a wedge into the NPC's unity, helped to form the Kano People's Party (KPP). This party had as its main goal the reinstatement of Sanusi as Emir. Such a move was particularly interesting in that Sanusi was notorious as one of the most vicious oppressors of NEPU over the previous decade. The KPP also called for the formation of a separate

---

72. Post, *Federal Elections*, p.53.

Kano state, which would be free from "Sokoto/Fulani" dominance. Further, this incident served as a catalyst to rally Tijaniyya support behind Sanusi, as well as the KPP and NEPU parties.[73] While this conflict did not lead to the downfall of the NPC as the NEPU leaders hoped, it did help weaken the party's hold on the Kano area. Anti-Sokoto feelings certainly ran high, as a letter to the NPC from the Kano Ex-Serviceman's Union illustrates.

> We the Kano Ex-servicemen has this date succeeded from the NPC. We are here now plain to tell you that the NPC was built to destroy the goodness of our Fatherland KANO. We have proved the Government of the Sokoto peoples projected by the Sardauna is filled with Evils, Treacherous, Boastings, Arrogant, Liars, etc. You Sokotos took the point in overthrowing our God-given Emir Sir Ahmadu Sanusi Sarkin Kano, so that you could still dominate here. Our new political party can aid us and not the government of any Sokoto man. Your government is bad and stinking. We own Kano and Kano owns us. We are not slaves to Usman dan Fodio.[74]

This quote points up the extreme complexity and unpredictability of politics in the Northern Region during this period. While both parties had spent much of the previous decade attempting to associate themselves with their own particular vision of Usman dan Fodio and his jihad, the period was to close with a political movement in the region's most important city that rejected the Shehu's legacy altogether.

CONCLUSIONS

The above discussion clearly shows that the conflict over the position of the Native Authority System was deeply rooted in the two parties' perspectives on the

---

73. The religious and political implications of this incident are discussed in detail in Chapter Six, "Brotherhoods and Politics."

74. NAK, KanoProf., Agency Mark PLT/8, 18 May, 1963.

region's history. Indeed, each party sought to present a vision of history that supported its own political agenda. To do so, each party developed a particular image of the jihad of Dan Fodio, the Sokoto Caliphate, and of the role of the British in the region. The result was no less than a conflict between two opposing visions of the region's self-image. Whether one party or the other was "right" is beside the point. The real issue is how both parties looked to the region's own history to supply a political and ideological model which would justify their own contemporary vision of the (Northern) Nigerian state.

Such a process is similar to that posited by Benedict Anderson in *Imagined Communities*.[75] Anderson states that the development of national consciousness and nationalism is a result of the creation of "imaginary" historical communities. Writ large, the NPC and NEPU's constructions of opposing histories seem to support Anderson's thesis. At a deeper level, however, the case study of Northern Nigeria contrasts with Anderson's thesis in two important ways. First, this chapter highlights the ways in which religious factors can play heavily into the forging of national consciousness -- a factor which Anderson largely discounts.[76] More importantly, Anderson's characterization of nationalism in Africa largely as "a response to the new-style of global imperialism" very poorly describes the situation in Northern Nigeria.[77] Indeed, the conflict of historical images waged by the NPC and NEPU is remarkable in regard to the degree to which it ignored (rather than responded to) the issue of colonial rule. Conflicting images Northern Nigeria's own past were much more central to the conflict between the NPC and NEPU than was anti-colonial rhetoric. British rule was far more often discussed in terms of how it had fit into pre-existing themes of governance in the region, rather than how it had radically

75. Benedict Anderson, *Imagined Communities* (New York, 1991).

76. Ibid, pp.10-12.

77. Ibid, p.139.

changed the political process and the relationship between state and society. Such a situation suggests that the "creation" of national consciousness in the African context was sometimes far more complex than Anderson gives it credit.

Finally, this case study points up the continuing importance of the Sokoto Jihad itself. Not only did the Sokoto Jihad serve as a model for other West African jihads during the 19th century, as suggested by Murray Last, but its significance has extended to the modern era as well.[78] As will be seen in the following chapters, the parties' conflicting visions of the Sokoto Jihad and Caliphate colored even those political debates which did not overtly deal with the region's history.

---

78. Murray Last, "Reform in West Africa: The Jihad Movements of the Nineteenth Century" in Ajayi and Crowder, eds. *History of Africa*, Vol. II. (New York, 1973) p.14

CHAPTER TWO:

THE LAWS OF GOD AND THE NATURE OF THE GAME: SHARI'A COURTS AND POLITICS

During the course of the 1950's and early 1960's the conflict between the Northern Peoples' Congress and the Northern Elements Progressive Union was not only fought in the political arena but extended to include the region's judicial system as well. Because of the party's close ties with the Native Authorities, the NPC wielded <u>de facto</u> control over the Shari'a courts (also known as the "native" or "<u>alkali</u> courts").[1] This situation gave the NPC a powerful political tool, and the party frequently sought to use this institutional control to limit the activities of their adversaries NEPU responded to the NPC's use of the courts in a number of ways, ranging from attacks on the NPC's interpretation and alleged abuse of the Shari'a to strategies by which they sought to manipulate the legal system to their own ends.

As the final arbiters of justice in the region, at least up to 1960, the British colonial administrators, too, were deeply embroiled in this situation. As previously noted, these administrators were generally pro-NPC, and were happy to see the activities of NEPU curtailed. The conflict within the courts, though, often threatened to expose this pro-NPC bias. As such, the British administrators were frequently torn between their investment in the existing legal system (via Indirect Rule), their desire

---

1. <u>Alkali</u> (pl. <u>alkalai</u>) is the Hausa word for "judge."

to see NEPU's "subversive" activities curtailed, and the need to develop a legal system that could more effectively handle the demands of modern party politics.

In the following chapter, a number of questions regarding the interaction of politics and religious law will be addressed. How did the legal system become embroiled in the conflict between the NPC and NEPU? How did each party seek to manipulate the legal situation to suit its own political ends? More specifically, what was the impact of the NPC's institutional ties to the courts and how did NEPU seek to combat this advantage on the part of their opponents? What were the parties' views on the nature and position of Islamic law in Nigeria? How did the political conflict between the two parties influence the structure and practice of law in the region? Given the fact that adherence to the Shari'a is a standard yardstick by which Muslim governance is judged, these questions are central to any examination of religion and politics in Nigeria's Northern Region.

BACKGROUND: THE LEGAL SYSTEM AND ITS IMPLICATIONS

The form of the legal system of the Northern Region during the 1950's and 1960's is important to the issues at hand.[2] At its most basic level, the legal system of the Northern Region represented a combination of both Shari'a law, under the control of the Region's traditional rulers (through the Native Authority system), and British Common law, as executed by the British colonial officers. Shari'a law in the region was dominated by the Maliki school of Islamic jurisprudence, and was applied to cases regarding civil, criminal (Haddi), and state affairs (Siyasa).[3] Shari'a courts were, except in the cases of the Emir's courts, under the guidance of an alkali

2. For a detailed history of the legal system in the Region, see Tijjani Muhammad Naniya, "The Transformation of the Administration of Justice in Kano Emirate, 1903-1966" Phd (Bayero University, Kano, 1990).

3. Paden, *Religion and Political Culture*, p.61.

("judge"). These courts were graded "A", "A limited", "B", "C" and "D", with the grades corresponding to the seriousness of the cases which they could hear. The grade A courts were those of the major Emirs and were certified to try even capital offenses. The grade A limited courts were those of lesser Emirs and of the most highly trained alkalai. The remaining courts were headed by lesser alkalai and were often found in rural areas.[4] During the latter 1950's, the Moslem Court of Appeals and the Shari'a Court of Appeals were established to hear cases from these alkali courts. The details of the creation of these appeals courts will be discussed in Chapter Three.

Not surprisingly, it was the British who had graded and organized the alkali courts within the Native Authorities that were the basic blocks of Indirect Rule in the region, and who later established the Moslem Court of Appeals. Such a policy was of great advantage to the colonial administration, since it freed them from creating and maintaining an extensive court system staffed by British personnel. By limiting their overt role within the legal system, the British were able to increase their own legitimacy in the region by stressing that they had not interfered with the practice of the Shari'a. Further, this situation helped protect the legitimacy of the Region's traditional rulers, whose duty it was to uphold Islamic law. This "promise to respect Moslem customs and religion" had its origin with Lugard himself.[5] With their own legitimacy at stake, the traditional rulers were willing partners in the British effort to play down the impact of colonialism on the region's legal system.

The British did maintain their own distinct legal system within the Northern Region. While by no means as extensive as the alkali court system, the British

---

4. KSHCB, "Native Court Specific Cases and General Correspondence, 1948-1960," ACC/45, Agency Mark R-256, 10 September, 1958.

5. NAK, "Survey of Islam in Northern Nigeria, 1952," ZarPrOf C/68, p.22.

Magistrate courts did act as the ultimate arbiters of justice in the colony. These institutions served as courts of the first instance only in cases involving British citizens or of grave concern to the colonial state (such as cases of sedition or rebellion). Far more often, the Magistrate courts heard appeals from the higher (grade A) alkali courts, when such action was deemed necessary. It is of central importance to this chapter to note that such appeals almost always involved cases of political nature. Further, as the highest courts in the region, the Magistrate courts could invoke a wide range of legal doctrine, including Nigerian Statutory law, Common Law, Doctrines of Equity, and the laws of England. They were also empowered to invoke native laws and customs when necessary "to prevent the commission of injustices."[6] Not surprisingly, this situation gave the British jurists a high degree of latitude in the hearing of cases and the rendering of judgements -- the utility of which was not lost on the colonial administrators.

Of more immediate importance, though, is the question of the relationship between the legal system and the NPC. It has already been noted that the NPC was in many respects a party of the traditional rulers for the traditional rulers. Because the Native Authorities were built around the traditional Emirate structure that traced its origin back to the Sokoto Caliphate, this meant that the Native Authorities, and the courts overseen by them, were under the control of the Emirs and their associated Masu Sarauta. The close relationship between the NPC and the Native Authorities gave the party a remarkable degree of influence over the court system. Indeed, in many cases the NPC was able to wield almost absolute control over the courts. As was stated by Sklar in 1963:

> In practice, the alkalis are political appointees controlled by the emir who generally works closely with the district heads, or principle

---

6. Sklar, *Nigerian Political Parties*, p.355.

agents of the NA. It is notorious that in the rural districts, the district heads and the alkalis together wield virtually absolute political power over the peasantry. Collusive political intolerance on their part renders opposition party activity extremely difficult if not hazardous.[7]

A similar point was made by Malam Lawan Danbazau, a legal adviser for NEPU:

> The police were in the hands of the chief, the prison was in the hands of the chief, and the court was in the hands of the chief, and the chief was an NPC member. So you see, if you had a political disagreement he [the chief] would put his police to arrest you, take you to his court and, if convicted, you were taken to his prison.[8]

THE NPC AND COURT CONTROL

Clearly, the NPC was able to gain great advantage from its de facto control over the alkali courts. Because the alkali courts were governed by the practice of Shari'a, any long-term advantage that the NPC was to gain by control over the courts had to be justified in terms of Islamic law. More to the point, for the NPC to attack NEPU via the alkali courts, NEPU members had to be charged with some violation of the Shari'a. Such a situation had the effect of further heightening the religious nature of the conflict between the NPC and NEPU, since within the alkali courts political charges were expressed in terms of violation of Islamic law.

At the most basic level, the NPC could rely on the courts as a deterrent to the political opposition. The fact that the courts and the NPC leaders were closely allied was certainly common knowledge among the regions populace, since the NPC was

---

7. Ibid, p.363. For more detail on the connections between the NPC and the Alkalai, see M.G. Smith, *Government in Zazzau, 1800-1950* (London, 1960) pp.284-286.

8. Shawalu, *Gambo Sawaba*, p.66.

formed around the <u>Masu Sarauta</u> who had always controlled the courts. As Post has stated "It was in this tradition that the elector had been brought up, not in that of an independent judiciary."[9] Just to be sure, though, it was a not uncommon practice, particularly in such NPC strongholds as Sokoto Province, for the <u>alkalai</u> to appear in court wearing NPC badges.[10] Such a situation could be of advantage to the NPC even in cases that did not involve political matters. The period saw frequent allegations of NEPU members being asked by <u>alkalai</u> to choose between membership in the NPC and prison terms. On other occasions <u>alkalai</u> allegedly reduced sentences and fines for NEPU members who agreed to cross the carpet to the NPC.[11] Some NEPU members even claimed that the judges were asking them to swear on the Qur'an that they would no longer support any party other than the NPC.[12]

In some cases, the NPC abuses of the court system were even more overt than those listed above. In his autobiography, Shaykh Abubakar Gumi (who at one point served as the Grand Khadi of the Shari'a Court of Appeals) relates a story "confessed" to him by a close friend who was a senior NPC official.

> He [Alhaji Gumi's friend] had gone out on a campaign tour for the NPC. In the course of the tour he visited a town in Sokoto Province with his entourage where the district head complained publicly against a prominent leader of the NEPU whom he said had become a bother to him. As my friend confessed to me, he simply gave orders

---

9. Post, *Nigerian Federal Election,* p.294.

10. Lawan Danbazau, 21 January, 1993.

11. These allegations are common fare in sources from the period. See for example *Daily Times,* 17 August, 1959; KSHCB, "NEPU Complaints and Court Cases." KanoPrOf, 2/73, PLT/5, 8 August, 1957; NAK, "NEPU File" PRE/3, ASI.I/918, 29 October, 1958. See also interviews with Lawan Danbazau, 21 January, 1993 and Hajiya Jumai Wool, 5 July, 1993.

12. Malam Ibrahim Heebah, *Nigerian Citizen,* 2 December, 1959.

and the NEPU leader was immediately arrested and sent to jail.[13]

While such cases as those related above show the extent of the NPC's influence over the courts, they do not give an altogether accurate depiction of the way in which the courts were utilized by the NPC. To use the courts effectively in the long run, the NPC could not afford to be too overt or to appear too high-handed, for to simply throw opposition leaders in jail without charges and trials would have been unacceptable not only to the populace, but to the overseeing British colonial officers as well. Thus, as mentioned before, charges against NEPU members needed to be justified in terms of violations of Islamic law.

It was under the aegis of Siyasa that NEPU supporters most frequently found themselves charged in the alkali courts. The most common charges against NEPU supporters usually fell into three types: slanderous utterances against individuals (particularly NPC and traditional leaders); utterances or actions likely to cause a breach of the peace; and violations of conditions imposed by rules and permits regarding political meetings.[14]

Charges regarding "slanderous utterances" provided the NPC with a valuable weapon with which to restrict the political activities of opposition parties -- particularly NEPU. As a basis for such charges, the alkalai frequently cited the Maliki law book *Tabsirat al-Hukkam*, which stated that "any person who makes abusive proclamation against any Moslem ruler should receive a very severe

---

13. Sheikh Abubakar Gumi, *Where I Stand*, (Kaduna, Nigeria: 1992) p.83.

14. Sklar, *Nigerian Political Parties*, pp.360-361.

punishment plus one month's imprisonment."[15] Almost any attack on NPC leaders could be construed as slanderous if the court so chose. As observed by Sklar:

> Prohibitions of slander and defamation of character in Muslim law have been stretched by certain Native Authorities and alkalis into virtual proscriptions of any derogatory mention of the names of individuals in political addresses.[16]

In some instances, it was not even necessary for a NEPU member to insult a member of the NPC, but merely to mention the names of certain prominent NPC leaders was enough to bring charges. During a local election campaign in Sokoto province during 1957, it was declared illegal for members of the opposition to mention the name of either the Sultan or the Sardauna.[17] Gambo Sawaba, head of the NEPU Women's Wing, was arrested and sentenced to three months imprisonment merely for showing a picture of the Sardauna while speaking against the NPC government.[18] Indeed, "abuse of the Sardauna" in particular became a ready-made charge that was nearly guaranteed to send the NPC's opponents to jail.[19] Further, the above mentioned "severe punishment plus one months imprisonment" could be widely interpreted. Some NEPU members received sentences at hard labor for up to three years for "abusive statements." Insults to such highly placed officials as the

---

15. KSHCB, "Punishment of Offenders in Native Courts in so-called Political Cases," KanoPrOf, ACC/1206, Agency Mark NCT/79, 7 September, 1957. Copies of this passage were circulated to all Native Authority courts to insure that the Alkalai were familiar with their ability to convict such actions.

16. Sklar, *Nigerian Political Parties*, p.361.

17. Ibid

18. Shawalu, *Gambo Sawaba*, p.81.

19. Muhammad Sani Umar, "Islam in Nigeria: Its Concept, Manifestations and Role in Nation Building," in *Nigeria Since Independence, The First 25 Years*, J.A. Atanda, et al, eds. (Ibadan, 1989), p.82.

Emirs could bring punishment of up to eighty strokes with a cane and imprisonment, although such extreme cases were rare.[20] Further, interpretation of the *Tabsirat al-Hukkam*, by the Wazirin Zaria (who often advised the British on matters relating to the Shari'a) declared that the Native Authorities in Muslim areas were corporate bodies and should be considered as a Muslim individual for certain legal purposes. As such, insults or "slanderous accusations" against the Native Authorities could bring charges just as could attacks on individuals. Even attacks on the NPC could lead to similar charges. For example, one member of the Action Group was arrested for calling the NPC a "Pagan party."[21]

In addition to charges of verbal abuse and slander, NEPU members were frequently charged with "conduct likely to cause a breech of the peace." For example, in 1955 one Rabo Maroki was arrested for leading a group of NEPU supporters to shout slogans at and disturb a wedding made up largely of NPC supporters. Malam Maroki was arrested and charged with "disturbing the peace and annoying people" and sentenced to three years imprisonment (later reduced to one year on appeal). The conviction was based upon the *Liya' al-Hukkam*, Ch.5, Sect.2, P.59, which was quoted as stating "In order to protect people a ruler can impose punishment upon anyone who has uttered abusive language against other people."[22]

The fact that Maroki was not specifically charged with "conduct likely to cause a breach of the peace" is in itself important.[23] There was actually a fair degree

---

20. KSHCB, "Native Courts Policy and Instructions," KanoPrOf, R256/46, 26 January, 1956. See also *Nigerian Citizen*, 15 October, 1958.

21. *Northern Star*, 3 September, 1959.

22. KSHCB, "Northern Court of Appeal Findings, Maroki Vs. Kano NA," Criminal Appeal #K/58A/1955.

23. This is the formal terminology for the charge according to the British-Authored Nigerian Code of Law which was in force in the Western and Eastern Regions.

of doubt on the part of some senior Muslim jurists in the North regarding the basis for such charges in Islamic law. Such an interpretation of the law was not in the interest of the NPC or the British. This topic will be examined in detail in the next chapter. In any event, charges such as the example above became increasingly common throughout the period in question.

The final type of charge commonly faced by NEPU regarded the rules and regulations regarding political meetings. Such charges include holding political meetings without permits or of violating the conditions stipulated in permits that had been previously issued. Such conditions might include the time, place or size of a meeting, or even the topics to be discussed during the meeting. One permit issued to NEPU by the Misau Native Authority in 1958, for example, stipulated that "If the members of NEPU spoke against the Northern Nigeria government they should be arrested and taken to an alkali court."[24]

Again, it must be noted that while such cases do not immediately seem to involve what would be considered religious law by those not familiar with Islamic jurisprudence, they were tried as violations of Siyasa. In 1955, an alkali made the following remarks regarding a charge of meeting without a permit. "Since the case involves rules and orders they will be charged according to Siyasa. They have done what is prohibited without a permit." Those accused were convicted and each sentenced to 12 lashes before being released.[25]

While the charges discussed above make up the great majority of the type of cases which involved the political parties, the legal influence of the NPC was

---

24. *Daily Times*, 3 March, 1958. (Quoted from Sklar, *Political Parties*, p.361).

25. KSHCB, "Native Courts, Specific Cases and General Correspondence, 1948-1960," KanoPrOf, ACC/45, Agency Mark, R255, 27 October, 1955.

expressed in other ways. Charges such as that of heresy were sometimes leveled in courts, once against Aminu Kano on the grounds that he wore a NEPU emblem on his shirt while before an alkalai.[26] Further, the influence of the NPC extended not only to the courts but also to the writing of laws. For example, during the 1950's, the NPC was successful in passing laws in many parts of the North that restricted women's mobility by making it illegal for women to move about in public. This law, which was defended on the grounds that Islam required women to remain in kulle (seclusion) and also that it was needed to halt "declining morality" also helped the NPC in its goal of denying women suffrage in the Northern Region -- if women could not go out, they certainly could not be expected to vote.[27]

NEPU STRATEGIES AND COUNTERMEASURES

Clearly, the NPC's influence over the legal system of the region as discussed above provided the party with a powerful means by which to restrict the activities of its political adversaries. Members of NEPU (and other opposition parties) found their ability to meet, speak and act freely greatly limited by the NPC controlled courts, especially when the Native Authorities' control of the police and prison systems is also taken into account. NEPU, while certainly disadvantaged by the NPC's control over the region's legal institutions, made the best of the situation. Not only did NEPU seek to minimize the harm done by the courts via a number of maneuvers within the system, but the radicals also sought to use the NPC's abuses of the courts against the conservative party.

For the most part, the ability of NEPU members and supporters who were

---

26. Alan Feinstein, *African Revolutionary*, p.150

27. NAK, KanoPrOf, 2/73, PLT/5/154, "NEPU Complaints and Court Cases." The issue of women's political rights is discussed in detail in Chapter Four.

faced with charges to prove their innocence was rather limited.[28] Because the decision of the court was based solely upon the alkali in charge, and because these judges so frequently were slanted in favor of the NPC, there was often little that could be said or done by the accused to alter his or her fate. This dilemma was compounded by the fact that the alkali courts did not allow the presence of council, so defendants could only rely upon their own knowledge of the Shari'a for their defense. While those members of NEPU who possessed such skills, such as Aminu Kano and Lawan Danbazau, sometimes were able successfully to argue their own innocence, few rank and file NEPU supporters had such skills -- though members facing trial were often coached in relevant legal strategies. Still, the evidence of two witnesses was generally sufficient to convict the defendants of most of the sort of charges already discussed. Given the influence of the NPC, it was probably of little difficulty for two NPC supporters willing to accuse NEPU members of "slander" to be found. More to the point, NEPU members were often guilty of making none-to-favorable comments regarding various members of the NPC, since the party was famous for showing little respect towards those in power.

In such a situation, frequently the only hope for NEPU members was to appeal beyond the alkali court system. Up to 1958 this meant appeal to the British District Officer and Magistrate. From 1958 to 1960 appeals would first be heard by the Moslem Court of Appeals and after 1960 by the Shari'a Court of Appeals. When granted, these appeals had notable advantages. First, those hearing the appeals, whether the British or later the Khadi of the Shari'a appeals court, were often somewhat more removed from the immediate political conflict than were the alkalai of the lower courts. At the very least, those charged stood a good chance that their sentences would be reduced upon their appeal being heard. At best, those making the

---

28. On those rare occasions when NEPU members were acquitted of political charges, the party was careful to give the case as much publicity as possible. See for example the case of M. Garba Kano, *Daily Comet*, 12 May, 1960.

appeal could hope that their charge could be thrown out on the basis of some procedural error on the part of the _alkali_ court. The odds of such an outcome were further bolstered by the fact that the Magistrates' courts allowed the presence of council. In such events, NEPU made good use of its alliance to the Eastern-Based NCNC to garner the services of barristers well acquainted with the British Common Law system.

The fact that the British Magistrates generally judged their cases according to British Common Law was also of great significance to those making their appeal, since offenses were not always translatable from Shari'a (as practiced at the time) to Common law.[29] For example one NEPU member, Malam Adamu Gaya, was arrested and convicted on the charge of passing in front of the Gaya District Head (The _Hakima_ -- the head of the local Native Authority branch). According to local practice, Gaya should have bent at the waist and held his fist up in salute while waiting for the District Head to pass. To do otherwise, much less cut across the District Head's path, was a show of disrespect. On appeal to the British Magistrate, this case was quickly overturned.[30] Similarly, charges such as "abuse of the Sardauna," had little basis in the British legal system. On the other hand, a charge of "conduct likely to cause a breach of the peace" frequently met with steeper penalties under Common Law and as such appeals on such grounds were not so likely to be successful. There can be little doubt that NEPU members were well aware of how the different courts viewed most charges, and planned their defense and appeals accordingly.

The situation did change somewhat with the establishment of the Moslem

---

29. The British Magistrates could invoke either the Nigerian Criminal Code, the Shari'a or Common Law, but generally bowed to the latter, perhaps due to their greater familiarity with it.

30. *Daily Comet*, 20 June, 1960.

Court of Appeals and the subsequent Shari'a Court of Appeals. No longer were Shari'a-based cases to be heard by the Magistrate, but rather they were sent to a special appeals court in Kaduna. Up to 1960 this greatly limited the success of appeals, and many NEPU members favored "opting out", of the Shari'a courts rather than face trial or appeal within them. This issue will be discussed in more detail shortly. Upon the establishment of the Shari'a Court of Appeals in 1960, though, NEPU experienced a change in fortune. Perhaps due to the fact that it was institutionally separate from the Native Authority system, the Shari'a Court of Appeals showed marked independence from political control, and frequently upheld the appeals of NEPU members. As stated by Shaykh Abubakar Gumi, who served as the Court's Deputy and later as Grand Khadi:

> NEPU too used the courts against the traditional rulers whenever it favored it to do so. This became more frequent particularly when the party discovered the impartiality of the Shari'a Court of Appeal. NEPU was almost always willing to provide undercover support to have an appeal sent to us in Kaduna, especially where the case was first heard in the Emir's court and there were good grounds for appeal.[31]

As can be seen from the above examples, appeals sometimes offered NEPU an opportunity at least to blunt the impact of the NPC's influence over the alkali courts. In the great bulk of political court cases appeals were generally not an option. This was largely because cases that originated with junior alkalai (less that grade A and A Limited) could not be appealed beyond the Emir's court unless the fine exceeded twenty-five pounds or the sentence was greater than six months. Since most political offenses did not exceed these levels, many active NEPU members found themselves faced with recurrent low-level convictions with very few avenues

---

31. Gumi, *Where I Stand*, p.83.

of recourse.[32] In many cases the process of appeal was so cumbersome that by the time the necessary documents, such as transcripts of the original trial, had been collected, the accused had often already served his or her sentence.[33] Further, as NEPU became more adept at overcoming such obstacles, the alkalai modified their sentences to render appeals less effective. For example, caning became increasingly common as punishment for political offenses over the course of the 1950's. Since punishment was given immediately after conviction, appeals were of little use in such circumstances.[34]

In such a situation, particularly during the period of 1958-1960 (when appeals went to the Moslem Court of Appeals in Kaduna), appeals offered little hope for NEPU members faced with trial in the alkali courts. It was during this period that the tactic of "opting out" became common. This tactic had its origin in the Minorities Commission Report of 1956 and the Panel of Jurists Report of 1958, both of which had suggested that non-Muslims be given the right to "opt out" of the Shari'a court system and have their cases heard either in a "Mixed Court" (which judged cases based on the Nigerian Criminal Code) or by the British Magistrate.[35] Upon the enactment of the option, all alkalai were required to enquire the religion of defendants in their court and ask if they consented to their case being judged according to Shari'a law.[36] NEPU members were quick to take advantage of this situation, and shortly after the option became official, NEPU defendants, some as

32. Sklar, *Nigerian Political Parties*, p.357.

33. *Daily Comet*, 20 June, 1960.

34. Such practices on the part of the alkali courts were not always undertaken with the approval of the British colonial officials. The practice of caneing political offenders in particular met with British disfavor. The conflict between the British and traditional authorities regarding this topic will be examined in detail in the next chapter.

35. KSHCB, "Native Courts, Policy and Instructions, 10 September, 1958.

36. KSHCB, Native Courts Policy and Instructions, 21/2/206, 13 August, 1959.

prominent as Malama Gambo Sawaba, head of the NEPU women's wing, were claiming to be Christians so as to have their cases heard by the British Magistrate rather than by the alkali.[37]

The NPC and the alkali courts were greatly frustrated by NEPU's "opting out" tactics, often to the amusement of the NEPU members. Doubtless, most alkalai were familiar enough with the local NEPU members to know who were Muslims and who were not. Lawan Danbazau, one of NEPU's advisers on Islamic Law, stated:

> [Many] people pretended to be Christians in the Emirs court. Certainly he knew that the plaintiffs were lying just to escape judgement. It was very funny to see somebody with a beard and babbar riga [traditional Hausa dress] calling himself a Christian.[38]

Some alkali tried to dissuade the defendants from such a strategy by pointing out that if they were no longer Muslims they could not inherit from their Muslim parents.[39] Such tactics do not seem to have been very effective, though. In frustration, some alkalai went ahead and sentenced the defendants, even after they had claimed to be Christians. Such cases were almost always overthrown on appeal.[40]

One story from the period involves nearly a dozen NEPU members who were all faced with charges in the Emir of Kano's court. All but one "opted out" and that

---

37. *Daily Times*, 7 August, 1959. Interestingly, the British Resident of Kano Province had foreseen the potential for just such a strategy on the part of the NEPU. The British role in this issue will be dealt with in detail in the next chapter.

38. Lawan Danbazau, 20 January, 1993.

39. Alhaji Baba dan Agundi, (Sarkin Dawaki Mai Tuta), 4 April, 1993.

40. *Daily Comet*, 6 April, 1960.

individual, himself a <u>malam</u> (religious scholar) was released by the Emir for being so forthright. The NPC later made the most of the situation by writing a song that stated 'the NEPU is no more, all the members have converted to Christianity save one.'[41]

Certainly, the decision to claim to be a Christian was not to be taken lightly by devout Muslims. NEPU members justified the action on the grounds that they feared for their lives at the hands of the <u>alkalai</u>. As one NEPU legal adviser stated:

> Allah has even said that if one wants to make you suffer and wants to kill you, you may hide your religion. So that is why we pretended to be Christians, because if not we may have been killed.[42]

While it is possible that the practice of "opting out" was in some ways damaging to NEPU in that the party gained a great deal of its legitimacy from its claim to superior piety, during the latter 1950's the party seemed to have few other options within the legal system other than to the undesirable course of simply accepting what the <u>alkali</u> courts dealt out. Those in power certainly found the tactic to be very troublesome. In August of 1960, the Native Courts Amendment Law gave the Resident of the Province the

> power to send back, for trial before any <u>alkali</u>, any person has made any false statement about his religion with the purpose of obstructing or delaying the course of justice or for any other improper purpose.[43]

---

41. Interview with Alhaji Mudi Sipikin, 12 January, 1993.

42. Alhaji Baba dan Agundi (<u>Sarkin Dawaki Mai Tuta</u>), 4 April, 1993.

43. *Daily Comet*, 30 August, 1960.

This development effectively ended the period of "opting out." Perhaps as a means of warning its members, NEPU printed the text of the new law in the party paper, the *Daily Comet*.[44]

The above examples make it clear that while at a distinct disadvantage at the hands of the alkali courts, NEPU was not altogether helpless. Still, such tactics as appeals and "opting out" were really merely defensive strategies that only served to blunt the advantage the NPC gained from its institutional influence over the Shari'a legal system. Outside of the legal system, though, NEPU did its best to utilize the alleged NPC abuse of the Shari'a to its own advantage. As already stated, adherence to and support for the Shari'a is a standard yardstick by which Muslim governments are judged. As such, a central theme of NEPU speeches and editorials were the abuses of the alkali courts. By calling attention to the NPC's alleged misuse of the Shari'a and alkali courts, NEPU could hope to undermine the party's religious legitimacy.

NEPU focused a great amount of energy at attacking the alkalai themselves. Many of these judges, stated NEPU, had only a cursory knowledge of the Shari'a, and as such were not making judgements in proper accordance with Islamic law.[45] Heavy play was given to such accusations in the NEPU party newspaper. As one editorial stated:

> These days you can scarcely find a Judge who is using the divine laws (Islamic Laws) as his source of adjudication, so as such we are calling on those in authority to please sew fine robes for the alkalai just like the robes of the [British] Magistrates.[46]

---

44. Ibid.

45. NAK, "NEPU File, 1957-1962," PRE/3, ACC/121, Agency Mark ASI/918.

46. Mohammad Danjani Hadejia, *Daily Comet*, 28 April, 1960.

NEPU also made use of public forums to make legal arguments that could not be made (at least not effectively) in court. For example, in an editorial entitled "In the Case of the Shari'a," Aminu Kano stated that while one Rabo Marokin Sawa had been sentenced to three years imprisonment on the charge of insulting the Emir, if his case had been tried according to the *Muwadda Malik*, he would have been acquitted.[47] Indeed, NEPU frequently made the argument that Muslim leaders were not above public remonstration as was suggested by the alkali courts' rulings. Rather, if traditional and NPC leaders could not tolerate criticism, they had no place in politics.[48]

NEPU also sought to draw public attention towards the harsh sentences imposed by many of the alkalai. One judge in Katsina was dubbed "Malam Bulala" (Mr. Whip) in *Daily Comet* headlines in an attempt to scandalize his frequent use of lashing for seemingly minor political offenses. A lecture on the subject of this judge was even organized at the Rex Cinema in Kano.[49] A similar case, where a leader of the Bornu Youth Movement (which was allied to NEPU up to 1958) was sentenced 80 strokes for a political offence, was also taken up by NEPU. After NEPU members distributed photographs of the BYM leader's wounds at the 1958 Nigerian Constitutional Conference, the alkali was reportedly suspended.[50]

NEPU was willing to take advantage of just about any means to threaten the

---

47. *Daily Comet*, 18 November, 1958.

48. Aminu Kano, *Daily Times*, 19 November, 1957. Taken from Sklar, *Nigerian Political Parties*, p.262, fn#78.

49. *Daily Comet*, 23 November, 1960.

50. *Daily Service*, 8 October, 1958 and *Nigerian Citizen*, 15 October, 1958. Taken from Sklar, *Nigerian Political Parties*, p.364, fn#83.

position of alkalai who they viewed as slanted towards the NPC. When an alkali in the service of the Hadejia Native Authority divorced a couple and then "proceeded to live in adultery with the woman" NEPU publicized the scandal in its mass meetings. Eventually, the Emir of Hadejia dismissed the judge and the court had to be closed temporarily.[51]

NEPU did not only attack the practitioners of the law in the region, though, but also directed their attack on the very interpretation of the law. The NPC, stated NEPU, was only maintaining a long-standing practice of abusing the law for the benefit of the ruling class of Masu Sarauta. The more repressive and conservative an interpretation of the law, the better it was for those in power. Thus, claimed such NEPU legal advisers as Lawan Danbazau, the abuse of the Shari'a, and in particular the Maliki school of law, could be traced back to the moral decay of the leaders of the Sokoto caliphate.[52] Further, stated NEPU, the British had encouraged the traditional leaders in their abuse of the Shari'a, as long as it helped consolidate their power -- particularly against radicals such as NEPU. As one insightful editorial stated:

> The government of Northern Nigeria under the NPC party seized the opportunity to promulgate obnoxious laws in the name of tradition and religion with the full cooperation of the European Colonial administration, with the sole objective of eliminating the opposition parties. They took the opportunity to use the alkali courts and the [Native Authority] police to intimidate and harass political opponents. All these criminal acts were done under the cover of Islamic tradition. This led to the direct involvement of the alkalai in the giving of biased judgements in order to safeguard their continued employment.[53]

---

51. KSHCB, Northern Region Intelligence Survey, February-March, 1958.

52. *Daily Comet*, 15 June, 1960. For more information on this topic, please see Chapter One.

53. *Daily Comet*, 16 June, 1960.

Such practices on the part of the NPC, maintained NEPU, were causing severe damage to the prestige of Islam, by convincing many that Islam was a cruel and oppressive religion rather one of justice. Malam Lawan Danbazau, one of the NEPU's key advisers on Islamic Law, laid out this argument in a series of editorials entitled "Musulunci Ya Hadu Da Sharrin NPC" (Islam Confronts the Evil Machinations of the NPC).

> The continued oppressive rule by the NPC has lead to a general atmosphere of insecurity in the whole Northern Region. Many Northerners, especially the non-Muslims living in the former provinces of Plateau, Benue, and Kabba soon started to hate Islam and its system of administration. They thought that the alkali courts are honestly applying the Shari'a. They seriously fear and hate anything to do with Islam, since Islam seems to mean automatic conviction without trial. They think that Islam condones all the wicked acts of the NPC-dominated Islamic courts, especially since the leaders of the system claim to be devout Muslims.[54]

Not only did such actions hurt the reputation of the NPC among non-Muslims, but Malam Danbazau even suggested that the oppressive tactics of the NPC were leading people to turn away from Islam. In a clear reference to the practice of "opting out," a NEPU editorial stated:

> The only way one can safeguard his life and property now in the North is to declare openly that he is a Christian... only non-Muslims can walk anywhere in the country without fear of intimidation by supporters of the ruling party.[55]

Such a situation was leading some individuals to renounce Islam altogether, claimed Malam Danbazau. "All these things are on the head of the leaders of this country

---

54. *Daily Comet*, 17 January, 1960.

55. *Daily Comet*, 18 January, 1960.

who call themselves Muslims."[56]

CONCLUSIONS

This chapter provides a particularly telling view of the theme of conflict between the NPC's control over religious institutions and NEPU's control of the ideological high ground. Clearly, the advantages gained by the NPC in using the courts against its political enemies are much more easily identified and quantified than is the ideological benefit garnered by the NEPU in their attempts to highlight the abuses and use them to undermine the conservative party's claim to religious legitimacy. Perhaps of greatest disadvantage to NEPU was the fact that the <u>alkali</u> courts were probably acceptable to the bulk of the population as long as the cases were not political in nature. Only when one challenged those in power were the courts a threat. Such a situation, of course, perfectly served the needs of the NPC and traditional rulers.

The polyvalent nature of justice in the Northern Region, though, was certainly a mixed blessing for the NPC and the colonial rulers. Within these multiple systems of justice, the legal acumen and maneuvering of the NEPU caused a great deal of trouble for those in power. Still, NEPU also found itself disadvantaged by the multiple systems of legal codes. The numerous systems of legal ideology operating in the North muddied the political waters by giving all the parties and colonial rulers multiple sets of values to draw upon and to invoke. In such a setting, the various systems of law became tools which the various players drew upon and invoked depending on which system provided the greatest immediate advantage -- rather than reflecting the norms and values of the society.

---

56. *Daily Comet,* 19 January, 1960.

Such a situation was increasingly unsatisfactory for all concerned, and steps were taken to establish a single legal code. These changes to the system of Shari'a law in the North had very real impact on the position and practice of Islamic law in the North, and will be examined in detail in the next chapter.

CHAPTER THREE:

POLITICS AND THE SHARI'A:
REINTERPRETATION AND REORGANIZATION

As evidenced in the previous chapter, the structure of the North's legal system created a situation wherein the courts became a major arena in which the political conflict between the NPC and NEPU was waged. This conflict though, revealed many of the inherent flaws in the region's dual legal system. The fact that NEPU was frequently able to use the dual court system to its own advantage was of no small concern to the NPC and the British colonial government. As a result, the period from 1950 to 1966 saw numerous changes in the legal system of the North, both in terms of the very nature of the law and the judicial structure. This chapter examines how the British colonial government, the NPC and NEPU viewed and interpreted the Shari'a and how these interpretations, combined with each group's political agendas, led to extensive reorganizations of the region's legal system and a redefinition of the place of the Shari'a within that legal system.

FLAWS IN THE SYSTEM

Each of the groups involved with the legal system during the period in question, NEPU, NPC and the British, considered that legal system to be deeply flawed, albeit for very different reasons. NEPU viewed the system as primarily serving the entrenched interests of the Masu Sarauta in general and the NPC in particular. The NPC, on the other hand, was greatly frustrated by NEPU's ability frequently to utilize the dual court system to evade control by means of such techniques as appeal and "opting out." For their own part, the British were also unhappy with the legal system they oversaw. The British were concerned with the ability of NEPU to continue its "subversive" activities despite the efforts to constrain them via the alkali courts. The use of the traditional courts helped insulate the British from the actual repression of the NEPU party. When NEPU successfully won appeals or forced its cases to be heard by the British Magistrate via such techniques as "opting out," the colonial rulers were forced either to act in a repressive manner themselves or to grant NEPU a court victory. Generally, the later course was taken, much to the distaste of the British officers. To further complicate the issue the British could not afford to allow the alkali courts to become too overtly oppressive of dissenting political voices. In order to maintain the ideology of Indirect Rule, the British colonial administrators sought to appear both impartial toward and outside of the Shari'a legal process. Thus, the colonial officers frequently found themselves walking a tightrope of their own making -- encouraging the alkali courts to limit disruptive political activity, but trying to keep them from doing so in a manner that might undermine their legitimacy. The frustration of the British is well described in the following passage by the British Resident of Kano regarding a case where NEPU had brought charges of assault against a NPC supporter.

> This case was typical of the inability of the Hadejia Native Courts to deal impartially with cases of a political background. [The alkali] had been told by the NPC that if he convicted the accused he would gain the displeasure of the Emir and myself [the British Resident of Kano province] and he had also been told by the NEPU that if he did not impose the most fearful penalties he would be in trouble with NEPU's lawyers. His court had developed into a political debating society

rather than a Court of Law.[1]

The fact that the British resident stressed the inability of the courts to deal properly with political cases is important. As previously noted, the alkali courts were probably relatively effective in dealing with civil and criminal cases that made up the bulk of their duty. The region's traditional judges were no doubt well-versed and in general agreement regarding the place of such matters within the Shari'a. Political cases, though, concerning such elements as the right of opposition politicians to attack verbally those in power or hold spontaneous political meetings, were well outside the range of experience of the region's alkalai. Prior to the formation of the NPC and NEPU, these Islamic judges had not been called upon to deal with Western-style competitive politics with all its related accusations and character assaults. Given that the alkalai clearly shared many interests with the NPC and the Masu Sarauta, it is hardly surprising that they reacted to the NEPU's attacks on these groups with an interpretation of the Shari'a that was decidedly conservative in that it helped to preserve the political status-quo of the region.[2] Still, there were cases where the alkalai and other legal scholars were not willing to provide convictions for the opposition party members accused of political offenses. Such a situation, however, did not always meet the needs of the British colonial rulers, who took steps to amend the situation in their own favor.

BRITISH ROLES AND PERSPECTIVES

It should be noted that the British were initially reluctant to undertake any radical reorganization of the region's legal system. Because of their ideological and institutional investment in the system of Indirect Rule, the British colonial officers

---

1. KSHCB, "Northern Region Intelligence Survey," October-November, 1958.

2. See Chapter Two for a detailed discussion of such matters.

were at great pains to show the efficacy of the traditional courts (and their parental Native Authority structure) in dealing with all the demands that could be placed upon them. To admit that the <u>alkali</u> courts could not effectively or objectively deal with political cases was to admit that the system was not really able to function in a modernizing Nigeria -- and in so doing admit the failure of Indirect Rule. As such, the British took various steps to react to the complications brought on by the dual court system and the advent of party politics. The first step taken by the British was to try and provide the region's <u>alkalai</u> with a framework for dealing with political cases under Shari'a law, though with a bias towards the sort of interpretation that suited the needs of those in power. Later, the British undertook institutional reforms that sought to amend the flaws inherent in the dual court system through the establishment of appeals courts which ruled according to the Shari'a and later with the creation of a comprehensive Penal Code.

One of the first and most basic steps taken by the British to deal with the problems created by NEPU was to monitor political cases carefully and guide the proceedings as they saw fit. Thus, the Colonial rulers hoped to limit the ability of NEPU to manipulate the system. This practice is illustrated in the following memo issued to District Officers.

> His Honour [the Civil Secretary] wishes the greatest care to be exercised in handling cases in Native Courts where persons are charged with crimes connected with the flouting of rules or orders of Native Authorities. It should be made known to Native Authorities in suitable terms that where prosecutions of this sort are imminent, the advice of the District Officer must be sought and if necessary, of the Resident with regard to the legal aspects of the case in terms of Nigerian Law. This particularly concerns the present campaigns being organized by such bodies as NEPU. Unless a case is handled correctly, there is always the possibility that a conviction will be upset on appeal or on a technical point. These subversive and semi-

subversive bodies normally have legal advice available to them.[3]

A common problem for the British involved the granting of bail to accused NEPU members. The alkalai were often unwilling to grant bail to members of the opposition while awaiting appeals to be heard. As such, even if their cases were overturned, NEPU members were often spending periods of some weeks in jail. It was difficult for the British not to recognize such examples of NPC abuse of the court system, and NEPU followed up such cases with numerous demands for redress from the British officers. Only by carefully overseeing the practices of the courts could the British hope to avoid such predicaments.[4]

British colonial officers, though, could not afford the time to oversee every single political case. One alternative was to prepare the alkalai better for the task at hand. Central to this goal was the Kano School for Arabic Studies (SAS). Though originally established in 1934 (under the name of the Kano Law School), the School for Arabic Studies took on ever-expanding duties to educate the region's judiciary, particularly during the 1950's. Interestingly, the teaching staff was imported to Kano from Khartoum.[5] By overseeing the education of the region's alkalai, the British were able to influence the nature of that education. There is little doubt that the British encouraged a rather conservative and state-friendly interpretation of the Shari'a in relation to political matters.[6] One document in particular is illustrative of this tendency on the part of the British. Assembled under the direction of C.V. Wilson, the Resident of Zaria Province, and entitled "The Provisions in the Criminal Code for

---

3. KSHCB, "Native Courts, Specific Cases and General Correspondence, 1948-1960." ACC/45, Agency Mark, R-256, April, 1953.

4. NAK, "NEPU Complaints and Court Cases," KanoPrOf 2/73, ACC/1299, Agency Mark, PLT/5, 23 June, 1955.

5. Paden, Religion and Political Culture, p.63.

6. NAK, "School for Arabic Studies, Policy," MakPrOf/1, Acc/48, Agency Mark, 72, Vol.II.

the Punishment of Subversive Activities and their Equivalent in Moslem Law," this classified circular was little more than a guideline for the alkalai on how to prosecute NEPU for political offenses under Shari'a law. The format of the document is laid out for easy reference. Broadly defined categories of undesirable behavior, such as "uttering seditious or near-seditious words," are cross-listed with the suitable charges under both British Common Law and the Shari'a. Examples of actual cases involving NEPU are given for each of the charges. One such example of "uttering seditious or near-seditious words" that was cited by Wilson was a statement by Aminu Kano on 10 March 1953, when Kano "advised anyone arrested by Police to retaliate violently against any violence by Police."[7] All such broad offense categories, case examples, and British legal charges were provided to the Wazirin Zaria (the Adviser on Islamic Law to the House of Chiefs), who was asked to fill in the appropriate charge under Shari'a law.[8]

Wilson was very much aware of the implications of this document, both in regards to its clear bias against NEPU and in terms of their approach to the Shari'a. On a cover letter attached to copies distributed to the provincial Residents he stated

> This compendium is to be used with discretion; that is to say, Administrative Officers must be circumspect in handling each case as it occurs. His Honour wishes to emphasize that there is no necessity for it to become obvious that alkali (sic) or Native Authorities are referring matters to the Administration to an excessive degree. Quite apart from this, Administrative Officers have powers of review at any stage of proceedings and, the objective being to see that justice is done and that peace is maintained, it is not considered that we need be over-nice.[9]

---

7. NAK, ZarPrOf., C.68, Security, 276/103, 26 April, 1954.

8. Ibid.

9. NAK, ZarPrOf., C.68, Security 276/103, 14 June, 1954.

There can be little doubt that once widely circulated (the compendium was eventually translated into Hausa and distributed to higher-level <u>alkalai</u>) this document was instrumental in influencing the interpretation of the Shari'a in respect to political matters.

Not all went to the liking of the British colonial authorities in the creation of the compendium, though. In particular, the staff of the British Civil Secretary's office were dismayed when informed by the Wazirin Zaria that no real charges existed for certain offenses that had been targeted by the colonial rulers. Among these include "Incitement to Disobedience," "Undermining the Lawful Power of Native Authority," "Incitement not to pay Tax," and "Incitement to Refuse Orders of the N.A." Rather, the Waziri stated that:

> NEPU members have committed no crime in this case, since they did not themselves commit any offence nor did they force anyone else to commit an offence.[10]

The Waziri made similar comment regarding the issue of Aminu Kano's call to meet police violence with violence.[11]

> Whoever follows his advice and resists should be punished for treating court assistants with contempt. But Aminu has committed no offence.[12]

The Waziri's comments reflects one of the basic themes of the Shari'a -- a strong emphasis on personal responsibility. Thus, the only party responsible for a

---

10. NAK, ZarPrOf., C.68, Security, 276/103/s./1-8.

11. See page 8.

12. Ibid.

crime is the one who commits the crime, and incitement to commit a crime is in itself not a valid charge. Thus, such common NEPU tactics as encouraging the populace to ignore orders issued by the Native Authority, to refuse the obligation of aikin tilas (forced labor) or not to pay taxes, could be undertaken without fear of prosecution under the Shari'a. Those individuals who took the advice of NEPU could be held accountable, but the NEPU members themselves could not.

The motivations of the Wazirin Zaria are not clear in the document. Certainly he would have improved his position with the British administration had he been more cooperative (see below). There is no evidence of NEPU sympathy on the Waziri's part. Some evidence does suggest rivalry between the Zaria Native Authority and the largely Sokoto-based power of the NPC during the early 1960's, but this does not adequately explain the Waziri's actions in 1954.[13] Most likely, the Waziri was motivated first and foremost by a dedication to a strict interpretation of the Shari'a as he understood it.

Whatever the Waziri's reasoning, such a situation was clearly undesirable to the British and the NPC, who would much rather have dealt with the problem at the source by forcing the NEPU to refrain from such activities. The Sardauna issued a public statement which made the NPC's stand on "incitement" perfectly clear.

> I feel that some Native Authorities do not at present realize their full
> responsibilities for the maintenance of Law and Order. Individuals
> occasionally make subversive statements or remarks likely to lead to
> a breach of the peace and too often these are ignored by the Native
> Authority.[14]

---

13. The Zaria Native Authority was audited by the Northern Region government in 1961. This was a standard technique by which the Native Authorities could be disciplined, since few could account for all their financial expenditures. A similar inquiry led to the resignation of Emir Sanusi of Kano in 1963 (see Chapter Six). See Amune, *Work and Worship*, pp.161-166.

14. *Nigerian Citizen*, 10 June, 1954.

Within a week of the Sardauna's statement, a member of the Civil Secretary's staff, J.C.H. Farmer, took the matter up personally with the Waziri.

> Realizing that the Waziri's comments as they stand would be very disappointing to the [Civil Secretary], I discussed the whole matter at length with him in an attempt to arrive at something more helpful, but the result was not encouraging.[15]

Farmer was disturbed to hear that at best an individual charged with such examples of "Incitement" could only be punished "provided that the offence is a particularly serious one" and that even in such cases the punishment will be slight -- possibly no more than a reprimand.[16] Faced with such a situation, the Civil Secretary's office issued a memo to all District Officers outlining their dilemma. Having established (and lamented) that there existed no clear provisions for prosecution of "incitement" under the Shari'a, the memo closed with the following statement:

> From this note it appears best to deal with cases of incitement or action liable to cause a breach of the peace under the relevant sections of the Criminal Code rather than under Moslem Law.[17]

In other words, British officers (who had the right to invoke either Shari'a Law, the Nigerian Criminal Code, or British Common Law) were simply directed to charge NEPU members by an additional set of rules in order to assure conviction in such situations. This opportunity, though, was available only to the British when hearing appeals or when Officers chose to review cases that were sub judice in the alkali courts (the latter being undesirable in that it was rather a transparent example of the

---

15. NAK, ZarPrOf, C.68, Security 276/121, 17 June, 1954.

16. Ibid.

17. NAK, ZarPrOf., c.68, Security 276/144, 24 September, 1954.

British anti-NEPU bias). As the decade of the 1950's progressed, though, such tactics proved increasingly unnecessary. Over the course of this period, the alkalai showed an increasing willingness to convict NEPU supporters on grounds of "incitement" despite the rather weak basis for such charges under the Shari'a. Such a tendency was likely a result both of the closeness of the alkalai to the NPC and Native Authorities as well as the tacit approval of the British for such steps. Speaking on this subject, Tanko Yakasai, a NEPU leader, states:

> [The British officers] were inspecting the courts and they had the power to review judgements passed by the courts. The alkalai, including the Emirs, were very much sensitive to what the reaction of the British officers would be. They had in mind whether what they would do would meet the approval of the British officers or not. The British were in a position to influence matters directly and indirectly.[18]

It was not always necessary for the colonial administrators to encourage a more conservative interpretation of the Shari'a. Indeed, in some political matters the British officers found themselves trying to mute the sometimes harsh tendencies of the alkali courts. The use of lashings as punishment for political offenses was a case in point. While the British did not absolutely oppose the use of lashing, they did become embroiled in a conflict with the Kano Native Authority (headed by Emir Sanusi) regarding how many lashes were allowed under the Shari'a. No doubt the concerns of the British were made all the more pressing by the fact that such punishments were given heavy play by NEPU as examples of the harshness of NPC rule. One case in particular, where five NEPU members were given up to two dozen lashes each after being convicted of "holding a political meeting without a permit and of flouting the authority of the district head" was heavily publicized by NEPU. The case prompted a call on the Emir by the British Resident of Kano, R.E. Greswell.

---

18. Alhaji Tanko Yakasai, 19 May, 1994.

I spoke to the Emir about this case and pointed out to him that he had no power, except in the case of Haddi [criminal] punishments, to award more than twelve strokes to a single person at any one trial. He said that he and his advisers had looked up the laws and had deduced from them that they were empowered to award twelve strokes on each charge. I warned the Emir about how careful he should be and how a false move on his part would lay him open to a suit for damages in the Supreme Court.[19]

The Emir, in response, protested that he was in no legal danger, at least not under Islamic Law, and cited the *Tabsirat al-Hukkam*, Vol. 2, Ch. II, in his own defense.[20]

Should the Emir punish a man and the man dies consequent to the punishment there will be nothing against the Emir and neither Blood Money nor atonement. This is contrary to penalty (Haddi). Should the man die consequent to penalty there will be nothing against the Emir [Emir Sanusi's emphasis] for he has carried out the command of God.[21]

This exchange makes clear that while the British were the ultimate arbiters of justice in the region and had clear influence over the way in which the Shari'a was interpreted and applied, their authority was by no means complete or without question in such matters. The above example is, though, an exception to the general theme of interaction between the British and the NPC. For the most part, there was little conflict between the colonial officers in Nigeria and the NPC in terms of their approach to the Shari'a. Both groups had basically the same goal, which was to equate disrespect for the traditional authority with disrespect for Islam, and to enforce this association by way of the Shari'a courts. With the assistance of the British, the alkali courts became the apparatus through which the NPC could limit opposition

---

19. KSHCB, "Native Courts Policy and Instructions," 29 June, 1956.

20. A text of Maliki Law.

21. KSHCB, "Native Courts Policy and Instructions," 29 June, 1955.

activity and punish those who attacked the party's claim to religious legitimacy.

It should be noted that the influence of the British regarding the interpretation of the Shari'a was not limited only to political matters. The closeness of the British officers to the various Native Authorities (engendered by decades of Indirect Rule), combined with the officers' duty of reviewing the activities of the Native Authority councils, had the potential for drawing the British into even the most mundane of affairs involving the Shari'a. A particular case in point occurred in Maiduguri Province in the middle 1950's, when the Divisional Officer of Bornu Division, M.J. Bennion, and his staff became embroiled in a dispute over the nature of punishment suitable for Muslims convicted of drinking beer. After extensive consultation with the Waziri of Bornu, and despite none-to-favorable press accounts, the British Resident's office supported legislation placing strict controls on those establishments serving alcohol and extremely harsh punishments for Muslims convicted of drinking.[22] Interestingly, while the British were concerned about the harshness of penalties dealt out to political offenders, they had no problem with Muslims convicted of drinking alcohol being given up to eighty lashes by alkali courts.[23] This case highlights the British tendency to live up to their official laissez fare approach to religious issues only when no political issues were at stake.

MODIFICATIONS TO THE SYSTEM

Despite the efforts of the colonial administration in Nigeria and the NPC in promoting a very state-friendly interpretation of the Shari'a in the alkali courts,

---

22. See for example, *Daily Service*, "80 Strokes for Drinking," 18 August, 1954; *Daily Times*, "No Beer in Islam," 16 March, 1955; and *Nigerian Citizen*, "Do Not Sell Beer to Muslims," 17 March, 1955.

23. NAK, "Drinking of Beer by Muslims," MaidugariProf., ACC/6237 Agency Mark, 106/40, 25 October, 1955.

NEPU was still not completely silenced. NEPU's ability to force appeals and hearings in the Magistrate courts in particular created problems for the British, since to avoid seeming openly hostile to the opposition party, the British Residents were forced frequently to overrule the decisions of the traditional judges. Such cases only provided NEPU with valuable political ammunition and a greater inclination to seek further appeals in the future. What was needed by the British administration and the NPC was a means of making the NEPU's appeals more difficult without undermining the position of the alkali courts or the Shari'a.

The embodiment of this desire was established in July of 1957 in the institution of the Moslem Court of Appeals. The new appeals court was "to hear appeals from Moslem Courts in Moslem cases."[24] Thus, appeals from the alkali courts no longer moved straight to the British Magistrate, but rather were handed over to the Moslem High Court of Appeals, based in Kaduna. The Moslem Appeals Court generally judged cases by the same conservative standards as did the lower courts and also did not allow the presence of council, as had the Magistrate courts. Not surprisingly, NEPU's ability to win cases on appeal was greatly reduced. In vain, NEPU called for the abolition of the Moslem Court of Appeals, on the grounds that the Magistrate courts had better served the needs of the people.[25] Only through the practice of "opting out" could Muslim members of NEPU avoid having their cases tried under the Shari'a as practiced in the region.

The most radical change in the region's legal system, though, was to come in 1960, on the eve of Nigerian independence. This change was the institution of the Northern Nigerian Penal Code. The Penal Code, which was proposed in January of 1958 and implemented in September of 1960 and which was based largely on the

---

24. *Daily Comet*, 27 July, 1957.

25. *Daily Times*, 3 March, 1958.

Code in force in the Sudan, brought several major changes to the structure of law in the region. In particular, only cases of civil nature were to be tried according to the Shari'a, with criminal and political cases being covered by the newly created Penal Code. The main goal of the Penal Code as stated was "to guarantee justice to all, despite diversity of racial origins and religious beliefs."[26] The Northern government took great pains to justify the Penal Code to the region's Muslim majority: "the code is acceptable to Moslems because it contains in it nothing that is offensive to or incompatible with the injunctions of the Holy Qur'an and Sunna."[27]

While the Penal Code was, no doubt, in many ways a reaction to the legitimate concerns of non-Muslims in the North (the great deal of attention given to this topic by the Minorities Commission Report in 1956 was probably largely responsible for the move), there were more immediate political concerns which the Code addressed. Not the least of these was the ongoing problem created by the region's dual legal system. Finally, only one legal system was in force in the region (except in civil cases, as stated above).

The Penal Code also brought about changes in the structure of appeals. Since Shari'a was only formally in force in civil cases, the Moslem Court of Appeals was restructured and renamed the Shari'a Court of Appeals. Likely in part because it was not expected to hear political cases, the new appeals court was institutionally separate from the Native Authority system. As such, NEPU found that the Shari'a Appeals Court was much more open to their arguments than had been the Moslem High Court of Appeals. Though the cases heard by the Shari'a Court of Appeals were supposed to deal only with civil matters, NEPU was still able to bring forth cases that could

26. *Nigerian Citizen*, 11 January, 1958.

27. NAK, "Statement of the Government of the Northern Region of Nigeria on the Reorganization of the Legal and Judicial Systems of the Northern Region. 1958," Policy Papers, ACC/334, Agency Mark, NCT/96.

prove embarrassing to the NPC and Native Authorities. One such case involved the seizure of an individual's house and land by the Hadejia Native Authority, on the grounds that they had been abandoned. The individual, who had been away two years, appealed to the Emir's court, but the case was upheld. NEPU, however, assisted the man in forwarding his case to the Shari'a Court of Appeals, which upheld his appeal on the grounds that land cannot be seized until it has been left vacant for ten years. Sheik Abubakar Gumi, deputy Grand Khadi of the court, commented on the political nature of this case as follows:

> Unfortunately, some powerful interests must have been involved in the case because someone promptly ran to complain to the Sardauna even as we were preparing our ruling. It was suggested to him that if we should be allowed to review the previous judgement given at the Emir of Hadejia's Court, we would not only put the Emir into ridicule, but all the other Emirs in the region as well. The Sardauna invited me to his house and wanted to know whether it was possible not to reject the Emir's ruling. My response was to ask him his reaction if the Magajin Gari of Sokoto had confiscated his own house in Sokoto and given it away. He understood and from then on made no further attempts to interfere again.[28]

The NPC was not completely disadvantaged by the new system. "Opting out," for example, was no longer possible under the unified Penal Code. Further, because of the complexity of the new system, a "interim period" of indeterminate length was declared during which time the alkalai would be "guided but not rigidly bound" by the new Code.[29] Such a situation clearly offered pro-NPC alkalai a great deal of latitude in their judgements -- particularly crucial as the parties vied for power on the eve of independence.

---

28. Gumi, *Where I Stand*, pp.84-85.

29. NAK, "Reorganization of the Legal and Judicial System of Northern Nigeria, 1958," Policy Papers, ACC/334, Agency Mark NCT/96.

NEPU REACTIONS

As has already been seen in the previous chapter, NEPU did not passively accept the NPC's control over and abuse of the legal system. While the in-court strategies of NEPU have already been examined in some detail, it is important to note that NEPU also attacked the very nature of the court system (particularly prior to the implementation of the Penal Code). Some within the NEPU camp even called for the alkali courts to be abolished as had been done in Nasser's Egypt (a common model for NEPU's vision of a progressive Islamic State). NEPU's leadership, particularly individuals such as Aminu Kano and Lawan Danbazau, recognized that such a move would be unacceptable to most of the region's populace and therefore stated that the courts should be placed under regional control (rather than under the control of their respective Native Authorities).[30] The alkali courts, as an institution, were not really to blame, stated NEPU, and a somewhat more liberal interpretation of the Qur'an was all that was needed. Such an approach, stated the party, would lead to very different conclusions regarding political issues.[31]

NEPU was realistic enough to accept that there was little chance of there being a major ideological shift on the part of the region's alkalai. Thus, the party placed much emphasis on calling for institutional changes that would limit the ability of the NPC to control the courts. As already mentioned, one such call was for the removal of the courts from the direction of the Native Authority system. Another common demand on the part of NEPU was for the codification of Islamic law as

---

30. *Nigerian Citizen*, 10 November, 1955. See also *Daily Times*, 7 March, 1957.

31. Paden, *Religion and Political Culture*, p.205.

practiced in Nigeria. NEPU hoped such a step would help end the courts' rather arbitrary approach to the Shari'a by forcing the <u>alkalai</u> to cite specific charges in each case.[32] As one NEPU editorial stated

> Those who call for [a uniform legal code] insisted that they are not against Maliki law, but against crooked interpretation of the Law. They want a uniform code for all the courts in Northern Nigeria under the great umbrella of Imam Maliki.[33]

Whenever possible, NEPU took the offensive against the NPC and accused the government of not being dedicated to the upholding of the Shari'a. An excellent example of such a case occurred in 1960, when an article appeared in the March 23rd edition of the Kano Native Authority's newspaper, *Sodangi* quoting a speech made by Emir Sanusi at the opening of a training course for the Kano area <u>alkalai</u>. On this occasion the Emir allegedly stated that the Maliki code of law was not suitable for the needs of the Northern Region in the modern era. Clearly, the speech and article were intended to help pave the way for the soon-to-be implemented Penal Code. NEPU, however, seized upon the Emir Sanusi's statement as evidence that the NPC was not loyal to the Shari'a. A NEPU editorial on the subject, entitled "What Stops Islamic Laws from Being in Conformity with Modernity?" stated as follows:

> In the address his Excellency [the Emir] said that the Maliki school of law does not conform with modern times. I was highly disgusted when I read what his Excellency wrote. As far as I am concerned, uttering such words will make the followers of other religions think that the Islamic religion is not able to be modern like other religions.[34]

---

32. *Daily Times*, 3 March, 1958.

33. *Daily Comet*, 22 June, 1960.

34. Mohammad Danjani Hadejia, *Daily Comet*, 27 April, 1960.

Indeed, this editorial was well in line with one of the NEPU's most common themes, that being the progressive nature of Islam. According to the NEPU's position, the laws of Islam were well suited to any time and situation, and any suggestion otherwise was an insult to the religion. Seemingly, the NEPU's attacks on the *Sodangi* article were effective. The NPC reportedly sought to buy up as many copies of the edition as possible (at prices of up to two shillings each) in order to limit the ability of NEPU to popularize the affair. Regarding such attempts, NEPU stated tauntingly

> We hereby pledge to hold firmly the newspaper called *Sodangi* of 23 March. We are holding it and we shall read it to those who cannot read. Nobody will ever tell us anything about NEPU being unIslamic again. It will expose the NPC's nonchalant attitude towards the religion of Islam.[35]

As the date for the implementation of the Penal Code drew near, a common theme for NEPU editorials was to attack the proposed legal system because it was not based wholly on the Shari'a.[36]

While NEPU was able to make some advantage of the move towards the Penal Code, the party was not prepared to condemn the Code outright. No doubt this was because the Code did indeed provide NEPU with one of its demands -- a unified and codified system of law for the Northern Region.

> One cannot say that the [Penal Code] system is completely bad and unjust to Northern Nigeria, especially when one thinks that when it is in effect it will be uniformly used throughout the region. There

---

35. Ibid.

36. See for example, "Penal Code Laws not in Conformity with the People of the Federal Republic of Nigeria, *Daily Comet*, 29 September, 1960.

will be no differences in judgements. More so, when it is in effect
where shall be no more judgements based on unwritten documents or
on the judge's instincts.[37]

As such, NEPU did its best to portray the Penal Code, once implemented, as a victory
for their party.

> [The Penal Code] is not strictly Islamic law, but can cover all aspects
> of ethics. We are happy. We are proud of our struggle. We achieved
> our objectives. In the future, no alkali will hide behind the smoke-
> screen of Islam to cheat and oppress people and declare he is doing
> it in the name of Islam.[38]

In general, the Penal Code seems to have been remarkable in terms of its
popularity with all of the parties involved, perhaps because each had, for their own
reasons, been dissatisfied with the old system to the point where any change was
likely to be considered an improvement. As Sklar stated in 1963, "These reforms,
achieved under conservative auspices, were a most hopeful augury for the future of
political democracy in the North."[39] Indeed, with the implementation of the Penal
Code, the level of competition between the NPC and NEPU in the region's courts was
greatly reduced.

CONCLUSIONS

Several points are evident from the preceding discussion. First, it is clear that
while the British colonial administrators took great pains to maintain an appearance

---

37. *Daily Comet*, 29 September, 1960.

38. *Daily Comet*, 22 June, 1960.

39. Sklar, *Nigerian Political Parities*, pp. 364-365.

of impartiality regarding the practice of the Shari'a in Northern Nigeria (an endeavor in which they were assisted by the NPC and Native Authorities), their influence was quite pervasive, particularly in political matters. Wherever possible, the British administrative officers sought to promote an interpretation of the Shari'a that supported their own political objectives -- most importantly the maintenance of the Northern Nigerian political status quo. Such tactics allowed the British to appear both removed from the contest for power in the North and sensitive to local religious concerns. When deemed necessary, such as in the cases of "incitement" examined in this chapter, the British officers were willing to intervene directly to further their own agendas. Such actions show dedication to neither political objectivity nor religious non-interference. Further, the difficulties of the colonial rulers in dealing with both the NEPU and NPC's desires to interpret and utilize the Shari'a as they saw fit points to the very real limitations on British power within the system of Indirect Rule in the latter colonial period.

The issue of British interference in religious issues (political or otherwise) has not been well addressed in the scholarly literature. No doubt this is largely due to the fact that the documents utilized in this chapter, being subject to the "thirty year rule," have only recently become available. Further, both the NPC and NEPU had their own reasons for downplaying the role of the British in legal matters.[40] As such, works based largely on oral data, such as most texts produced in the 1960's and 1970s, shed little light on the role of the British in the legal conflicts between the two parties. However, the efforts of the British colonial administration and the NPC in encouraging a particularly conservative and state-friendly interpretation of the Shari'a did not blunt the activities of NEPU as much as was hoped. Thus, it was necessary for those in power to pursue institutional changes that would further limit the range

---

40. The reasons for this downplaying of British influence are discussed in Chapter One "Party Politics and the Legacy of the Sokoto Caliphate" and Chapter Two "Courts and Politics."

of action of NEPU within the legal system. The introduction of the Penal Code presented something of a compromise, in which each party was able to claim a victory and many of the inherent failings of the dual court system were corrected. This case is one of the few examples during this period of the NPC and NEPU actually reaching a mutually acceptable middle ground on such a contentious political and religious issue.

CHAPTER FOUR:
ISLAM, POLITICS AND WOMEN'S RIGHTS

While the competition between the NPC and NEPU took many forms, perhaps no particular area of conflict brought the parties' ideological differences into such sharp contrast as did the question of women's political rights and roles. Although the debate was most vehement regarding whether women should be granted political rights such as suffrage and the holding of political office, it expanded to involve women's wider social roles and their status within society. Not surprisingly, the conservative NPC resisted the granting of real political rights to women and called for the maintenance of women's "traditional" roles. In contrast, NEPU declared that the time had come in Northern Nigeria for women to be freed of traditional roles and to take up new (political) responsibilities.

Although this conflict dealt with a contemporary political question, the debate itself was carried out almost completely in terms of Islamic ideology. The NPC maintained that Islam forbade women from taking part in most aspects of politics, while NEPU claimed that Islam allowed them a variety of political roles. In the course of this chapter, several questions will be addressed. First, what roles did women play in each of the political parties? What was each party's stand on women's suffrage and on such topics as women holding office? How was each stand justified in terms of Islamic ideology? What were the implications of each stand in terms of women's wider position within society? How did the debate reflect on the construction and perception of women's "traditional" roles? To answer these questions, this chapter examines both women's participation in various political activities and each party's stands on the issue of women's political rights during this time.

THE SETTING: WOMEN'S POLITICAL ROLES

Although the issue of women's political rights did not come to the forefront of political debate in the region until around 1956, both parties had established "women's wings" by the early years of the decade. The structure and activities of these organizations were very telling of the parties' coming stands on women's political rights. NEPU was the first party to involve women in the political process, with its women's wing being opened in Kano in 1953.[1] Even two years prior to this date, in 1951, a woman by the name of Gambo Sawaba was giving lectures at NEPU rallies in the city of Zaria, in part due to the fact she was fluent in Hausa, Ibo, Yoruba and Nupe. Even when not lecturing, she would frequently serve as an interpreter for other speakers.[2] The fact that NEPU gave such a prominent role to women in party activities helped draw other women into the political process. Because of the practice of kulle (purdah or wife seclusion), many women in the region could not attend such political rallies. Early female members of NEPU sought to overcome this barrier by moving from house to house in the region around Zaria and other cities to speak to secluded women.[3]

Such activities helped NEPU recruit female political activists in numbers

1. Sklar, *Nigerian Political Parties*, p.419.

2. Shawulu, *Gambo Sawaba*, pp.46-48.

3. Ibid, p.48.

great enough to warrant the formation of a NEPU women's wing within a couple of years of the party's founding. Alhaji Tanko Yakasai, an early NEPU organizer, states that wherever there was a NEPU branch, there was also a women's wing, which had its own compliment of leadership. The women members elected their own Chairman, Vice-Chairman, Secretary, Treasurer, etc. Each of these groups then elected representatives to the National women's wing.[4] In general, the women attracted to NEPU were young. Hajiya Jumai Wool, one of the first members of the NEPU women's wing in Kano reports that there were no members in her group over the age of thirty.[5] Many of the more promising members of the women's wing were schooled, in practical as well as political subjects, at the party's newspaper office in Zaria, where the *Daily Comet* newspaper was produced.[6] This practice was also indicative of NEPU's wider stance in favor of female education.

Largely because of their resistance to the idea of women taking active political roles, the NPC did not follow the NEPU's lead in actively seeking to recruit women into the party. Still, the leadership of the NPC recognized that NEPU was attracting the sympathy of a number of the region's women. As such, the party formed its own women's wing, complete with local branches. For the most part the membership of this wing was made up of relations and associates of the party's leaders. For example, in Kano, one of the leaders of the NPC women's wing was Ladi Kara, a "slave" of the Emir.[7] Another informant reports that the general procedure of the NPC was to appoint prominent local women as heads of the various branches of the women's wing, but that actual meetings among the wing's members

---

4. Alhaji Tanko Yakasai, 6 June, 1993.

5. Interview with Hajiya Jumai Wool, 5 June, 1993.

6. Shawulu, *Gambo Sawaba*, p.49.

7. Hajiya Jumai Wool, 5 June, 1993. The informant here used the word bawa, which is generally translated as "slave." It may very well be that Ladi Kara was one of the Emir's concubines.

were rare.[8] A 1957 newspaper article stated that the women's wing of the NPC in Maiduguri had collapsed when its membership fell to only two.[9]

As a result of the party's conservative stand towards women, members of the NPC's women's wings were not to be found lecturing at rallies or canvassing for support from house to house. The NPC's lackluster support for any kind of women's organization lasted through to the end of the First Republic. In 1963, the Sardauna of Sokoto was contacted by the Jamiyar Matan Arewa (Northern Women's Congress), a group of 60 women who sought to "bring together all women in the North in order to teach the reading and writing of English and general domestic science," and who explicitly foreswore any interest in politics. Despite these none-too-radical goals, the Sardauna agreed to patronage of their group only after they had sent repeated letters. Even so, a private note to his secretary stated that he did so "with reluctance." [10]

It should be noted that membership in women's wings was not the only political role played by women during the period. Women were a common fixture at political rallies for both parties, though the relationship between the parties and the women varied considerably. The mere presence of a number of women could help attract spectators to a political rally. As one NEPU supporter stated "we sang and danced and clapped our hands -- since we were young everyone was interested when we sang for NEPU."[11] The fact that the presence of young women tended to attract young men was not lost upon the leaders of the political parties. Though the activity seems to have been pioneered by NEPU, both parties made use of goge dancing to

---

8. Alhaji Tanko Yakasai, 6 June, 1993.

9. *Gaskiya,* 5 July, 1957.

10. NAK, "Northern Women Organizations,:" PRE/2, ACC/471, Agency Mark PRE/291, 8 September, 1963.

11. Hajiya Jumai Wool, 5 June, 1993.

attract potential party converts and raise funds. These dances, which centered around the goge, a single-stringed bowed instrument, were popular during the fifties and sixties. The parties sponsored concerts and charged admission. Hajiya Jumai stated that before the NPC copied the practice, they at first complained, because young male NPC supporters were being drawn to the NEPU events when "they saw the young women dancing and having fun."[12] This information was corroborated by Tanko Yakasai, who said "we used the goge dance to mobilize and recruit, and the younger elements of the women actually assisted in this work."[13]

The relationship between women and politics was not always as simple as having women act as a lure for potential male party members, for the parties often hired or coerced prostitutes to serve their supporters' sexual needs. Renee Pitten's research revealed that the NPC had an officer known as the "party manager," whose duty it was to see that prostitutes "complied with party directives." Further, it was his job to see to the women's transport, food and accommodation during political tours. Pitten continues on to state:

> Almost all the karuwai [prostitutes] were involved in the political campaigns (there was little choice), and the campaigns were in support of the NPC. Women who supported other political parties, such as NEPU or NCNC, were usually induced to change their alliances or move elsewhere. The party provided tangible support for the karuwai, although periodically it would express condemnation of the women, and withhold the largess the women had come to expect, and for which they worked. There was generally an understanding between the karuwai and the NPC organizers that if the karuwai cooperated with the Party, the Party would show its appreciation in terms of financial support and positive social sanctions. It was an article of faith of the time that "siyasa sai da mace" (Politics cannot

---

12. Ibid.

13. Alhaji Tanko Yakasai, 6 June, 1993.

exist without women).[14]

It is important at this point to examine just exactly what is implied by the term "karuwai." The most common translation for this word is indeed "prostitute" as utilized by Pitten above, but it is also frequently applied to women who chose to live outside contemporary social mores. Hence, women who attended party rallies or goge dances were almost certainly regarded as karuwai. As one newspaper editorial commented: "If one visited any public political meetings, he would see no respectable female, neither the wives of the NEPU or NPC leaders. He would see only karuwai."[15] Such a designation, though, does not necessarily mean that all the women in question were exchanging sex for money or had been coerced to serve the party in such a capacity. Certainly some women did find themselves in such a situation, while others, simply by taking part in politics, found themselves characterized as "karuwai".

The ambiguity between women who were indeed prostitutes and those who sought to break out of traditional roles worked to the advantage of the NPC. Anti-prostitution sweeps of entire towns were common during the period of the fifties and sixties. These actions were frequently declared as moves to "restore morality" and stop "anti-Islamic activities". Such occasions were a prime opportunity for the authorities (who almost always supported the NPC) to settle scores against those who supported their opponents. Editorials in the NEPU *Daily Comet* complained that, while they of course supported the idea of anti-prostitution campaigns, it seemed that

---

14. Renee Ilene Pitten, "Marriage and Alternative Strategies: Career Patterns of Hausa Women in Katsina City," PhD, Anthropology, (SOAS, 1979/1980).

15. Alhaji Durimin Iya, *Gaskiya*, 2 November, 1956.

only those prostitutes who supported NEPU were being arrested.[16] Indeed, all female members of NEPU were threatened by such campaigns. As one NEPU member stated: "They arrested the NEPU women and the prostitutes and every woman in NEPU was called a prostitute. If you were arrested they might imprison you for up to three years."[17] Such risks seem to have been very real. Hajiya Jumai Wool stated that she was arrested for the first time when she was fifteen years of age.[18] Hajiya Gambo Sawaba alleged in 1958 that the forty women present at the first meeting of the NEPU women's wing in Kano were all arrested and imprisoned for one month each.[19] On the occasion of one NEPU rally in Katsina which coincided with an anti-prostitution campaign, the NEPU women's wing had to travel hiding under tarps in the back of a truck, for fear that they would be arrested by the Native Authority police.[20]

Clearly, there were extensive barriers to women's political participation in northern Nigeria. Women who sought to break out of social boundaries such as kulle and overcome barriers to the acquisition of education were faced with constant repression, as mentioned above, and even threat to life and limb. Gambo Sawaba's biography includes several instances of beatings and assaults, all attributed to the NPC's Yan Mahaukita (Sons of Madmen). One such attack represented a clear attempt at murder where she was left for dead in the bush, to be found several days

---

16. See, for example, *Daily Comet,* 16 July, 1959, "Any Politics in Raid of Kano Prostitutes?". See also, *Daily Comet*, 17 July, 1959, "N.A. Police and Prostitutes."

17. Hajiya Jumai Wool, 5 June, 1993.

18. Ibid.

19. Hajiya Gambo Sawaba, *Nigerian Citizen*, 5 March, 1958. See also Sklar, *Nigerian Political Parties*, p.419.

20. Ibid.

later.[21] For those women who did participate in the political process, particularly on the side of NEPU, it is obvious that they were willing to take great risks for what they saw as right.

THE EDITORIAL DEBATE: "The Position of Women in Islam"

Up to late 1956, the conflict over women's political roles was one of actions. The members of NEPU's women's wings pushed the limits of women's accepted political roles simply by taking an active part in political activities. The NPC effectively showed its disapproval by harassing these women by way of the party's control over the courts and police.

The announcement of a Constitutional Conference to be held in London in 1957 brought a new aspect to the conflict over women's political rights and roles. The Constitutional Conference provided an opportunity for parties in opposition to the NPC (not only NEPU but also the Western-based Action Group) to push for women's suffrage in the North in front of an international audience. The NPC leaders at the conference followed a staunch party line which stated that female suffrage was simply unIslamic. When interviewed by the BBC (in London) and asked why his party resisted women's suffrage, the Sardauna simply replied "Because of our religion." This comment was given front-page treatment by several northern Nigerian newspapers. In support of the Sardauna's position, the President of the NPC branch in Jos, Alhaji Audu, stated that "It is unthinkable for anybody to suggest that

---

21. Shawulu, *Gambo Sawaba*, pp.80, 94, 99. Such attacks were by no means limited to female NEPU members. Both the NPC and NEPU employed armed gangs (the NEPU's being the Positive Action Wing or P.A.W., who were know for wearing calabash helmets). The NPC's size and wealth, not to mention their influence over the courts and Native Authority police, tended to give them a distinct advantage in terms of political violence. Without exception, former NEPU members reported physical attacks -- ranging from simple beatings to hit-and-run attacks with automobiles to allegations of outright torture.

overnight the sacred traditions of the Northern Region should be abandoned."[22]

The comments of the Sardauna in London, though, were an extreme distillation of a debate which had already raged for several months in 1956 and early 1957. This debate had shifted the conflict over women's political rights away from one of actions (though this factor continued) and towards a public, ideological argument over the Islamic basis of women's political rights. During this period, speeches and editorials on women's political rights became a central focus of each party's activities.

The debate was opened when one Isa Wali wrote an eight-part editorial for the newspaper *Gaskiya* entitled "Makamin Mata a Musulunci" (The Position of Women in Islam). The articles dealt with all aspects of women's political and social rights. Wali's assertions were quite radical in the context of the northern Nigerian community. Wali stated that according to Islamic sources, women were the political, moral, and social equals of men. Indeed, these articles created such a stir that every single issue of *Gaskiya* for the next four months featured replies either rebutting or supporting the writings of Wali.[23] It was not uncommon for several replies to be published in each issue.[24]

It is important to note that Isa Wali was a closet NEPU supporter. Because he worked for the Northern Region government, he chose to maintain a guise of political neutrality. Still, his extensive editorials were the equivalent of a NEPU platform on Women's rights. Isa Wali's political tendencies were certainly not

---

22. *Nigerian Citizen*, 22 June, 1957.

23. Interestingly, this remarkable source has been largely untouched by scholars of women and Islam in Nigeria.

24. Given the length of this debate, only a small portion of the arguments can be presented here.

overlooked by the newspaper's readership. Witness an early rebuttal by an NPC supporter.

> All what Malam Isa is saying is in line with the manifesto of the NEPU party -- woman liberation. He should come out and tell us that he is now a propagandist of the NEPU party.[25]

Indeed, Isa Wali's argument that Islam did allow (and even encouraged) women to take political roles was a direct challenge to the NPC's stand against women's political and social rights.

> We want the female population of this great country to get their rightful place as permitted by Islamic law and as practiced in other Muslim nations. Our female population must be given all their rights. In fact, they are treated little better than in pre-Islamic Arabia. They remain illiterate and work like slaves.[26]

The comment comparing the region to pre-Islamic Arabia served as a subtle attack on the NPC's vision of Islam, which NEPU sought to identify as so reactionary that it drew upon pre-Islamic customs rather than the proper laws of Islam as introduced by the Prophet. In effect, NEPU was stating that the "traditional" role of women as defended by the NPC was not Islamic at all, but a hold-over from the region's pre-Islamic past. According to Isa Wali, it was not the religion of Islam that called for restrictions on women's rights, but rather the local (and pre-Islamic) traditions of Northern Nigeria.

My intention is to bring out clearly the real meanings of the Qur'an,

---

25. Malam Isa Katsina, *Gaskiya*, 4 December, 1956.

26. Isa Wali, *Gaskiya*, 16 October, 1956.

as opposed to the meanings given by our local Muslim Scholars. Another objective is to show clearly the difference between what is compulsory in Islam and what elements of our local heritage are passed off as Islamic injunctions.[27]

One of Wali's primary goals was to show that true Islam was not averse to women taking part in politics. He noted that the Prophet's fourth wife, Aisha, led a rebellion against the fourth Caliph, Ali. Further, he stated

> Nobody challenged the action of Aisha in leading a rebellious group against Ali. Her leadership role came out clearly. So you can see that if a woman, the wife of our Holy Prophet, could lead a war party, there is no leadership role which a woman could not hold. Throughout Muslim history, especially during the Abbasid period, females enjoyed esteemed public positions. One must see how women were so numerous in any field of human endeavor.[28]

In a later installment, Wali pointed out that the wives of the Prophet's companions were known to be wise and devout Muslims.

> Even among the companions of the Prophet, there were wives who were more clever than their husbands. For example, the wife of Saud ibn Musayyab was more knowledgeable and intelligent than her husband.[29]

While Wali conceded that physical conditions such as pregnancy might disqualify a woman from holding "the highest positions of government," (a direct answer to a common NPC argument that pregnancy prevented women from holding

---

27. *Gaskiya*, 11 September, 1956.

28. Ibid. It is interesting to note that this same argument regarding Aisha as an example of legitimate political leadership in the classical period of Islam is (independently) advanced by Leila Ahmed in *Women and Gender in Islam* (New Haven, 1992) p.75.

29. *Gaskiya*, 18 September, 1956.

government offices) other positions, such as that of <u>alkali</u> (judge), or holding positions local and regional councils, were certainly open to them.[30]

Also central to Wali's argument was the fact that other Muslim states did not restrict women's political activity as did the Northern Region of Nigeria. Countries such as Egypt, Pakistan, Syria, Turkey, and Malaysia were cited as examples of polities where women could vote and hold office even though the population of these countries was largely Muslim. Malam Wali went so far as to cite specific examples of women from these countries who held high political positions, such as Begum Sha Nawaz, the Pakistani Ambassador to the United States or Mrs. Makbul Dibian, a Turkish Minister of Parliament.[31] Such examples were given to show that Islam was indeed a progressive political force, and that only in the eyes of the NPC was it incapable of dealing with the demands of a modern world.

> It is the duty of the entire Muslim community of this great nation of ours to work hard and bring out clearly the true meaning of Islam. They should separate truth from falsehood or mere culture, as people are doing in other Muslim countries.[32]

Malam Wali's articles were not limited only to political matters, though. He expanded his argument to include such issues as women's mobility, right to education, and men's right to take more than one wife and to keep concubines under Islamic law. In so doing, Wali was attacking the real root of the conservative argument regarding the exclusion of women from politics – their inferior social status.

---

30. Isa Wali, *Gaskiya*, 18 September, 1956.

31. Isa Wali, *Gaskiya*, 19 October, 1956.

32. Isa Wali, *Gaskiya*, 11 September, 1956.

Wali also dealt directly with the issue of whether social restrictions such as kulle, and the nature of women's proper education should limit women's ability to take part in political activities. Echoing a common NEPU theme, Wali attacked the idea that wife seclusion was considered mandatory for all Muslims. Rather, he maintained that as long as a woman behaved modestly and was properly dressed, she was free to go about as she wished. Repeating his theme that Northern Nigeria was governed by local, rather than Islamic, tradition, Wali pointed out that other Muslim nations did not so restrict women's freedom of movement.[33]

> Nowhere in the whole Qur'an and the Hadiths is there clear indication that we should isolate our female population as we are doing in Northern Nigeria. Certainly the verses are misunderstood by our Nigerian Ulama. What is required is to keep themselves covered when they are to go out. [34]

Isa Wali even questioned the relevance of the action of the Prophet in secluding his wives -- the fact that Mohammad had "secluded" his wives being a central argument for those who supported the contemporary practice in Nigeria. The passage of the Qur'an which deals with this topic, Wali maintained, was clearly addressed only to the wives of the Prophet, and was a result of Mohammad's desire to protect himself from those who sought to gain influence over or to attack him through his wives. Hence, stated Wali, in this case the actions of the Prophet were relevant only to his own (very unique) situation, and were not to be emulated by his followers.[35]

---

33. *Gaskiy*a, 9 October, 1956.

34. Isa Wali, *Gaskiya*, 9 October, 1956.

35. Isa Wali *Gaskiya*, 9 October, 1956. Again, it is interesting to note that this same argument is advanced by Ahmed in *Women and Gender in Islam*.

The issue of <u>kulle</u> was of particular interest to many of the region's women, since it did not only limit women's general mobility, but in many cases also led to a restriction on women's economic activities and even access to medical care. On this latter issue, Hajiya Jumai Wool stated:

> [Aminu Kano] said women could go to the hospital if they were pregnant, but they [the NPC] said this was contrary to Islam. Women should stay at home and use traditional medicines. The NPC members used the Hospital for themselves.[36]

As for education, NEPU had long maintained that there should be no distinction between male and female education as dictated by the Qur'an. This was a policy that NEPU acted on directly in the Islamiyya schools which they founded throughout northern Nigeria.[37] There was a well-known event in Kano when Aminu Kano publically presented a seven-year old girl who had memorized the entire Qur'an -- as a means of showing the effectiveness of the Islamiyya school's blending of Western and Islamic educational techniques. This event was designed not only to highlight the school, but also the intellectual potential of females. Echoing the NEPU support for women's education, Wali stated that Islam called for women to be educated equally to men -- in all areas of scholarship.

> It is compulsory in Islam for women to be educated. There is no question about it. There is no difference in the form of education between male and female.[38]

Showing little fear, Malam Wali even went so far as to call into question the

---

36. Hajiya Jumai Wool, 5 June, 1993.

37. For more information on the Islamiyya schools, see Chapter Five "Services to the Muslim Community."

38. *Gaskiya*, 18 September, 1956.

practice of polygamy in Islam. While he recognized that the Qur'an did state that up to four wives were allowed, he argued that the restrictions placed on this practice, particularly the Quranic injunction to treat all wives equally, made the institution of polygamy beyond the reach of all but the most extraordinary men (such as the Prophet himself).[39] In support of this fact, he cited that the third Caliph had only married a single wife.[40]

As stated previously, the most basic argument advanced by the NPC was simply that Islam prohibited political activity by women. In their replies to Isa Wali, NPC supporters made their arguments in more specific terms. One Hadith cited in support of the NPC's stand was "People will rarely triumph if a woman is assigned as leader."[41] The logical extension, claimed members of the NPC, was that if you could not have female leaders, you could not give women the vote, since in a democracy, the voters are the true leaders.[42] Alhaji Abubakar, Dokajin Kano, requested that Wali "check his sources" regarding his statement that women had similar rights to positions of leadership to men, and pointed out that there were no "female heads of state" during the period of the Rashidun. He went on to say

> There are simply duties and functions which Islam clearly forbids to women from pursuing. Things such as political leadership, judging court, leading prayers and others. Any society that gives such functions to women is not an Islamic society.[43]

---

39. Isa Wali, *Gaskiya*, 25 September, 1956.

40. Ibid.

41. *Gaskiya*, 18 September, 1956.

42. Alhaji Tanko Yakasai, 17 April, 1993.

43. Alhaji Abubakar, Dokajin Kano, *Gaskiya*, 30 October, 1956.

Along a similar line, another writer attacked Wali's claim that other Islamic states were granting political positions to women.

> I wish to draw the attention of Malam Isa Wali to the fact that we do not wish our government to copy what is done in Persia, Tunisia or Egypt. They are following the example of Western Culture. We are Muslims. Our culture is Islamic.[44]

During an interview in 1993, Nasiru Kabara recalled the debate, and attacked Malam Wali by stating that he never showed textual evidence that Islam supported women in positions of authority.

> But he could not show a line in the tradition of the Prophet. He and his supporters could not show one single tradition which shows that women can do this. It was just foolishness and ignorance to say otherwise.[45]

The NPC, though, did not rely solely upon their argument that Islam prohibited political activity by women specifically. Rather, the most common argument put forward by the NPC supporters was that it was Islam's restrictions on women's social rights and roles that necessitated women's exclusion from the political realm -- kulle in particular, but also issues of education.

Several writers attacked Malam Wali's assertion that kulle was not supported by Islamic ideology. Alhaji Durumin Iya, an NPC member and stalwart from Kaduna, stated that voting, for example, would require that women leave their homes. Such an activity would be a violation of kulle, and would necessitate that women "mixed freely with men." Both actions which ran contrary to Islamic

---

44. Alhaji Salihi Durmin Iya, *Gaskiya*, 20 November, 1956.

45. Sheik Nasiru Kabara, 27 June, 1993.

injunction. Malam Iya continued on to state: "Muslims should not allow their wives to come out of their houses, because if a woman leaves her house, <u>Shaidan</u> (Satan) will certainly beautify her structure and many men would be attracted to her" and that "there is nowhere that it is lawful for both male and female to mix together."[46] In closing his commentary, Malam Iya attacked Wali's knowledge of Islam by stating:

> The above quoted Hadith clearly expose the shallowness of the Islamic knowledge of the one who said there is no single Hadith to support <u>kulle</u> in Islam.[47]

In a very interesting rebuttal to Wali's claims that <u>kulle</u> was unIslamic, one Musa Bojude stated:

> In our society our greatest Caliph was the famous Shehu Uthman dan Fodio. We know that he kept his wives in his house. We also know that the Shehu was <u>Sheiku Kutab</u> -- that he communicated with the Prophet on a daily basis while he lived among us. If keeping women in houses is wrong the Prophet would have directed Uthman dan Fodio to stop doing so.[48]

Some individuals took an even more extreme line than those scholars quoted above. Malams Awwad and Sha'abon, Hausas living in the Gold Coast, were so moved by the issue that they wrote from abroad to cite a Hadith from the book *Ibn Adi Aid Anas* which they cited as follows: "A woman is allowed out of her matrimonial home on two occasions -- when she is being taken to that house and when she dies."[49]   Others stated that it was permissible for some women to go

---

46. Alhaji Salihu Durumin Iya, *Gaskiya*, 30 October, 13 November, 1956.

47. Ibid.

48. Musa Bojude, *Gaskiya*, 20 November, 1956.

49. *Gaskiya*, 7 December, 1956.

outside of their homes, but only if they were old and ugly, and even they must be modestly clothed.[50]

Not all of the NPC's arguments in favor of kulle and against female suffrage and political activity were so grounded on religious ideology. In addition to his ideological arguments in favor of kulle, Alhaji Salihi Durimin Iya also put forward an esthetic argument.

> I wish to draw the attention of M. Isa Wali to the fact that women who are put "behind bars" -- in kulle -- are softer and more lovely. That is why people wish to see them. They are true females. Those not under kulle have lost all their feminine characteristics, they regard themselves as equal to men and Allah makes them coarse and unattractive.[51]

Another writer stated that women should not hold political office simply because of their character.

> Women should not hold public office because they can be easily deceived or cheated. Their hearts are weak. They are sympathetic and can be quickly governed by emotion rather than reason.[52]

The issue of women's education was also frequently cited as a reason for denying women political rights. In the words of one writer:

> It must not be forgotten that the population of women in the Region exceeds that of men, and about 99% of the women are not only

---

50. Musa Bojude, *Gaskiya*, 20 November, 1956.

51. Alhaji Salihi Durimin Iya, *Gaskiya,* 15 November, 1956. This particular editorial is in interesting contrast to Iya's earlier claim (30 October) that 'Satan beautifies Women who leave their homes.'

52. Mohamad Sagir, Dokajin Kano, *Gaskiya*, 30 October, 1956.

illiterate, but are uninformed and uneducated in every way. Women's franchise at this stage and under such appalling circumstances merely means putting the destiny of the country into the hands of an illiterate, uninformed and uneducated public -- you can imagine how disastrous that would be. That would be democracy indeed![53]

Such commentary as this was, of course, made with disregard for the fact the male population of the North was itself largely uneducated. Further, the Native Authorities (largely staffed by NPC supporters) had consistently resisted the idea of female education in the Northern Region for much of the twentieth century, a situation frequently lamented by the British colonial government in the region.[54] While the NPC was not necessarily opposed to the idea of education for women, they did have very particular ideas about what sort of education was suitable. In an article entitled "Appeal to Women," the Sultan of Sokoto called upon women to

wake up and be prepared to march in line with their menfolk [because] as future mothers they should learn how to be clean and keep their homes in order.[55]

In a similar vein, the Sardauna of Sokoto stated "no country can develop properly without good housewives, teachers, nurses, and other occupations that require the services of women."[56]

Several writers, though, directly rebutted Isa Wali's claims that women could and should be educated equally to men.

---

53. *Nigerian Citizen*, 20 July, 1957.

54. See, for example NAK, "Girls education in Sokoto," SokPrOf. C. 145/46-56, 20 January, 1955. Also see, NAK, KanoPrOf., AR2/15, 1957.

55. *Nigerian Citizen*, 8 January, 1958.

56. *Nigerian Citizen*, 20 February, 1965.

The quest for knowledge for a woman is compulsory provided there is no danger of breaking the laws of Allah in seeking that knowledge -- that is, like the mixing of men and women in the name of education. If females can be educated without mixing with the opposite sex, then all is well and good.[57]

and

Getting education is compulsory for both male and female in the Islamic religion. However, the sort of education is that which would allow women to perform domestic duties properly -- cooking, cleaning, child raising, etc. Education for other duties is, I fear, unIslamic.[58]

Hence, the logic for the more conservatively minded members of the northern populace was clear. It was basically a good thing for women to be educated, but only when it did not require mixing with men and only in a fashion that facilitated their role as mothers and housekeepers. Wider education was not suitable for women, and without this education they were not qualified to vote.

As previously noted, the NEPU leadership staunchly advocated women's education. In response to the above-quoted editorials one Audu Danladi lamented the absence of a women's voice in the ongoing debate over women's rights.

No woman has responded to the writings of Isa Wali, either for or against. This is a very serious matter. People just go ahead and discuss the affairs of those who cannot defend themselves. This is very unfair as far as I am concerned. It seems there are two reasons for why our female population have refused to comment on such a matter that affects them so directly. The first and most important is ignorance. How many women can read or respond to these debates? How many even know about the articles? The second reason is fear --

---

57. Alhaji Abubakar, Kokajin Kano, *Gaskiya*, 30 October, 1956.

58. Saidu Ahmed, *Gaskiya*, 13 November, 1956.

fear of the sort of condemnations that have been leveled against Isa Wali for telling the truth. We are cheating our female population by not sending them to school. We allow them to live in ignorance.[59]

Throughout the period of the fifties and sixties, the NPC stood by its stand that Islam prohibited women's political involvement. In 1957, they were successful in blocking a motion to give women special representation in the Northern Region House of Assembly.[60] The following telegrams were exchanged in 1962 between Sarkin Dawaki Bello (NPC representative to the Nigerian Parliament, Lagos) and the Sardauna of Sokoto.

> 21 August, Sarkin Dawaki to Sardauna:
> Have followed with deep interest and appreciation your stand on women Franchise. Your stand is right. Be firm. God will always be with you."
>
> 22 August, Sardauna to Sarkin Dawaki:
> Your much respected telegram received with respect. You know I should and did it for NPC and Muslim cause. We will never be dictated to by any brute.[61]

THE WIDER IMPLICATIONS: THE POLITICAL DEBATE AND WOMEN'S POSITION WITHIN NORTHERN NIGERIAN SOCIETY

With a debate that frequently touched upon such topics as whether or not women should be secluded in kulle and what type of education women should receive, it is clear that the question of whether or not women should have a political role was only one aspect of the conflict between the NPC and NEPU. What was actually at stake was whether or not women were to be relegated to "traditional" roles

---

59. Audu Danladi, *Gaskiya*, 30 November, 1956.

60. NAK, PRE, R2219 "Political Rights of Women."

61. NAK, PRE/97 "Premier's Personal File."

(as perceived by the parties) in all aspects of life, or whether they were to have a choice to pursue a more progressive lifestyle if they so desired. The statements by the NPC that such institutions as kulle, restrictions on women's interaction with men and limitations on female education required that women's participation in politics be limited, were tantamount to Government sanction of these same institutions and practices. Indeed, this was the case. For example, during the 1950's the NPC succeeded in placing laws on the books of some parts of the Northern Region that made it a crime for married women to go out of their houses -- even to attend traditional ceremonies such as naming ceremonies, weddings and funerals. NEPU reacted strongly to this law. A letter to the Kano Resident stated:

> Not only is this a terrible precedent but a shocking retrogressive step in the emancipation of northern women... This we see as an act that will certainly bring about confusion and make us look ridiculous and primitive in the eyes of the modern world... [it] goes beyond the law, Islam and common sense.

The acting Resident, M.C. McClintock, was shocked by NEPU's letter, and replied that the law had been "designed to arrest progressive deterioration in Moral Standards," and had been arrived at in consultation with a committee "most qualified to advise on this point."[62] Those consulted were none other than the Emir of Kano and his advisers, all staunch backers of the NPC.

THE POLITICS BEHIND THE DEBATE

It should be noted that the successful resistance of the NPC to women's suffrage was in some ways counter-intuitive. The Northern Region was the only one of Nigeria's three semi-autonomous regions not to extend the vote to women, and in

---

62. NAK, "NEPU Complaints and Court Cases," KanoPrOf, 2/73, PLT/5/154,

doing so it limited its potential to overwhelm the other regions with its significantly larger population. The answer to this quandary, though, lies in the politics of the Northern Region itself. While the NPC frequently played upon the "Islamic" nature of the North, the truth was that the region was home to several million non-Muslims, a point frequently cited by opposition parties in calling for women's suffrage. These parties, such as the Western region based Action Group (AG) and the Eastern-based National Council of Nigerian and the Cameroons (NCNC) often requested that if Islam forbade women from voting, then non-Muslim women within the North should still have the right to vote if they so desired.[63] As one opponent of the NPC stated in the course of a House of Representatives debate on the subject:

> As you are aware, the Northern Region has a diverse population, speaking different dialects, having different customs and traditions. In my humble opinion, I beg to suggest that the Government should relax this rule and allow Christian and Pagan women to vote. It is understood that the reason why women in the extreme North are not allowed to vote is due solely to religious reasons. But in places like the Tivs, the Idomas and so on, women are allowed to do things equally as men. I see no reason why women in our own country should not be allowed to vote. If the Northern Government wants women in the extreme North not to vote, they should allow our women to vote for us.[64]

Such a situation was, indeed, exactly what the NPC feared. In truth, the very restrictions which the NPC cited as reasons for limiting female participation in politics (perceived religious strictures, seclusion, poor education) would probably have kept the great majority of the female Muslim population from voting if the vote had been extended. These restrictions, though, would have had much less effect on non-Muslim populations. Estimates conservatively placed the non-Muslim female

---

63. See, for example, *Nigerian Citizen*, 3 August, 1957.

64. P. Deem Kpumm, House of Representatives Debates, 24 February, 1959, p.1114.

population at over one million.[65] This situation could have given a significant boost
to the Middle Belt Christian and Pagan vote that largely supported the United Middle
Belt Congress (UMBC), a party that sought as its main goal to carve a new region out
of the southern section of the North. If the UMBC were to have attained its goal, the
Northern Region would have been in dire danger of losing its political dominance
over the smaller and less populous southern regions -- and hence the nation as a
whole.[66] Similarly, if any Muslim women were to vote, it is likely that they would
have been of the better educated and more progressive type that was drawn to NEPU
-- helping that party in its resistance to NPC rule. Indeed, the NPC was very
aware of the national political contest as well as that within the Northern Region. It
is interesting to note that those northern women who resided in either of the southern
regions were encouraged to take advantage of women's right to suffrage in these
territories and vote for parties in alliance with the NPC.[67]

By keeping the discourse on the topic of women's political rights limited to
a debate over Islamic ideology, the NPC was able to direct attention away from the
issue of the internal politics of the Northern Region. For its own part, NEPU could
not avoid the focus of the debate without appearing that it could not meet the NPC's
arguments based on their own interpretation of religious ideology. Such a situation
would have been a serious setback for a party that in large part based its legitimacy
on a claim to greater Islamic knowledge. Similarly, by limiting the argument largely
to a question of Islamic interpretation, the NPC kept the potential for British

---

65. *Daily Times*, 1 May, 1958.

66. Demands for a Middle-Belt region were a common facet of politics in Nigeria up to the end of
the First Republic, with the UMBC and AG being the primary proponents of the creation of the new
region.

67. The NPC never contested seats outside of the Northern Region, instead preferring to operate
through small opposition parties. The reliance on this approach shows to what degree the NPC relied
on their dominance of the North as the key to national political power.

interference to a minimum, since official British policy was to remain neutral in religious matters. When interviewed regarding the British stance on women's suffrage in Northern Nigeria, Alan Lennox-Boyd, Secretary of State for the Colonies replied "This is clearly a matter for the Northern Region themselves."[68] Further, since the British were themselves not in accordance with the U.N. Convention on the Political Rights of Women (they did not allow women into the House of Lords), they were unlikely to force the issue on the Northern Region.

CONCLUSIONS

Clearly, the issue of Women's political and social rights was a very telling one, as the conflict between the NPC and NEPU serves both to show us how religion was central to the politics of the period, and also to offer considerable insights into women's status during the period -- offering considerably greater historical depth to our understanding of the status of women during this critical period in Nigerian history. Contrary to the perspective of most contemporary literature on women in Northern Nigeria, it is clear that the debate over women's political and social roles has been raging for some time, and that debate has been deeply intertwined with discussions of the region's religious and historical self-identity. A familiar component to the debate, though, is the desire of conservative elements to assign women the role of "repositories of culture."

It would seem that the NPC's strategy of limiting the political participation of women in the Northern Region by reference to a conservative interpretation of Islamic ideology and tradition worked greatly to the party's advantage. The NPC was successful in keeping the right to vote out of women's hands throughout the First Republic -- despite the continuous demands of all opposition parties. While the NPC

---

68. *Nigerian Citizen*, 20 May, 1959.

was successful in the short run, it was NEPU that saw its goals achieved in the long run. With the collapse of the First Republic, northern women, Muslim and non-Muslim, were to be given the vote. Further, the attention NEPU commanded in the course of the debate helped improve the awareness of a great portion of the northern populace regarding the rights of women in Islam and helped weaken the hegemony of the conservative interpretation of Islamic sources. These factors did not seem to have been lost on the female voters of the region, who were said to have been a decisive block in helping to give the Peoples Redemption Party (NEPU's Second Republic incarnation) a strong showing in several key northern states in the 1979 elections.[69]

---

69. Hajiya Jumai Wool, 5 June, 1993. See also Barbara Callaway and Lucy Creevey, *The Heritage of Islam: Women, Religion and Politics in West Africa* (Boulder, 1994), pp.148-149.

CHAPTER FIVE:

SERVICES TO THE ISLAMIC COMMUNITY

Previous chapters have examined in some detail the ways in which both the NPC and NEPU drew upon religious ideology, history, and institutions to bolster their political positions. While such factors were clearly politically expedient and served in many ways to improve each party's standing with their supporters, such tactics did not necessarily draw the attention of those individuals who were less concerned with politically or ideologically complex issues. Perhaps in part due to the region's low rates of literacy, intellectual issues were often secondary to the question of just what sort of concrete religious services the parties could offer. Such expectations were not out of place. Governments in predominantly Islamic regions have long been expected to provide for the spiritual well-being of the Muslims under their administration. This situation, though, was complicated by the presence of the British, who sought to limit the overt presence of religion in politics as Nigeria moved towards independence. To the British colonial rulers, religion and politics did not belong together, at least not openly, in the Western-style democracy which they hoped to bequeath to Nigeria. While the parties both gave lip-service to this division of religion and politics during the 1950's, their own agendas, and the expectations of the populace, nonetheless necessitated that the parties' obligations as (would-be) Muslim rulers be recognized. After the granting of independence in 1960 the role of the parties in offering religious services to the populace became much more visible.

An examination of the processes by which the parties offered religious services will reveal many aspects of the role of Islam in the conflict between the NPC and NEPU. Several specific questions will be addressed in this chapter. Exactly how did each party envision, justify, and play out its role as a provider of religious services to the region's Islamic community? How did non-Muslim groups react to such activities on the part of the parties? What do the parties' strategies tell us about how they envisioned the role of government in a modernizing Islamic region? Further, the sort of services each party offered is telling of just how that party viewed the religion of Islam itself.

THE PARTIES AND RELIGIOUS SERVICES DURING THE 1950'S

Throughout the course of the 1950's there existed a tension between the basic tendency of politics in Islamic regions to take on a religious aspect and the desire of the British to limit this tendency as much as possible, or at least restrict such activities to areas of governance which were deemed "proper." Indeed, largely due to the ideology of Indirect Rule, the British were caught between trying to limit the overt inclusion of religious elements in the political process and their recognition of the legitimate duty of Islamic governments to provide certain religious services, such as the upholding of the Shari'a. Clearly, the NPC, as the party of government, was provided with a distinct advantage by this dynamic, since by being in power the provision of these "legitimate" religious services became a part of their activities. No doubt the generally pro-NPC British were aware of this fact. While disadvantaged by their lack of access to the institutions of governance, NEPU still undertook to offer religious services to the region's Muslim populace. Such activity, though, often had to be undertaken in very carefully constructed "apolitical" settings so as to avoid action by the British.

During the 1950's, the NPC seemed content to limit their religious activities to those which were tied to the administration of the region. The close association between the NPC and the Native Authorities was of advantage to the NPC in this case, since the traditional rulers had many religious roles. Still, these traditional rulers were considered civil servants, and as such were expected to refrain from open political activity in the course of their duties as "impartial administrators." Emirs, almost all of whom belonged to the NPC, frequently led prayers at the Friday Mosques in each of the region's major towns. Many alkalai (Islamic judges), all of whom were employees of the Native Authorities, also belonged to the NPC and many ran for office on the party's ticket. Such connections to the region's Islamic institutions certainly aided the NPC in promoting the party's legitimacy among the Muslim populace.

Not surprisingly, NEPU was greatly disturbed by the role of traditional leaders -- the Masu Sarauta -- in the politics of the 1950's. Throughout the early period of party politics, NEPU protested that traditional leaders were taking unfair advantage of their role as religious leaders to make political statements. The following article was published in the NEPU Daily Comet after the Emir of Kano allegedly made political comment prior to leading Friday prayers.

> The NEPU has protested to His Excellency, the Governor of [the] Northern Region Sir Gawain Bell, in the strongest terms against the alleged use of mosques as pulpits by Emirs in the Region to campaign for votes for the party they support. Now not only is it a flagrant attempt and a clever royal move on the part of the Emir to make use of religion to further the ends of the party he supports, but also a direct participation in partisan politics.[1]

---

1. Daily Comet, 10 March, 1959. See also "Are Emirs Used For Campaign Purposes?" Daily Comet, 11 September, 1959.

While the NPC did indeed receive a certain amount of legitimacy from the Party's organic linkages to the region's Islamic institutions, the NPC did not limit its strategy to passively reaping such benefits. The upholding of the Shari'a, for example, was one area in which the NPC actively sought to draw attention to itself. Certain examples of this practice were of immediate political expedience for the NPC, such as in the case of the debate over women's political rights. Here was a case where the NPC could cast itself as the 'defender of the Shari'a' and also protect itself from a potentially hazardous political situation.[2] The NPC, though, also took stands on issues relating to the Shari'a when there was not a particular political issue at stake. The matter of the legality of the drinking of alcoholic beverages by Muslims was one such issue that was given wide play by the NPC government. During August of 1959, for example, a series of speeches by NPC leaders such as the Sardauna and Isa Kaita (then Minister of Education) spoke vociferously against the proposed absence from the new legal code of a law which would specifically forbid Muslims from drinking beer or other alcoholic beverages. In one such speech, the Sardauna stated bluntly "As long as my party, the NPC is in power in the region, it will not legislate what God has forbidden."[3] Elaborating somewhat, Isa Kaita stated that such a law would "help to safeguard and nurture the faith of the teeming Muslims in the region."[4]

The timing and political context of such remarks as these are worth noting. During much of 1958 and 1959, the issue of the Northern Nigerian Penal Code was being widely debated by the NPC and NEPU. A common tactic used by the NEPU leadership was to attack the Penal Code on the grounds that it was not based wholly

---

2. See Chapter Four, "Islam, Politics, and Women's Rights," for a detailed discussion of this issue.

3. *Daily Comet*, 5 September, 1959.

4. *Daily Times*, 21 August, 1959.

on the Shari'a.[5] There can be little doubt that the NPC's drive to protect northern Muslims from the potential legalization of alcohol was largely a means by which the party was able to take a highly visible stand in defense of the Shari'a and to show that the Penal Code would have the interests of Muslims at heart. This is particularly likely in light of the fact that there was no strong support for the legalization of alcohol consumption by northern Muslims, the proposal having come from the western-region based Action Group.[6]   Indeed, no northern-based party, including NEPU, supported the legalization of alcohol for Muslims.

Far more important than the issue of beer-drinking, the case of the pilgrimage to Mecca is an example of one area where the NPC government actively sought to provide a new service to the populace of the region. Several factors encouraged or even necessitated state involvement in the Hajj. As Muhammad Sani Umar has stated:

> The observance of certain religious rites were such that by their very nature they must attract the involvement of the state. For example, the performance of the Hajj involves immigration, foreign exchange, custom and excise as well as diplomacy. These were issues that could not be treated by religious agencies; the state, no matter how secular, had to be involved.[7]

Up to the period of the 1950's, the great majority of pilgrims journeying to

---

5. See, for example, "Penal Code Laws not in Conformity of the People of the Federal Republic of Nigeria", *Daily Comet*, 29 September, 1960. For a more detailed discussion of this issue see Chapter Three, "Politics and the Shari'a."

6. Western Region Muslims who lived in the North had long chaffed at that region's prohibition of drinking by people of the Islamic faith. Western Muslims frequently complained that, not being from the North, they should not be so restricted. See NAK, "General Correspondence on Liquor for the Northern Provinces, 1948-1956," SokPrOf, ACC/1502.s.1,

7. Muhammad Sani Umar, "Islam in Nigeria,", *Twenty Five Years*, p.79.

Mecca from Nigeria had no choice but to undertake an arduous overland journey that could last up to several years. Over the course of the twentieth century, this process became increasingly difficult as the states between Nigeria and the Hejaz sought to exert greater control over their international boundaries. By the middle of the twentieth century, pilgrims were faced with demands for passports from border officials and other functionaries where none had previously been sought. This difficulty was also exacerbated by longstanding colonial fears that Nigerian pilgrims were being exposed to anti-colonial propaganda from Sudanese Mahdists and "Bolshevik Agents" during the long overland journey.[8] Between the 1920's and 1950's, the British sought to streamline and routinize the Hajj by requiring pilgrims to show that they had enough cash to pay for motor or sea transport to the Hejaz. Such transport was much faster, and thus served to reduce the potential for contact with corrupting influences along the way. Further, the British were perfectly happy if their activities actually limited the number of Nigerians who undertook the Hajj.[9]

The NPC, too, was to take an active role on behalf of Nigerian Pilgrims. The first major step was taken in 1952, when the NPC made arrangements with West African Airways Corporation to carry pilgrims to Mecca by air.[10] The actual air transport to the Hejaz at this time was run by the wealthy Dantata family, and as such the credit for assisting pilgrims did not accrue to the NPC government alone. A new company, Hajair of West Africa, was established in May of 1957 with the assistance of the Northern Region Government, but was bought out by the Dantatas for £11,000 within a matter of weeks. In January 1958, yet another publicly-assisted company,

---

8. See AH, K.281, 13 October, 1926 and AH K.4797 Vol.1, 1927. See also NAK, ZarPrOf, C.68, 1953.

9. Jonathan Reynolds, "Good and Bad Muslims: Islam and Indirect Rule in Northern Nigeria" Presented at the African Studies Association Conference, 3 November, 1995.

10. Paden, *Ahmadu Bello*, p.283.

Alharamaini Limited, was established to facilitate pilgrim transport, both overland and by air. The Northern Region government took out £45,000 in debentures in this venture.[11] The NPC was careful to insure that their role was not missed. When the first pilgrims traveled under the aegis of Alharamaini in May of 1958, the Sardauna traveled to the Kano airport to see them off.[12]

Leading members of the NPC took an active role in the pilgrimage as well. In 1954, Isa Kaita was sent on pilgrimage by the Sardauna with the goal of researching a report on the pilgrimage.[13] Traveling with Kaita, some three hundred "official pilgrims" made the trip from Nigeria to Mecca by air. Reflecting a continuity in Colonial perspectives on the Hajj from Nigeria, this trip delighted the British administrators because the new mode of transport served to isolate the pilgrims from potential contact with political radicals such as might be found in Nasser's U.A.R.

In July of 1955, the Sardauna made his first journey to Mecca -- by air. From this time on, the Sardauna made the Hajj twice each year, once during the month of Zulhajj (major Hajj) and the Umra (lesser Hajj) at some other time of the year. The nature of the Sardauna's semi-annual trips to Mecca is worth noting. A number of prominent members of the NPC always accompanied the Sardauna on pilgrimage. Being invited on Hajj with the Sardauna became a major sign of favor among the members of the NPC and was a key means by which the party rewarded supporters. Extensive press coverage of the Sardauna's trips to Mecca insured that popular attention was focused on the activities of the Sardauna and his followers. Front-page announcements of each trip were common fare in such Northern papers as the

11. Paden, *Ahmadu Bello*, p.285.

12. NAK, "Premier's Touring Notes, 1958-1965," PRE/2, ACC/178-191. Agency Mark PRE/99.

13. Paden, *Ahmadu Bello*, p.280.

Nigerian Citizen and *Gaskiya Ta Fi Kwabo*, as were daily reports of the Sardauna's activities while abroad. These articles frequently included pictures of the Sardauna and his companions in the course of their prayers.[14] While abroad, the Sardauna sent back regular telegrams detailing the trips' religious and political events. Designed for popular consumption, these telegrams were printed in northern newspapers.[15] By focusing attention on the Sardauna's frequent pilgrimages, the NPC no doubt sought to improve their image as a devout Muslim party.

The benefits of accompanying the Sardauna on pilgrimage were not lost on Nigeria's Islamic and political leaders, as the following letter addressed to the Sardauna from one Lasisi Atandu, a Muslim leader from Oyo, illustrates.

> I am now willing to affiliate my Religion (sic) Organization with your party simply because you are a Godly man and a Muslim leader of no equal. The only other thing that I am now urging you to do for me at present is that I want you to send me to Macca-Medina in the next pilgrimage and I want this to be announced in the Radio and in the daily news in particular should my humble letter be acceded.[16]

By the early 1960's, the number of "companions" who traveled to Mecca with the Sardauna had grown from a dozen in 1955 to nearly a hundred. Indeed, requests to be taken on pilgrimage with the Sardauna became so frequent that the Premier's Office designed a form letter stating as follows:

> Sir,
>
> I am directed by the Honorable Premier of Northern Nigeria Alhaji Sir Ahmadu Bello, Sardauna of

---

14. See, for example, *Nigerian Citizen*, 1 July, 1956.

15. See, for example, *Nigerian Citizen*, 24 June, 1959.

16. NAK, PRE 240, Vol. II/259, "Matters Affecting Pilgrims"

Sokoto, to acknowledge the receipt of your letter dated _____ and to advise you to be patient until you can afford to pay your own passage to Mecca.

Wassalam.[17]

Clearly, the NPC was successful in drawing popular attention to the pilgrimage and heightening the populace's expectations regarding the potential of actually making the pilgrimage themselves. The fact that a great number of the region's populace sent requests for assistance regarding the pilgrimage directly to the Premier's office is in itself important, and reflects the success of the NPC in creating an image of itself as a provider of religious services to the Muslim populace of the North.

Unable to fund frequent pilgrimages for its own members, much less for members of the general populace, NEPU tried to throw doubt on the motives of the NPC members who traveled to the Holy Land. Members of the NPC, stated NEPU, were traveling to Mecca not for the purpose of worship, but rather were doing so just for the opportunity to travel and meet with friends abroad. Further, such trips were taken at the expense of the Nigerian taxpayers, as was stated in the following NEPU poem.

NPC's ambition has perished,
they have appropriated the whole of the people's property
to pay their fares to Mecca
to pray for glory
but in fact they have overlooked that they are really
praying for hell-fire.[18]

---

17. NAK, PRE 240 Vol.II, "Matters Affecting Pilgrims." The fact that Lasisi Atandu was from Oyo is worth noting. Because the NPC did not actively contest seats in political contests outside of the northern region, alliances with such southern organizations were a major source of influence outside of the North.

18. "We recognize those who have wronged us," by M. Abba Maikwaru. From Whitaker, *Politics of Tradition*, p.395.

Such accusations brought in return an unusually vociferous defense by the
Sardauna.

> One further point that requires clarification is the unwarranted
> propaganda that is being spread by some non-God-fearing,
> unscrupulous and iniquitous people both in Nigeria and abroad that
> I and some of my colleagues go on pilgrimage every year in order to
> meet political friends from Arab countries. I want to make this quite
> clear that pilgrimage is a religious matter. It is a matter that you
> cannot force a man to go or to stop him from going. I would like to
> assure those who seem to agree with this propaganda that we go on
> pilgrimage because we have the means of going, we are healthy, and
> we want to go. I am not trying to call any witnesses for what I do
> when I go on pilgrimage. My only witness is God Who has created
> me and Who has ordained that Moslems should go on pilgrimage if
> and when they can. I would like further to make it clear that if I have
> anything to do politically I shall never hide it.[19]

Whether or not NEPU allegations had any truth behind them, the fact that the
NPC did take actual steps to streamline and routinize the Hajj cannot be denied.
Indeed, these efforts only increased over the course of the NPC's tenure in power.
In 1955, the Northern government appointed representatives to advise pilgrims on
customs, immigration and finance matters at the Kano airport. In addition, three
representatives of the government were sent to Saudi Arabia to oversee similar
matters there. A new Hajj camp was financed for pilgrims arriving at Jeddah by
sea.[20] During this same year, the Sardauna made an official trip to Saudi Arabia to
examine the problems faced by Nigerian pilgrims.[21] In combination with this trip the
Sardauna made arrangements with Saudi officials to allow Nigerian pilgrims to enter

---

19. NAK, "Premier's Speeches, 1962-1963," PRE/3, ACC/57, Agency Mark A.S.

20. Paden, *Ahmadu Bello*, p.284.

21. Ibid, p.283.

Saudi Arabia with "pilgrims' documents" only, and not to require them to have international passports. This move allowed several hundred Nigerian overland pilgrims to enter Saudi Arabia from Port Sudan, where they had been held up for some time due to their lack of formal documentation.[22] Such efforts showed the ability of the Sardauna to work on behalf of Nigerian Muslims even outside of Nigeria. In years to come, arrangements were also made to repatriate Nigerian pilgrims who were stranded in Saudi Arabia. In 1963, for example, planes returning to Nigeria to pick up pilgrims bound for Mecca carried some 1255 "destitute" pilgrims back to Nigeria. This effort was given high-profile coverage in the region's papers.[23]

The efforts of the NPC government in drawing attention to, facilitating, and streamlining the Hajj had significant impact on the practice. By the early 1960's, the number of Nigerians making the pilgrimage had increased more than tenfold. The NPC government was careful to insure that it received credit where credit was due. An article in the widely circulated *Nigerian Citizen*, entitled "The Holy Mission" read as follows.

> We have in mind the difficulties previously encountered by these Alhajis and would-be Alhajis in the hands of some unscrupulous, get-rich-quick and so-called businessmen.
> Through the vigilant efforts of both the Federal and Northern Governments these difficulties have been considerably minimized. Several top-level missions, sponsored by the two governments have, on several occasions, traveled to Saudi Arabia to see things for themselves, with a view to bringing about some improvements, which will not only minimize the pilgrim's difficulties but will also ensure some measure of comfort and security.
> We are happy things have begun to improve. The intending

---

22. *Daily Times*, 3 March, 1958.

23. See, for example, *Nigerian Citizen*, 27 April, 1963.

pilgrims have begun to enjoy some measure of relief and confidence under the present arrangement.[24]

Given the importance of the Hajj to Muslims, it being one of the Five Pillars of Islam, there can be little doubt that the efforts of the NPC government on their behalf were noted.

NEPU AND RELIGIOUS SERVICES

NEPU, for its part, could take no part in the assistance that went to Nigerian pilgrims. Without access to the institutions and capital assets that came with control of the government, NEPU could not hope to undertake the provision of such services to the region's Muslim populace. This did not mean, though, that NEPU was unable to offer any sort of religious services, just that the smaller party's approach had to differ significantly from that of the NPC. Not surprisingly, NEPU drew upon one of the key strengths of its leadership, their high level of education, both Islamic and Western, in order to offer a religious service to the region's Muslims. A great proportion or NEPU central leadership were teachers, either at the region's new government schools or at traditional Makarantar Allo (Qur'anic schools). Many members of the NEPU knew one-another through the Northern Teachers' Association before NEPU was founded.

The course taken by NEPU was to offer "modern" education to the region's Muslim populace in the form of the "Islamiyya" schools. These schools combined traditional Islamic subjects, the memorization of the Qur'an for example, with subjects such as mathematics and presented them in a "Western" academic setting. The students sat at desks facing a blackboard, rather than gathering around the malam

---

24. *Nigerian Citizen*, 10 April, 1965.

while sitting on the ground. In an interview with John Chamberlain in 1971, Aminu
Kano stated that the original idea for the Islamiyya schools started among the "Bauchi
circle" of NEPU organizers -- in particular Sa'ad Zungur.[25] Early plans to establish
an Islamiyya school (before 1950) were not successful, largely owing to the fact that
the local District Head in Bauchi, Alkali Ibrahim, "didn't want to modernize
traditional schools."[26]

The first documented opening of an Islamiyya school was on 8 July, 1951 in
Maiduguri, Bornu province. Even before the school's opening, though, it had
attracted the attention of both the local Native Authority and of the British Resident.
NEPU, operating under the guise of the Jamiyyar Islamiyya (the Islamic Congress),
had sent out leaflets throughout the area outlining the goals of the school. Copies
were even sent to the British Resident and the members of the Shehu of Bornu's
council. This action immediately resulted in a file being opened to maintain records
of the school's activities.[27] The maintenance of this file led to regular visits to the
school by members of the Native Authority and by British officers. The pamphlet,
entitled "The Aims of Jamiyyar Islamiyya" read as follows.

1) To build Arabic Schools for young boys and adult people i.e.
Elementary Schools, Colleges and Universities.
2) To improve the present Kuranic (sic) schools in existence.
3) To improve reading-rooms and provide them with good Arabic
books for the sake of Arabic Students and Tutors.
4) To send students and teachers to countries in the East for visiting
sake and to learn further Arabic Studies.
5) To maintain and run the religion of Islam in the proper way set
originally.
6) To build quarters for students coming outside the town in which

---

25. Chamberlain field notes. Interview with Aminu Kano, 4 June, 1971.

26. Ibid.

27. NAK, "Islamiyya School, Maiduguri," MaiPrOf, 5732/2.

the school is in order to relieve tutors of the burden of feeding students.

Entrance fee 2/-, Monthly contribution 1/-.

The school teaches in the Elementary schools, religion (general), practical teaching with demonstrations, the Koran, reading and writing in Arabic, History of the Prophet Muhammad and his followers and those of the Khalifas, Arabic songs, good manners and respect, sanitation and feeding.[28]

Such stated aims of the Jamiyyar Islamiyya reflect many key themes in NEPU's approach to religion. Immediately apparent in the pamphlet is its authors' dissatisfaction with the status of Islamic education in the North. This fact reflects the strong emphasis placed by the NEPU leadership on education at all levels -- witness the plan to establish not only elementary schools, but also "colleges and universities." Further, the education was for adults as well as children.

Seemingly, the Jamiyyar Islamiyya's efforts to publicize the opening of the Maiduguri Islamiyya school were a success. Setima Adamu, the member of the Shehu's council who was sent to observe the opening ceremony on 8 July, 1951, estimated the number of people in attendance at about two thousand.[29] At the time of its opening, the school had some 25 children enrolled. By 20 August the number of children had grown to 80 (ten of whom were female). Also by this later date, the school could boast some 90 registered adults, who attended in the afternoon for both "basic and advanced study."[30] The fact that 12% of the children enrolled were female is worth noting. Young girls were generally excluded from traditional Qur'anic education and were left to be trained at home, if at all. The school's acceptance of female students was in line with one of the key NEPU platforms, which was equal

---

28. NAK, MaiPrOf, 5732/1, May, 1951.

29. NAK, MaiPrOf, 5732/2, July, 1951.

30. NAK, MaiPrOf., 5732/4, August, 1951.

education for males and females -- in addition to equal political rights for both sexes. Interestingly, the school's willingness to take on female students was not outlined in the "Aims of Jamiyyar Islamiyya" pamphlet sent out prior to the school's opening. Perhaps the school's founders were fearful that advanced warning of such a radical move would lead the local Native Authority to act harshly towards the new institution.

As seen above, the Jamiyyar Islamiyya did not attempt to hide their presence from the local authorities, rather preferring to announce most aspects of their activities openly. Still, an effort was made to distance the activities of the Jamiyyar Islamiyya from those of NEPU. Indeed, the British Resident wrote the following note after he quizzed the teachers of the school regarding their ties to NEPU.

> The Jamiyyar Islamiyya has nothing to do with the NEPU, or so I am told, but several of its members are also members of the NEPU. The two teachers are Mallam Bukar, the President, and one Malam Lawal, a Kano man who just happened to be here but on no definite business at all. He is a member of NEPU.[31]

Indeed Malam Lawal was a NEPU member -- none other than Lawan Danbazau, one of the party's founders and later its key adviser on Islamic Law, operating under a sort of academic nom de guerre. A *Gaskiya Ta Fi Kwabo* article noted the work of one Lawal Danbazam at the Bornu Islamiyya school.[32]

While the British officers in the region may have been, for the moment, taken in by NEPU's Jamiyyar Islamiyya cover, the local Native Authority (likely much more familiar with NEPU personalities) was not. The Native Authority reported to

---

31. NAK, MaiPrOf, 5732/6A.

32. *Gaskiya*, 19 September, 1951.

the District Officer that "The Shehu and his council will arrange to watch the movements and activities of the Jamiyya very carefully."[33] Throughout the early period of the school's operation, the Native Authority and Shehu's council called for frequent inspections and reviews of the school by the British Resident. For his own part the District Officer seemed content with the school's activities.[34] Indeed, the District Officer seemed much impressed with the way in which the Islamiyya school was operated. Following an inspection of the School on 25 October of 1951, it was reported that

> The headmaster of the school asked one tiny pupil to state the five heads of Islam, and the pupil without stumbling stated them in good order. Some pupils were also asked some religious and historical questions and they gave clear answers quoting some verses from the Qur'an and the Hadith.
> The School is not only strict on the teaching of the Qur'an but useful subjects are also taught. The methods of teaching Qur'an differs greatly to the method used by local undeveloped schools in the town. I heard some children in the school quoting some Quranic verses with very good and clear pronunciation.[35]

Hence, for the British, who saw devout Muslims as good colonial subjects, the idea of Islamic education was always attractive -- particularly if it stressed elements such as "good manners and respect."[36] During the early 1950's the British sought to have religious instruction added to the daily activities of the region's (secular) primary schools. "We also suggest that every school should have a mosque

---

33. NAK, MaiPrOf, 5732/2, July, 1951.

34. NAK, MaiPrOf., 5732/26-31.

35. NAK, MaiPrOf, 5732/12, October, 1951.

36. NAK, MaiPrOf, 5732/1.

attached and the boys should be forced to attend every <u>Sallah</u> (prayer) time."[37]

Thus, the idea of more effectively teaching Islamic religious subjects seemed a perfectly good idea to the colonial rulers -- as long as the courses remained religious, and not political or secular in focus. Regarding the courses taught in the school the District Officer stated as follows:

> The secular subjects permitted to be taught in a class for religious instruction are Reading and Writing in the vernacular. I do not wish to interfere in a school whose main object is to teach religion, but they should be warned that they may not teach secular subjects other than the above. If they wish to do so they must first seek recognition as a school by the Director of Education. This can be done through me, but it involves full compliance with the regulations made under the Education Ordinance.[38]

Indeed, in general the British colonial government was hesitant to interfere with the school's activities, as the Shehu's council lamented in the following report.

> The Resident raised the matter of the application for a site for a [new] school by Jamiyyar Islamiya (sic). He said that in his opinion an application for the opening of a Koran school was a matter for the religious leaders of the community and that an application by a political party might, perhaps, be properly rejected as being outside their sphere. He doubted, however, whether an application by private persons could be properly rejected merely on the grounds that some of them happened to be members of a political party.[39]

NEPU was only able to maintain the cover of the <u>Jamiyyar Islamiyya</u> until

---

37. NAK, "Religious and Moral Instruction in the Northern Province, 1951-1952," MakPrOf, ACC/2062, Agency Mark 5676, 10 May 1951.

38. NAK, MaiPrOf., 5732/16, 12 Nov., 1952.

39. NAK, MaiPrOf. 5732/18, 29 November, 1952.

late 1952 and early 1953, when the party began to administer and fund the schools directly, as well as to open additional establishments. Of course, it was not in the interest of the party to remain in the background in respect to the Islamiyya schools. If the party was to collect any immediate political capital from the promotion of Islamic education, it was necessary for the NEPU to be clearly associated with the new schools. Given the political situation during the early 1950's, it is doubtful that NEPU could have been so successful in establishing the schools if they had been openly associated with the party from the very beginning. The following exchange between the District Officers of Bornu and Kano highlights the resistance the colonial and traditional leaders had towards NEPU's association with the Islamiyya schools.

> The NEPU branch in Nguru has applied for permission to open a Koran school, but before considering the matter further, the Bornu [Native Authority] is anxious to know whether similar requests have been received in other places.
>
> I should be grateful therefore if you would let me know whether any such applications have been made in your division and if so, what has been the [Native Authorities] reaction.
>
> (Reply)   With reference to your confidential memorandum #5583/s.1 of 5th May, no such applications have been received here. I mentioned the matter to the Emir confidentially, and he left me in no doubt that had any been received, his action would have been very unfavorable.[40]

In addition to showing the anti-NEPU collusion of the British colonial administration and the Native Authorities, the above passage is also very telling of the suspicion these groups held towards NEPU's taking on some educational role. Given such an attitude towards NEPU's educational endeavors on the part of the colonial and Native Authority powers, it is not surprising that the radical party opted

---

40. NAK, ZarPrOf., C.45 5/1/16-17.

to cloak their activities via the <u>Jamiyyar Islamiyya</u>. By 1953, though, the Islamiyya schools were well enough established that NEPU could step in. This end was achieved by the formal "dissolution" of the <u>Jamiyyar Islamiyya</u> and by NEPU taking over. Continuity was provided by the fact that the same administrators and teachers remained in their positions. However, teachers such as Lawan Danbazau were able to use their own names at last.

By 1954, NEPU boasted some 15 Islamiyya schools in the Northern Region. There was also a single school in Ibadan, in the Western Region. Even with the backing of NEPU now apparent, the British were hesitant to interfere with the schools as long as the subjects were religious rather than "secular."[41] Neither the British nor the NPC-backed Native Authorities could legitimately attack NEPU for providing religious instruction to the region's Muslim populace. Regular inspections of the schools were carried out to insure that the curriculum did not broach non-religious (particularly political) subjects.[42] The schools' administrators were frequently (and pointedly) reminded by the authorities that if secular subjects were introduced, the schools would be required to comply with the Federal Education Ordinance requirements for teacher certification, school construction, student accommodation, etc.[43] Because such requirements were clearly beyond the institutional and financial means of NEPU, this was no small threat.

The fact that the British hoped to maintain a division between secular and religious instruction only points up the degree to which the colonial administrators were ignorant of the degree to which these two spheres of thought are indivisible in Islam. The British may have been successful in keeping NEPU from including

---

41. NAK, MaiPrOf., 5732/34, 20 October 1954.

42. NAK, MaiPrOf., 5732/35, 3 May, 1955.

43. NAK, MaiPrOf., 5732/34/ 20 October, 1954.

overtly political courses in the Islamiyya schools' curricula, but they could not have hoped to restrict the teachers (themselves NEPU members) from offering their own interpretations of passages during instruction on the Qur'an, Hadiths or Sunna. The curriculum of the schools invariably included instruction in religious "Tradition" and "History." One inspection report stated that the history text for the Maiduguri Islamiyya school was "the teacher's own book".[44] As was illustrated in the first chapter, NEPU and NPC's interpretations of the region's history were at considerable odds with one another, and there can be little doubt whose version was presented in the Islamiyya schools.

Without more extensive knowledge of the day-to-day material covered in the Islamiyya schools, it is hard to judge just exactly how much "radical" material was being presented to the students. It was the strategy of NEPU, though, to start with what was most familiar to the populace, and introduce different ideas, methods and subjects gradually.[45] This was not always an easy task. In 1952 the Kano Islamiyya school at Bakin Ruwa attempted to introduce instruction in boko (Hausa written in Roman script), only to have the idea rejected by the students' parents.[46] Instruction in English, even if it had been acceptable to the parents, which seems unlikely, was forbidden by the colonial government unless the school conformed to the Education Code. Still, even in regards to more traditional subject matter, the Islamiyya schools were still radical in terms of their "Western-style" instruction and their admission of female students.

Even with the Islamiyya schools in an established position in most major towns throughout the North by 1954, NEPU was faced with serious opposition by

---

44. NAK, MaiPrOf., 5732/13, 25 October, 1951.

45. Chamberlain field notes, Interview with Aminu Kano, 4 June, 1971.

46. Ibid.

those who did not approve of the new schools' progressive nature. Not surprisingly, this resistance came in part from the NPC and the Native Authorities -- who were probably much more aware of the potential for "subversive" instruction even when courses were limited to religious subjects. In an interesting reverse of the generally more pro-Western NPC tendency, the NEPU's opponents launched a campaign that attacked the Islamiyya schools on the basis of their "Western nature" -- in particular their structural similarities to Christian mission schools. The Islamiyya schools were given such derogatory nicknames as "Makarantar Mission" (Mission School) "Makarantar Bible" (Bible School) and "Makarantar Dogon Gaimu" (The School of the Long Beard).[47]

The issue even became violent at times. During the opening of one Kano Islamiyya school, Aminu Kano was slapped by one of the Emir's dogonyaro (bodyguards). This was particularly significant because, as head of NEPU, Aminu Kano was generally immune to the physical attacks and harassment that the rank and file of NEPU members were more frequently victim to.[48] Even students who were enrolled in the school were allegedly harassed, though the long waiting lists for the schools kept such efforts from reducing the number of students actually receiving instruction at any given time.[49] In 1953, one of the Kano Islamiyya schools was broken into and badly vandalized.[50] Such resistance to the NEPU-run schools -- widely attributed to the Yan Mahaukita -- was indicative of how great a threat they were viewed by the NPC and the Native Authorities.

---

47. Saidu Balla, 17 January, 1993. Sule Gaya, 21 January, 1993. The latter reference to Makarantar Dogon Gaimu is probably a reference to the schools run by the Alsatian Catholic Missions. The Alsatians all wore long beards.

48. This story has become a famous tale in Kano political history, with almost all informants relating it when asked about the Islamiyya schools.

49. Chamberlain field notes, interview with Aminu Kano, 4 June, 1971.

50. Ibid.

In regard to education of the Muslim populace, NEPU seemed to gain a decided advantage over the NPC government. On the subject of religious education the NPC received an unusual amount of (apparently apolitical) criticism. The following letter is illustrative of popular commentary on the subject.

> The recent move by the Government of the Northern Region to upgrade the School for Arabic Studies is very commendable indeed. But while congratulating it on this move I would like to draw the attention of the government to the deplorable and outmoded system of acquiring infant religious education -- the Koranic schools system -- in this region.
>
> The Koranic schools are, to my mind, the most important institutions for the teaching of the Koran and religion to a child and is one of the fundamental 'musts' imposed on any Muslim parent: yet there is still no move to improve or better the standard of teaching in them.
>
> I therefore suggest to the government to urge the NAs [Native Authorities] -- those in Muslim divisions of course -- to establish infant schools for that purpose and recruit teachers from the School of Arabic Studies to run them. Once they are established the government should then support them by grants... I very much hope that in the interest of Islam, the Native Authorities concerned will endeavor to see that this suggestion is adopted.[51]

NEPU was careful to contrast their party's efforts regarding religion as opposed to those of the NPC, as seen in the following editorial.

> My question is what type of assistance does the NPC party give to Muslims and Islam? The NPC party has never established a single Islamiyya school for the improvement of the young ones throughout Northern Nigeria. If there is one, please point it out.[52]

---

51. Hassan Ahmed, *Nigerian Citizen*, 4 November, 1959 – Ahmed does not appear to have had any affiliation to the NEPU.

52. M.A.K. Abdulkarim Bature Dukawa, "It is the NEPU Party that has the Interest of the Progress of Islam in its Programme, not the NPC," *Daily Comet*, 13 June, 1959.

Even during the early 1960's, when the mixing of religion and politics was becoming even more overt, the NPC government still shied away from direct aid to religious schools. Perhaps members of the NPC were responding to (or relying on) the general resistance of much of the populace to changes in the educational system.[53] Still, the apparent lack of support for improved education in the North (religious or otherwise) was frequently pointed up by NEPU leaders and supporters, who maintained that the NPC was trying to keep the Northern populace ignorant as a means of continuing their corrupt rule. Indeed, a common theme for NEPU was to stress the centrality of education in Islam and the liberating effect of knowledge in general -- whether Western or Islamic. In addressing the issue of education in the North during NEPU's annual conference in 1955, Aminu Kano stated "Ignorance is the root cause of all the evils of our people."[54]

Time now allows a historical perspective on the issue of the Islamiyya schools. Since the 1950's, the schools have increased in popularity to the point where they are found in most wards of large towns and cities. Indeed, they have proven so effective and popular that even those who first attacked them, the conservative backers of the NPC and Native Authorities, now support them. Even more so, many former members of the NPC now claim that it was their own party that invented the Islamiyya schools, though the historical record, as seen in this chapter, does not support such a claim. Some former NPC members say that it was the NPC that created religious Islamiyya schools, and that the NEPU schools only dealt with secular subjects.[55] Quite to the contrary, it is clear from the evidence that those in

---

53. Even in contemporary Northern Nigeria, a large percentage of the population keep their children out of the secular public schools in favor of the traditional Makarantar Allo.

54. Presidential address to the Fifth Annual Conference of the Northern Elements Progressive Union, 1955. From Sklar, *Nigerian Political Parties*, p.373, fn.#101.

55. Interview with Sule Gaya, 21 January, 1993.

authority acted to keep the NEPU from teaching anything but religious topics. Despite NEPU's lack of institutional resources, the party was still able to draw upon its academic strength to offer the populace with a concrete religious service in the form of the Islamiyya schools -- a service that would outlive the party itself. The NPC, too, offered concrete services to the Muslim community in the North, particularly by drawing upon the advantages that come from access to the state apparatus -- an advantage that they would maximize with the coming of independence.

THE PARTIES AND RELIGIOUS SERVICES DURING THE 1960'S

With the coming of independence on 1 October, 1960, the combination of religion and politics began to become increasingly open. No longer did the presence of the British, with their Western-inspired division of religion and politics, serve to undermine the tendency of Islamic political bodies to combine religious services with their other political duties.

The withdrawal of the British influence did little to change the NEPU's approach to the mixing of religion and politics except to allow them to be more overt in some practices. NEPU's use of tafsir, the translation of the Qur'an into Hausa with accompanying interpretation, is a case in point. During the 1950's, tafsir readings by such NEPU leaders as Malam Aminu Kano helped to establish the scholarly credentials of the party's leadership by showing their extensive knowledge of Arabic and the Qur'an. Only the most educated of malams were considered competent to undertake tafsir.[56] Blatantly political interpretations of the Qur'an were frequently avoided during the 1950's. Such settings could still be used to draw large crowds, in order that more political speeches could follow the tafsir. During the 1960's, though,

---

56. Paden, *Religion and Political Culture*, p.298.

NEPU was able to undertake more overtly political religious interpretations. Paden makes the following comment regarding tafsir by Malam Aminu Kano.

> In recent years, many tafsir interpretations by Aminu Kano have stressed the centrality of justice in Islam (interpreting justice mainly in terms of equality), the centrality of education in Islam (the sixth pillar of Islam is regarded by Aminu as "read," a reference to God's command to Muhammad in the cave of Mount Hira when the Qur'an was handed down), and the need for tolerance between people of the book. The tafsir readings are not used to make specific references to the contemporary political scene, but rather to underscore certain principles of belief and action.[57]

Paden's comment regarding the lack of "specific references to the contemporary political scene" misses the point, at least in terms of the potential for politically charged tafsir interpretations of such subjects. Indeed, Paden follows the above quote with the following comment.

> The tafsir of Aminu Kano confirms the Hausa expression "there is no King except God" (ba sarki sai Allah), rather than the Hausa expression "the King is the Shadow of God" (Sarki zillullahi ne). Respect for human authority is implicit in the tafsir but a higher moral code is depicted that has precedence over anything human and hence fallible.[58]

Such commentary as this -- stressing the division between divine authority and the authority of Kings -- is a direct attack on one of the Masu Sarauta's key claims to legitimacy. For the NPC, who sought to associate respect for Islam with respect for traditional rulers, such tafsir was a very real threat, especially when one takes into consideration the popularity of such lectures. During one presentation in 1967, so

---

57. Ibid, p.299.

58. Ibid, p.305.

many people gathered to hear Aminu Kano that traffic on the street outside the house where the tafsir took place was blocked by the audience.[59]

In general, NEPU leaders were not able to take much advantage of the relaxing of the restriction of mixing religion and politics. The NPC, quite to the contrary, was in a better position to take advantage of the relaxed restriction on religious services to the region's Muslim populace. The highest office of the Northern Government, the Premier's office, became a major conduit for small (but numerous) services to Muslims resident in the North and even in Nigeria's other two regions. As discussed in the first chapter, the Sardauna had selected works of Usman Dan Fodio translated into Hausa and published. Beginning in the early 1960's, these works were distributed out of the Premier's office, and files were kept to record thank-you notes and process requests for additional copies.[60]

The works of Usman Dan Fodio were not the only materials and items distributed as religious favors by the NPC government. Copies of the Qur'an were frequently requested of the Premier, and these requests were generally met. The following is an example of a letter addressed to the Sardauna requesting a Qur'an.

> I have the honor most humbly and respectfully to submit this humble letter before you in order to ask for a Koran together with what you may give me as a gift. Why I request this is because I am now learning Koran and I have not got enough money to buy one. I have tried all my possibility to see that I possess one but every attempt of mine failed.[61]

---

59. Ibid.

60. NAK, "Requests for Religious Books, 1961-1966," PRE/2, ACC/404, Agency Mark PRE/222.

61. Ibid., 22 Dec. 1964.

This appeal was met, with a new Qur'an being placed in the mail to the requesting individual only six days later.[62] Requests such as this were common enough that the Sardauna's office once again prepared form letters, stating that the Sardauna hoped the gift Qur'an would help the recipient on the true path. Books were not the only items distributed through the Premier's office. Prayer mats and beads were also frequently distributed.[63]

It is worth noting that these requests were being addressed to the Sardauna of Sokoto, who was both the region's premier and the head of the NPC, and were being processed through the central office of the region's government -- not through the Sardauna's private residence or through some independent office or body. This situation brings up several points. First is the success of the NPC in using the Sardauna, the great-great-grandson of the Shehu, as the focal point of the party's religious legitimacy. Second is the fact that there was no hesitancy to combine this open distribution of religious favors with the highest office of the region's government, with the Premier's staff and institutional facilities being used to facilitate the process. Indeed, it was probably in the best interest of the NPC to associate these services as closely as possible with the government, just to insure that there was no doubt from whom the goods flowed. The point at which the record is incomplete, though, is from where the funds for such services came. Clearly, the payroll for the staff was coming from the government coffers, but the source of the funds for the religious books and items is not so easy to pinpoint.

Requests for religious goods and services made to the Sardauna were not limited to small items such as Qur'ans and prayer mats. In March of 1961, a letter

---

62. Ibid.

63. For numerous examples of such activities, see NAK, "Religious Affairs of the Muslim Community, 1960-1965," PRE/2, ACC/145, Agency Mark PRE/53.

was addressed to the Sardauna from Mahammadu Sokoto, a community leader in Samaru (near Zaria), stating that the community had attempted to build a new mosque, but had run out of funds before the construction process was complete: walls had been raised, but the Mosque was roofless. In response to this query, the Sardauna replied:

> I have already asked the Resident of Zaria to find out for me how much it will cost to finish the mosque. Once I get an answer I will get a contractor to finish the job.[64]

Here again there is no indication of where the funds for the completion of the mosque were coming. It is clear that the Sardauna did fund some mosque-building projects "out of pocket," such as in the case of the Kaura Namoda Jum'at Mosque which reportedly cost some £6000.[65] It is doubtful, though, that the Sardauna could have himself funded the dozens of small mosques that were constructed with government assistance during the early 1960's. Whatever the source of the funding, it is clear that the offices of government -- including the Resident of Zaria -- were being called upon to provide benefits to the region's Muslim populace. Duties such as helping to build mosques represented an expansion of the role of the state in the affairs of the Muslim community. This was not an issue that necessitated a state role -- such as helping to streamline the Hajj. This was a case of the government taking on a role that would not have been considered "proper" by the British colonial rulers.

The NPC, however, was destined to go far beyond such small projects as helping small communities to complete mosque-building projects already in progress. In the course of the early 1960's, the NPC was to undertake the renovation and

---

64. NAK, PRE A11/21, 27 March, 1961.

65. *Nigerian Citizen*, 17 February, 1965.

construction of some of the region's largest and most important mosques. Such programs gave the NPC frequent opportunities to trumpet the party's dedication to Islam and to draw connections between themselves and the region's religious forefathers.

In early 1963, the NPC sponsored an effort to rebuild two of the city of Sokoto's most important mosques -- those of the Shehu Usman dan Fodio and Muhammad Bello. Not surprisingly, the Sardauna of Sokoto was the person through whom the campaign was organized, since he was both the head of the NPC and a descendant of the Shehu and Muhammad Bello. Advertisements were taken out in major newspapers presenting the following statement by the Sardauna.

> You may remember that some time ago a fund was opened to enable the public to contribute, in the service of Islam, to the rebuilding of the mosques in Sokoto city, the Massalacin Shehu and the Massalacin Bello. The Sokoto NA [Native Authority], the sponsors of the appeal, have again asked me to undertake the responsibility for appealing to you. I am therefore once more appealing for your contribution for the completion of the work already started. I am your brother in Islam.
> (signed)Alhaji Sir Ahmadu Bello,
> Sardaunan Sokoto.[66]

Donations to the mosque campaign were to be sent to the Sardauna, care of the Premier's office, Kaduna.

The *Nigerian Citizen* carried full front-page stories announcing the opening ceremonies on the completion of the larger mosque projects, such as that of the Sultan Bello Mosque -- which reportedly cost some £100,000 to complete.[67] The

---

66. *Nigerian Citizen*, 2, 9, March, 1963.

67. *Nigerian Citizen*, 6, 10, July, 1963.

high level of media attention given to these occasions made them a perfect platform for the NPC to insure that their efforts in the service of the region's Muslim populace were not missed. Indeed, the speeches given by NPC leaders on these occasions cover almost all of the NPC's claims to religious and political legitimacy. The speech given by the Sardauna on the occasion of the opening of the Sultan Bello Mosque began as follows.

> Our fore-fathers were known for their building of Mosques, and on that we shall remain by the grace of God. The most excellent work a man can do is the one which he did for the sake of Allah. The most excellent part of the existence of a man is the one he gives to devotion. There is no higher devotion in being a Moslem than the upkeep of mosques. After God has revealed how his light is, that is Islam, which is the light of the Heavens and the earth, he commanded the building of mosques so that those people who are not engaged in trade or commerce should worship God in the mornings and evenings. In the Hadith of the Prophet, on whom be peace, he said 'everyone who builds a mosque for the sake of God, God will build a house for him in Paradise.' To us, however, if there is any mosque worthy to be honored anywhere in this country, it is this mosque.[68]

The political utility of such statements is readily apparent. The first line of this quote represents the common theme of connecting the NPC government to that of the Sokoto Caliphate -- in this case by stating that the NPC, like the early caliphate, was building mosques in the service of Islam. Further, the speech, by proclaiming that the building of mosques was the highest possible form of devotion, implied that the NPC was as devoted a party as was humanly possible.

In his speech, the Sardauna was also careful to insure that the populace of the region knew where to place the credit for the new mosque.

---

68. AH, SA/A, 34, "Text of Speech Delivered by The Premier of Northern Nigeria, The Honorable Alhaji Sir Ahmadu Bello, K.B.E., Sardauna of Sokoto, at the Historic Ceremony of the Opening of the Rebuilt £100,000 Sultan Bello Mosque." Friday, 5th July, 1963.

> There is one thing that has been the fundamental thing in laying the foundation of this great work and that was the faith, help and encouragement given by the Honorable Sultan Sir Abubakar and all the members of his council. I will not mention my own help as the Head of the Northern Region Government and my connection with the work in general. I pray that God may sanctify it, and make it what has been made for His sake. I must thank Mr. Gulwell who drew up the plan of this mosque and also to thank the Northern Region Government for sparing him to work on the mosque free of charge. I must also thank the Bank of West Africa for keeping the money subscribed without charge of any kind.[69]

Also stressed by the Sardauna was the role played by the international Islamic community in the building of the mosque. He was careful to state that the U.A.R. had donated not less than 20% of the mosque's total cost. Representatives from Saudi Arabia were on hand to donate religious books to the mosque's library and none other than the Imam of Medina was on hand to offer the opening prayer for the ceremony.[70] The presence of these dignitaries and the extent of their countries' contributions helped show just how important the efforts of the NPC were in terms of bringing Northern Nigeria into the mainstream, if not the forefront, of the Islamic world -- an effort that was not lost on the region's Islamic community.

Frequent references were also made to the grandeur of the mosque and to its expense. Such references also helped point out that only the NPC, with its access to the wealth of the region's traditional rulers and to the apparatus of the state (if not the state's funds), could afford to undertake such acts of benevolence. The fact that these undertakings were well beyond the means of NEPU was so obvious as not even to warrant mention. Such projects also had the benefit of being difficult for NEPU to attack, since it was difficult to argue with the benefit of improved places of worship.

---

69. Ibid.

70. Ibid. See also *Nigerian Citizen*, 6 July, 1963.

The best NEPU could manage was to argue that the idea to rebuild the mosques had actually been the radical party's idea.

> We welcome the news not because it is good and proper to reconstruct the mosque and bring it up-to-date with other mosques built in advanced Moslem countries but because it has vindicated the NEPU. In 1954 the NEPU at its Annual Convention held in Sokoto adopted a resolution calling for the reconstruction of the mosque by calling all Emirs and Chiefs of this country to support the resolution.[71]

There can be little doubt, though, that such claims by NEPU did little to sway the popular attention given to the NPC's efforts to build mosques and provide such concrete services as streamlining of the Hajj. Indeed, such efforts on the part of the NPC received much the same level of fanfare, if not actually more, as did major development projects such as the building of airports, dams, and factories. Elsewhere in Africa, or even elsewhere in Nigeria, such "development" projects were one of the main ways by which newly independent governments sought to insure their legitimacy. The fact that religious projects received at least equal attention in Northern Nigeria is an indication of the centrality of religious issues to the legitimacy of political parties in the region. Indeed, by the latter years of the First Republic, the leadership of the NPC government in the North was expanding their concept of the role of government to include the populace's eternal spiritual concerns as well as those of this world. To this effect, the Sardauna made the following statement.

> We are now fighting for development and all amenities for our people, we should therefore fight to brighten their future they will meet with God.[72]

---

71. *Daily Comet*, 2 September, 1959.

72. *Nigerian Citizen*, 6 October, 1965.

Such religious obligations on the part of the government, even a Muslim government, were far removed from those envisioned by the British during their tenure as colonial rulers. The role of the NPC in looking after the spiritual welfare of Muslims was to be further expanded during the course of the early 1960's, with the party, at least on the rhetorical level, broadening the scope of their "duties" to include the conversion of non-Muslims to the religion of Islam.

The Islamic conversion campaigns undertaken by the NPC under the Sardauna's leadership during the latter years of the First Republic are a prime example. These campaigns, which were undertaken as "a private matter" by the Sardauna were grandiose efforts to convert as many non-Muslims (mainly Pagans, but also Christians) to Islam as possible.[73] Beginning in 1964, and reaching their climax between April and July of 1965, these campaigns centered on the Sardauna, accompanied by the local NPC faithful, preaching to and converting non-Muslims.

Similar to the mosque-building projects, these conversion campaigns were given heavy play in the region's media. The *Nigerian Citizen* of 28 April, 1965, devoted not only the entire front page, but also a two-page center section to stories and photographs highlighting the Sardauna's efforts to convert people to Islam. Headlines included such statements as "Sardauna Launches Great Islamic Conversion Campaign;" "Thousands Accept Islam in the North: Total Elimination of Paganism in Northern Nigeria;" "In the Footsteps of Usman dan Fodio;" and "Sardauna's 20th Century Islamic Crusade in Northern Nigeria."[74]

Also similar to the mosque-building projects, the conversion campaigns

---

73. Interview with Inuwa Wada, 30 January, 1993. See also Muhammad Sani Umar, "Islam in Nigeria," in *Twenty-five Years*, p.82.

74. *Nigerian Citizen*, 28 April, 1965.

offered the NPC the opportunity to strengthen their claim to religious and political legitimacy by comparing their contemporary efforts to those of the founders of the Sokoto Caliphate. Comparisons between the campaigns and the jihad of Usman dan Fodio, as seem above, were common fare in the press.[75] In one interview, the Sardauna even suggested that his own campaigns were greater than those of his forbears.

> He explained that his ancestors did their jihad with the sword, spears and other crude weapons of the olden days, but that today, the position is different. It is his desire, he explained, that people become Moslems only out of their free-will, adding that those who have been converted to Islam have done so because they are convinced that the religion is the right one and not because of any other reason.[76]

The day-by-day and week-by-week progress of the conversion campaigns was given constant attention by the press and the Premier's office. Press releases from the Sardauna's office made sure that nothing was missed by the "independent" press -- as the following example shows.

> The Honorable Premier has had a most successful four day tour of Gashaka/Mabilla in the Southern Division of Sardauna Province. He was received **both as a political and spiritual head** [emphasis added] wherever he went. Thousands of enthusiastic crowds... gathered to welcome him and his colleagues. All of them were milling around in an attempt to touch his body, dress, or even vehicle. The Premier was presented with 120 heads of cattle by Mabilla Fillanis [Fulani] as a gesture of their tremendous affection for him and his great ancestor Shehu Usman dan Fodio.[77]

---

75. See, for example, *Nigerian Citizen*, 1 May, 1965.

76. *Nigerian Citizen*, 1 September, 1965.

77. NAK, "Press Releases, 1962-1965, PRE/2, ACC/433, Agency Mark PRE/255, 25 May, 1964.

Another common theme of the conversion campaigns was the keeping of a record of the number of individuals converted to Islam. Daily reports to this effect were common fare in the newspapers. An article in the *Nigerian Citizen* of 6 October, 1965, for example, was entitled "Another 1824 new Islamic Converts in Kano." By mid-1965, the NPC could boast such headlines as "Islamic Campaign, Sardauna Preacher: 187,216 converted to Islam."[78] Such numbers were instrumental in the NPC's claim to Islamic devotion and leadership, both in Northern Nigeria and abroad.

The fact that the NPC saw the conversion campaigns as a means of gaining further advantage over NEPU is clearly outlined in the following District Office report.

> The Honorable Premier, Sir Ahmadu Bello, Sardauna of Sokoto's two-day visit to this Division was looked upon as the most successful religious and political crusade ever known in this part of the Region. The Honorable Premier pronounced that he did not come to meet his party men only but to meet everybody has left the few NEPU followers in bewilderment as to whether they are following the right leader.[79]

The conversion campaigns, though, did not serve only to reinforce such well-worn NPC themes such as the party's institutional, ideological, and genetic links to the Sokoto Caliphate and its founders. The record also suggests that the conversion campaigns were in part an attempt to unify the North with Islam as the common bond. Just as the NPC had highlighted the unifying nature of dan Fodio's jihad and the Sokoto Caliphate that followed, the party also stressed Islam as a force that would

---

78. *Nigerian Citizen*, 19 June, 1965.

79. KSHCB, KanoPrOf, Monthly Intelligence Survey, Northern Division. June-July, 1965.

help to unify the Northern Region.[80] As noted in Chapter Four, the non-Muslim sections of the Northern Region, particularly the Middle Belt, presented a threat to the rule of the NPC -- on a national as well as regional level. This factor was especially true in light of the fact that such non-Muslim groups had little interest in the NPC's claim to legitimacy as the "true Muslim party." By converting such groups to Islam, the NPC could at least hope to draw them into the fold of the party faithful.[81]

The goal of converting non-Muslims was achieved in no small part by showing them the rewards that were to come by accepting Islam and with it the NPC's basis of legitimacy. During the campaigns, those who converted were frequently given not only religious items such as Qur'ans, prayer beads and prayer mats, but also valuables such as bolts of cloth, tailored clothes, and pots and pans. On some occasions, gifts of cash were even distributed.[82] On the community level, the regional government helped insure that educational services were extended to those areas where conversions had been particularly numerous.[83] Local leaders were also encouraged to assist in the conversion process. Those leaders who helped provide a good turnout were given substantial sums of money to continue "the propagation of Islam." After a successful campaign in Zaria in October of 1965, the Emir of Zaria was given a check for £2000.[84] The combination of goods given to converts and local authorities who helped arrange the conversion ceremonies in advance seemed to be effective. A *Nigerian Citizen* article dated 1 September, 1965

---

80. See, for example, *Nigerian Citizen*, 19 June, 1965.

81. This point has been raised by Muhammad Sani Umar, "Islam in Nigeria," in *Twenty-Five Years*, p.81-83.

82. *Nigerian Citizen*, 28 April, 1965. Interview with Alhaji Baba Daradara, 7 June, 1993.

83. Sule Gaya, 21 January, 1993. See also *Nigerian Citizen*, 28 April, 1965.

84. *Nigerian Citizen*, 6 October, 1965.

stated as follows:

> The Premier has also accepted an invitation to visit Karaye and Dutse Districts where about **4000 are awaiting him to convert them to Islam** [emphasis added]. The Premier said that he would visit the area on his return from a one week tour of parts of Ilorin Province late in September.[85]

The considerable rewards offered to converts and to those local leaders who helped facilitate the conversion process does throw some doubt on the sincerity of the conversions themselves. While the members of NEPU were largely powerless to attack the benefit of the conversion campaigns while they were being practiced -- devout Muslims could hardly complain about efforts to convert people to Islam -- the subject is a very sensitive one when raised with former NEPU members. Indeed, many NEPU members maintain that the only reason that the Pagan community was converting to Islam was to collect as many of the conversion gifts as possible -- sometimes by converting on more than one occasion. One member of the NEPU women's wing, Hajiya Jumai Wool, related the following conversation with a recent convert.

> [The Sardauna] went to the villages to convert the Pagans. He gave them cloth and other things to hold. I met one Pagan and asked him his name. He asked whether I meant his name at home or in town. He said in town his name was "Sani," but at home it was "Ranau." He said if he went to town he would wear the clothes he was given and his cap, but at home he did not wear them. When I asked if the Sardauna converted him he said yes, for the clothes and two Naira [about £2].[86]

---

85. *Nigerian Citizen*, 1 September, 1965.

86. Hajiya Jumai Wool, 5 June, 1993.

This account points up the way in which the converts were able to change "Pagan" and "Muslim" roles as easily as if they were changing clothes. These roles depended not only on location, but also upon the situation, such as a visit by members of the government who were more likely to extend services to Muslims than to Pagans.

The mention of the name "Sani," -- as seen above -- is worth further discussion. New converts were expected to take Muslim names. "Sani" is a common male name, meaning "second born." Seemingly, though, a disproportionate number of male converts took this name -- possibly over fifty percent. The explanation given for this statistical mystery is a pun on the meaning of "Sani." Sani, pronounced with a long "a" sound, sounds very much like the Hausa statements "sa a ni" ("give to me") and "sa'a ni" (lucky me). Hence, the new converts were taking a name that humorously expressed the basis of their conversions.[87]

Several other themes are apparent in the NEPU members' appraisal of the conversion campaigns. One is that the campaigns were a means by which the NPC hoped to offset the NEPU's attacks on the NPC as a party with a weak grasp of the scholarly and ideologically complex aspects of Islam. Alhaji Tanko Yakasai, one of the founders of the NEPU, made the following statement on this issue.

> Unfortunately for the Sardauna, he was not a scholar like Malam Aminu [Kano] or Sa'ad Zungur. As such he was advised to prove his religious zeal in a practical way which would compensate for his inadequacies in the theoretical knowledge of the religion. He could not give a speech and comment on verses of the Qur'an. [As a result] the way they decided to do it was to go out and covert people to be Muslims and then the Muslim community would believe that this is a committed Muslim.[88]

---

87. Ibid.

88. Alhaji Tanko Yakasai, 17 April, 1993.

While NEPU was not able to respond immediately (or at least openly) to the Sardauna's conversion campaigns, the same was not true for other groups based in the North, particularly those representing non-Muslims, the Northern Christian Association being a case in point. The Christian Association was much disturbed by the extensive role of the Northern Region government in the conversion campaigns -- particularly when combined with dramatic as headlines stating "Sardauna Declares Holy War." This particular newspaper article read as follows:

> The Premier of the North, Alhaji Sir Ahmadu Bello, Sardauna of Sokoto, has called on the Christians to change their faith to Islam. He said that this was necessary in order that they might have the glory of Allah on the doomsday. "Only through Islam is it that sin committed by man could be forgiven" Sir Ahmadu added.[89]

The Sardauna made a similar statement during an interview that year.

> I would very much like not only the Federation of Nigeria, but the whole world to become Moslem. If it does, many of the complicated problems that face it today will fall away. For example, since Islam does not permit lying and cheating and double dealing, a country that has Islam as its official religion would infinitely be a better country in which to live, it would be in which love were king, in which equal opportunity for all would be guaranteed, not by an act of legislation, but by the call of Islam. I will continue, both in my private and public capacities, to mix religion with politics. To me the two are inseparable.[90]

Not surprisingly, Christian groups in the North and South found such statements to be disturbing when they came from one of the Nation's most powerful political

---

89. *Nigerian Citizen*, 6 October, 1965.

90. Interview, 1965. Taken from Abba, *Sir Ahmadu Bello: A Legacy*, p.47.

leaders. To ease tensions, the Sardauna released the following statement, which was printed in newspapers under the title "No Persecution in North Says Premier."

> [The Sardauna] appealed to people not to get into their heads that they could be persecuted for their religious beliefs. The Premier was on Thursday speaking to the delegation of the Northern Christian Association who called on him. Sir Ahmadu, who is also the Vice-President of the World Islamic League, said he had never throughout his religious campaign said that he did not like Christians. "It is my wish to see that people become Muslims just as Christian missionaries will like to see that people become Christians."[91]

Whether these reassurances were taken to heart is doubtful, particularly when the calls to conversion were combined with the NPC's often vociferous anti-southern propaganda -- a common theme of which was the "Pagan barbarism" of the southern regions. There can be little doubt, though, that the conversion campaigns, under the leadership of the Sardauna and clearly undertaken with the interests of the NPC in mind, were seen as a threat by politically aware Christians and non-Muslims in the North and South. This situation could only heighten the tensions that already existed between Northern Nigeria and the Western and Eastern Regions.

All the reasons behind the NPC's activities in offering religious rewards and services did not lie within the boundaries of Northern Nigeria, or even Nigeria as a whole. Beginning with his first pilgrimage to Mecca in 1956, the Sardauna developed close ties with leaders of other Islamic governments. The Sardauna established a particularly close relationship with members of the Saudi royal family, and also became well known to leaders such as Gamal Abd al-Nasser of the U.A.R. During his semi-annual pilgrimages the Sardauna also frequently made side trips to

---

91. *Nigerian Citizen*, 27 October, 1965.

Iraq, Jordan, Kuwait and Pakistan.[92]

During the 1950's, these Islamic states were increasingly in conflict with the European powers over such issues as the establishment of Israel and the Suez crisis. With the largest Muslim population in Sub-Saharan Africa, Nigeria clearly presented an opportunity for these states to extend their influence. In the latter 1950's, the Northern Region government was sternly rebuffed by the British for its growing contact with Nasser's U.A.R. Eventually, the Sardauna was forced to refuse publicly the U.A.R.'s attempts to establish relations.[93]

After independence in 1960, though, the NPC was free to pursue whatever contacts it saw fit. Proving their political savvy, the NPC leaders did not immediately commit to either the socialist U.A.R. block or the more conservative Saudi-led Islamic contingent.[94] Rather, the party, under the Sardauna's leadership, sought to play the two blocks against one another in contest over Nigeria's allegiance. In the end, it was the Saudis with whom the Sardauna developed the closest ties, but only after substantial financial assistance had been donated by the U.A.R. (witness the £20,000 given towards the renovation of the Sultan Bello Mosque). The Saudis' donations to religious projects in the North were far more substantial than that of the U.A.R. In June of 1964, for example, Prince Faisal, on behalf of the Saudi government, donated £60,000 for the "promotion of Islam in Nigeria." According to Paden, the official and "unofficial" donations by the Saudis probably amounted to

---

92. NAK, PRE/52/17.

93. *Nigerian Citizen*, 24 March, 1956. See also *Johannesburg Sunday Times*, 7 October, 1956; *The Times* (London), 24 January, 1957; and House of Representative Debates (Kaduna), 24 February, 1959.

94. For information on this conflict see John Esposito, *Islam and Politics* (Syracuse, 1984), p.129.

"millions of pounds."[95] Even without such financial benefits, the NPC-led northern government likely found the more conservative Saudi government, particularly in respect to the Saudi defense of hereditary (royal) succession, more amenable to their own philosophy of Islamic rule.

Though no records are known to exist to account for exactly how the donations from Saudi Arabia, the U.A.R. (and other Islamic states such as Kuwait), were spent, it is likely that these funds provided a substantial source of the funding for the provision of the religious services discussed in this chapter. At gatherings of the International Islamic community, the Sardauna was careful to trumpet the efforts of his government in providing for and expanding the extent of Nigeria's Islamic community.

> I continue my personal work in building or rebuilding mosques in central places as that is a big propaganda for Islam and it encourages the people of the area to improve their religion. I published the local manuscripts which were written by my ancestors as they are accepted by the public as a whole, so that will encourage learning of both the religion and the Arabic Language.
> I and other Muslim personalities have joined hands in my country and are working vigorously in this field of conversion with the result that the pagans are being converted to Islam in groups nearly everyday and everywhere in the country. We thank God that through His help and guidance and in spite of the preoccupations which it is His will that we should have, 176,930 unbelievers were converted to Islam from December 1963 to March 1965. Not only the pagans are being converted to Islam but also some Christians are embracing it, among them some personalities of standing.[96]

---

95. Paden, *Ahmadu Bello*, p.543.

96. NAK, "Speech to General Islamic Conference, Mecca, 1965," PRE/280. The reference to 'personalities of standing' likely refers to the Prime Minister of Gambia, who converted to Islam while visiting the Sardauna in Sokoto.

International gatherings also provided the Sardauna the opportunity to make statements that would have raised a furor in Nigeria.

> I have earlier spoken of conversion of non-Moslems to Islam. I would like to say that this is only the beginning, as there are other areas we have not yet tapped. I hope that when we clean Nigeria we will go further afield in Africa.[97]

Doubtless, the two previous quotes were very much geared to the audience at hand, but this factor does point up that Islam was a tool that the NPC could (and did) employ both at home and abroad. Indeed, the national and international aspects of the NPC's policy of providing Islamic services and aggressively pursuing the conversion of the Northern Region's non-Muslim populace were interdependent. Contacts with the international Islamic community provided the NPC with capital resources to expand greatly the potential extent of the services that the party offered to the North's populace -- services that only served to enhance the NPC's religious legitimacy at home. Further, as long as the NPC presented its efforts to the Islamic community properly, it received still more funds to continue the process.

In addition to providing financial resources to the NPC, the Sardauna's contacts with the international Islamic community greatly served to bolster his own prestige with the Muslim populace of Nigeria. In 1965 the Sardauna was named Vice President of the World Islamic League -- a title that was frequently used with his name from that point on.[98] There can be no doubt that the Sardauna's increasing interaction with leaders from Muslim states helped Nigerian Muslims feel much more a part of the international Muslim community -- a fact bolstered by the increasing ease of pilgrimage.

---

97. NAK, "Speech by Sardauna at the Residence of the Pakistan Ambassador," PRE/280s.1.

98. *Nigerian Citizen*, 9 January, 1965.

The effect of such international linkages with the wider world Islamic community on non-Muslim Nigerians, of course, is much harder to judge, though certainly some found the situation threatening. In many ways, the close interaction between the leadership of the NPC (particularly the Sardauna) and leaders of other Islamic regions in the early 1960's can be seen as the starting point for the more contemporary debates regarding the propriety of Nigeria's membership in the Organization of Islamic Conference.

CONCLUSION

The proceeding discussion points up a number of important themes. At the most basic, this chapter further reinforces the theme of the NPC's control over and emphasis on institutional matters of governance, while NEPU drew upon and emphasized matters of a more intellectual nature. Hence, in their attempts to offer religious services to the region's Muslim populace each party drew upon their established strengths. The NPC provided concrete services such as the provision of religious goods, facilitation of the Hajj, building of mosques, and the undertaking of conversion campaigns. NEPU offered the populace a new system of Islamic education and religious instruction in the form of tafsir. The efforts of both parties point up the degree to which religious services were a critical component in the political economy of patronage during this formative period in Nigerian history.

This chapter is also revealing in terms of giving a much better picture of the chronological progression of the interaction between religion and politics during the 1950's and early 1960's. In particular this section points up the role of the British in restricting the overt practice of mixing religion and politics during the 1950's. Further, the NPC's expanding efforts to establish its religious legitimacy at home and abroad points up the way in which religion and politics interacted on the local, regional and international levels during this period.

The effect of the expanded linkages with the wider world Islamic community on non-Muslim Nigerians, of course, is much harder to judge, though certainly some found the situation threatening. In many ways, the close interaction between the leadership of the NPC (particularly the Sardauna) and leaders of other Islamic nations in the early 1960's can be seen as the starting point for the more contemporary debates regarding the propriety of Nigeria's membership in the Organization of Islamic Conference.

CHAPTER SIX:
BROTHERHOODS AND POLITICS

While previous chapters have examined the ways in which the NPC and NEPU drew upon various religious sources such as written texts, institutions, and historical reference to bolster their religious and political legitimacy, it is important also to examine the way the parties dealt with the existence of the region's Sufi turug, -- the Qadariyya and Tijaniyya in particular[1]. These two brotherhoods were significant to the political conflict between the NPC and NEPU for a variety of reasons. At the most basic level, the brotherhoods represented important power bases, since their membership made up a substantial portion of the region's adult population. Not only did the brotherhoods represent a potential source of votes for the parties, they also possessed important networks of communication and authority that could be used to mobilize and organize large numbers of people in support of party activities. The political value of such existing systems of organization and allegiance is not to be underestimated, particularly in a setting such as that of Northern Nigeria in the 1950's and 1960's, where systems of political mobilization and consciousness were far from extensive.

Sufism represents a more mystical approach to Islam. Eschewing the extremely textual and legalistic approach of orthodox classical Islam, early Sufis such

---

1. Turuq (sing., Tariqa) means "path" or "right way."

as al-Ghazali (1058-1111 AD) stressed that the individual could attain spiritual union with Allah in this world, through such mediums as self-denial and intense prayer. Over time individual Sufi's came together to organize brotherhoods or turuq The brotherhoods placed Sufi students under the spiritual guidance of a shaykh. Living shaykhs traced their authority not only to their own teachers, but to those who had previously been leaders of the brotherhood, back to the tariqa's founder. These chains of authority are known as silsila. Thus, by their very nature, Sufi brotherhoods are hierarchical in organization, with well defined paths of spiritual authority.

Of key importance to the examination of the role of the turuq in the conflict between the NPC and NEPU is the fact that the Qadariyya and Tijaniyya were organizations with their own corporate perspectives and agendas. Further, the two brotherhoods were in competition for the allegiance of the region's Muslim populace. Such was the intensity of this competition that it frequently turned violent during the first half of the twentieth century. Largely because of this conflict between the two brotherhoods, and because of other institutional and ideological factors, many scholars have maintained that they took similarly oppositional political sides during the 1950's and 1960's, with the Qadariyya siding with the NPC and the Tijaniyya siding with NEPU. This chapter seeks to show that there did not exist a "natural" alliance between the Qadariyya/NPC and the Tijaniyya/NEPU, but rather that the cooperation between these groups was constantly being renegotiated as necessitated by changing political conditions.

To determine the nature of the relationship between turuq and the political parties, several questions need to be addressed. What was the nature of the conflict between the brotherhoods and how was it relevant to the political conflict between the NPC and NEPU?   What was the basis of the "affinity" between the NPC/Qadariyya, and the NEPU/Tijaniyya? What political forms did this "affinity" take?   What factors/situations encouraged cooperation between the parties and brotherhoods?   What factors/situations discouraged cooperation?   How did these relationships change over the course of the period in question?   To answer these questions it is necessary first to examine the background of the conflict between the two brotherhoods and also to examine the historical aspects of each party's relationship to the state in the region of Northern Nigeria.   Next, the interaction between the parties and the turuq during the 1950's and 1960's will be analyzed in order to focus on the dynamics of the relationship between these important religious and political organizations.

BACKGROUND: THE TURUQ IN NORTHERN NIGERIA

First, it must be noted that both the Qadariyya and Tijaniyya brotherhoods have their origins outside of the region of Northern Nigeria. The Qadiriyya was founded in Baghdad by 'Abd al-Qadir Jilani during the 11th/12th century A.D., and spread into North and West Africa during subsequent centuries.[2] The Qadariyya is reputed to have been introduced to Hausaland by al-Maghili during the 15th century.[3] The Tijaniyya was a much more recent arrival, both to Islam and Northern Nigeria. This order was founded in the 18th century by Ahmed al-Tijani in Southern Algeria.[4] Reportedly, the Tijaniyya was introduced into Hausaland (Kano in particular) by Umar al-Futi in the early 1800's.[5]

---

2. Peter B. Clark, *West Africa and Islam: A Study of Religious Development from the 8th to the 20th Century*, (Edward Arnold, 1982), p.31.

3. Anwar, "Struggle for Influence and Identity, the Ulama in Kano, 1937-1987," MA Thesis, Maiduguri, 1989. p.20.

4. Ibid, p.21.

5. Paden, *Religion and Political Culture*, p.68.

The key step in the institutionalization of the Qadiriyya in Northern Nigeria was the jihad of Usman dan Fodio, undertaken in the first decade of the nineteenth century. Dan Fodio was himself a follower of the Qadiriyya, as were most of the Fulani scholars who supported him.[6] Indeed, there can be little doubt that Usman dan Fodio's position as a spiritual leader of the region's Qadiriyya was a means by which he was able to organize and rally his followers. Because of this relationship between the Qadiriyya and the leadership of dan Fodio's jihad, there existed strong ties between the leaders of the Sokoto Caliphate and the tariqa from the Caliphate's inception. With the establishment of colonial rule, the British recognized and supported the relationship between the brotherhood and the traditional leaders who had become the basis of the system of Indirect Rule. In no small part, the British favored the Qadiriyya because they found the "character" of the brotherhood favorable to their interests. As one British officer, Captain G. Callow, remarked on the Qadiriyya in 1926,

> It appears to be the most lenitive sect [found in the region], and perfectly harmless to the state; I think it would be quite impossible to arouse followers of this sect to any fanaticism.[7]

By the early 1950's, this situation had not changed profoundly, either in respect to the relationship between the Qadiriyya and the state or the perspective of the British regarding this relationship. The following statement was part of an extensive survey of Islam in Nigeria undertaken by the British Colonial government in 1952.

> The Kadiriyya here is an institution of the state and its following has been assured by the Sultans and Emirs who followed Muhamadu

---

6. Ibid, p.68.

7. NAK, "Notes on Muhammadanism," ZariaPrOf, K.2867/14, 25 September, 1926.

Bello and his companions.[8]

In contrast to the Qadiriyya, the Tijaniyya was not closely linked to the apparatus of state, at least not in most parts of the North. For roughly the first 100 years of its presence in the region, Tijaniyya followers were but a small presence found predominantly in the area of Kano. It was the conversion of Kano Emir Abbas to the Tijaniyya during World War One that gave the brotherhood its first tie to political power in the region.[9] Paden has stated that this step was in no small part an attempt by the Sarkin Kano to separate himself from the religious control of Sokoto, a fact supported by the spread of Tijaniyya among many non-Fulani malams in Kano around this same time.[10] During the next few decades, the Tijaniyya grew in influence not only in the region of Kano, but also in such areas as Zamfara, which had long chafed at control by Sokoto. In 1937, Emir Abdullahi Bayero renewed his silsila from Shaik Ibrahim Niasse of Senegal.[11] This step not only signified a break of the Kano Emir with the religious supremacy of Sokoto, but also showed the growing influence of Niasse in Northern Nigeria.

The fact that the growth of the Tijaniyya in Northern Nigeria was both a reaction and a threat to traditional authority was lost neither on the traditional leaders themselves nor on the British colonial officials who relied on these traditional leaders to carry out their objectives. Since most of the traditional rulers were themselves Qadiriyya, the expansion of the Tijaniyya threatened to weaken the ties of religious

---

8. NAK, ZarPrOf, C.68, 2425/15. 25 February, 1953.

9. Paden, *Religion and Political Culture*, p.218.

10. Ibid.

11. Paden, *Religion and Political Culture,* p.69.

authority between the rulers and the ruled.[12] The British, while also concerned with this dynamic, feared the Tijaniyya because of what they saw as the brotherhood's "radical" character. Particularly under Shaykh Ibrahim Niasse, the Tijaniyya made membership much more accessible to the wider populace -- having simplified the initiation so as not to require an extensive knowledge of Arabic. Further, Niasse taught that he had the power to extend his own <u>fayda</u> (state of divine grace) to his followers, thus sparing them from judgement on the last day.[13]

Perhaps because the brotherhood eschewed the "elitism" of the Qadiriyya in favor of a more open and populist approach to membership, the British feared that the Tijaniyya was a vector for the spread of "communist propaganda" via "Bolshevik Cells" in Morocco and Senegal.[14] Further, Niasse's international activities (he commonly traveled throughout West Africa and the Middle East to promote his brotherhood) had pan-African overtones. Finally, suspicions that some Tijaniyya had supported the abortive Mahdist uprising of 1944 compounded the suspicions of the Nigerian colonial administrators towards the <u>tariqa</u>.[15] Throughout their tenure of colonial rule, British administrators eyed the Tijaniyya with distrust.[16]

Even without Communist or Mahdist ties, the Tijaniyya were indeed a threat to the spiritual authority of the Qadiriyya in Nigeria simply because they sought to

---

12. Alhaji Tanko Yakasai, 6 June, 1993.

13. Hiskett, *Development of Islam*, p.288.

14. AH K.4797 Vol. 1. 1927. See also AH K.281, 13 October, 1926 and NAK Zarprof, c.68, 1953. The exact reasons for these fears of "communist Islam" are not well developed in the colonial reports cited. Nonetheless, such comments are common in colonial reports dealing with the Tijaniyya.

15. NAK, "Survey of Islam in Nigeria in 1952," ZarPrOf, Security 464/94, 17 April, 1953.

16. Jonathan Reynolds, "Good and Bad Muslims: Islam and Indirect Rule in Northern Nigeria," presented at the African Studies Association Conference, 3 November, 1995.

establish a new focus of religious allegiance. It is no surprise that those areas most likely to accept the Tijaniyya, such as Zamfara and Kano, had long histories of resistance to the authority of Sokoto. The fact that the Tijaniyya's focus of authority was on the person of Shaykh Ibrahim Niasse of Senegal, who made no attempt to hide his international and Pan-African aspirations, only made the situation more threatening to the British and NPC.

Thus, while the British took great pains to create an facade of impartiality towards the various Islamic groups in the region of Northern Nigeria, they actually had a vested interest in the maintenance of the "state-friendly" Qadiriyya in a position of power in the North.[17] This fact was to greatly color the British perspective on politics in the North up to the very end of colonial rule.

During the 1940's, the growing presence of the Tijaniyya in the North led to numerous clashes between the followers of the Qadiriyya and the Tijaniyya. In addition to the violence between followers of the turuq, the conflicts of the 1940's involved the state as well. Because of the close relationship between the Qadiriyya and the traditional leaders who formed the basis of the Native Authority system, it was not unusual for these traditional leaders to use the police and courts to suppress the activities of the Tijaniyya. Following clashes around Sokoto in 1949, for example, several Tijaniyya mosques were leveled on the orders of the Sultan of Sokoto.[18] Thus, the answer of the Native Authorities to the issue of conflict between the turug was to limit the visibility (if not the existence) of the Tijaniyya.

Malam Buhari, a Tijaniyya scholar in Kano city, reported that throughout the

---

17. See, for example, Lugard's statements in *Dual Mandate*, p.594.

18. Clarke/Linden 1984, pp.44-45. See also NAK, "A Survey of Islam in Northern Nigeria in 1952," ZarPrOf, C.68, Security 464/94, 17 April, 1953.

1940's and 1950's, the Native Authorities frequently prevented the Tijaniyya from building mosques, because "this would attract public attention to us."[19] The actions of the Native Authorities were not always directed at physical institutions, but sometimes, it is alleged, at the members of the tariqa itself. "The [Native Authorities] caught Tijaniyya followers and tortured them. They sent them to jail. Sometimes they even killed people."[20] Because of the British authorities' suspicions and fears of the Tijaniyya (as discussed above), the colonial rulers were willing to turn a blind eye, if not give active support, towards the repression of the Tijaniyya.[21]

Certainly, not all the steps taken against the Tijaniyya were overtly violent. A common tactic on the part of those in authority during the 1940's was to try and restrict the visibility of the Tijaniyya presence. A major component of this approach was to stop the Tijaniyya members from undertaking wazifa and kabalu in public. The issue of kabalu in particular deserves mention. Referring to the act of praying with arms crossed and hands clasped, this practice was favored both by the Tijaniyya and by the Mahdists. Qadiriyya followers practiced sabalu, praying with hands at one's side.[22] During the course of the early 20th century, the practice of kabalu had become a form of symbolic resistance to the religious authority of Sokoto -- being practiced both by the Tijaniyya and Mahdists. During a meeting with leading Tijaniyya malams in the late 1940's, the Sultan of Sokoto demanded that they stop

---

19. Interview with Malam Buhari, 23 May, 1993.

20. Malam Buhari, 23 May, 1993. British documents from the 1940's and 1950's make references to confrontations between the Tijaniyya and Qadiriyya. Such documents are rather vague on the actual actions of the Native Authorities. See NAK, ZarPrOf C.68 "A Survey of Islam in Northern Nigeria in 1952."

21. Alhaji Tanko Yakasai, 17 April, 1993.

22. Sabalu is typically practiced by followers of the Maliki school of law. Thus, it is all the more striking that the Tijaniyya and Mahdists, who both followed Maliki law, would choose to practice Kabalu.

their members from practicing <u>kabalu</u> in public.[23] As will be seen, the issue of <u>kabalu</u> continued to be an important one to the end of the First Republic in 1966.

POLITICS AND BROTHERHOODS IN THE 1950'S AND 1960'S

Thus, with the advent of party politics in the early 1950's, there existed a situation where most traditional rulers and the colonial authorities perceived the Tijaniyya as a religious and political threat. Not surprisingly, the conflict between the Qadiriyya and the Tijaniyya became an important element in the politics of the period. Scholars, though, are not clear exactly on how the <u>turuq</u> related to the NPC and NEPU. Many scholars, such as Sklar and Post, fail to address the issue of the importance of the brotherhoods to politics during the period. Other scholars, such as Whitaker and Paden, discuss the <u>turuq</u> in some detail, but never establish a clear relationship between politics and the brotherhoods. Finally, other researchers such as Cruise O'Brien, Hiskett and Umar do attempt to define a clear relationship but in so doing oversimplify the relationship by stating that the Qadiriyya supported the NPC and the Tijaniyya supported NEPU.[24]

The following discussion will focus on the interaction between the NPC and NEPU political parties and the Qadiriyya and Tijaniyya Brotherhoods to show that while some tendency does exist for the sort of cooperation identified by Cruise O'Brien, Hiskett and Umar, this cooperation was subject to constant renegotiation as demanded by the political climate at the time. In so doing, this chapter will provide a more textured perspective on the role of brotherhoods in the political conflict

---

23. Malam Buhari, 23 May, 1993. M. Buhari was not sure of the date of this meeting, but he suspects it was around 1949.

24. See Donald Cruise O'Brien "Brotherhood Abroad," *West Africa*, (11-17), January, 1993, pp.16-17. Umar "Islam in Nigeria," in *Twenty-Five Years*, pp.77-88. Mervyn Hiskett, *The Development of Islam*, pp.285-289. Hiskett, *The Course of Islam*, p.121.

between the NPC and NEPU during the 1950's and 1960's.

The case to be made for a clear NPC/Qadiriyya and NEPU/Tijaniyya alliance is an attractive one. First, there were considerable organic links between the Qadiriyya and the leadership of the NPC, since most of the NPC leaders belonged to the class of <u>Masu Sarauta</u> who traced their heritage back to the (largely Qadiriyya) leaders of the Sokoto Jihad. Indeed, many, if not most, NPC leaders were Qadiriyya. The link between the Qadiriyya and the region's traditional leaders is clearly evidenced by the fact that all Emirs' town criers would preface announcements with the statement "Oh you Qadiriyya, the Emir greets you and wants you to hear the following..."[25] Indeed, even Emir Sanusi of Kano, himself a Tijaniyya, would have his town crier make the same statement.[26] Support for the NPC by the Qadiriyya was at times overt, witness the following poem collected by Hiskett:

> We Pray God the Glorious, the King of Truth
> That NPC may rule Nigeria
> For the sake of the Lord 'Abd al Qadir al-Jilani
> My your rule [O Sardauna] last until the coming of the
> Mahdi.[27]

Unlike the case for the NPC and Qadiriyya, there existed no clear organic link between NEPU and Tijaniyya. Still the two groups' general tendencies would seems to call for alliance. Both were in positions of minority opposition to the region's political and religious elite. Further, both group's "radical" rhetoric appeared to be socialist and Pan-Africanist in its nature -- particularly offensive to the eyes of the British. Given such a situation, cooperation between the two groups seemed only

---

25. Interview with Shaik Nasiru Kabara, 27 June, 1993. Alhaji Tanko Yakasai, 6 June, 1993.

26. Shaik Nasiru Kabara, 27 June, 1993.

27. Hiskett, *Development of Islam*, p. 285.

natural. As Cruise O'Brien has commented on this presumed affinity:

> There is also a political dimension to the success of the Niasse Tijaniyya in Nigeria, which can be dated back to the associations of Ibrahim Niasse in Kano, in this case with Aminu Kano and the [NEPU]. A shared quality of populism can be observed in this association, a disposition to take up the cause of the commoner, of the talakawa, against aristocratic privilege.[28]

Indeed, there were numerous occasions during the 1950's and 1960's when NEPU spoke out regarding the "repression" of the Tijaniyya at the hands of the Native Authorities, which would seem to suggest that such an alliance existed.

Detailed examination of the role of the brotherhoods in the politics of the 1950's and 1960's, and their interaction with the two political parties, suggests that while certain commonalities of purpose did exist, there cannot be said to have existed any sort of "alliance" between the NPC/Qadiriyya and the NEPU/Tijaniyya during the period in question. Several factors point up the rather complex (but not indecipherable) relationship between the parties and brotherhoods during this period.

One of the facts that is most basic to the difficulty in ascribing any sort of clear party/brotherhood alliances is the fact that both parties had members of both brotherhoods in their leadership and among their followers. In terms of the leadership of the NPC, for example, Sir Ahmadu Sanusi, the Emir of Kano, was not only the leader of the Tijaniyya brotherhood for Nigeria, but was also considered one of the most powerful leaders of the NPC -- at least up to his break with the Sardauna and resignation from the emirship in 1963. Further, Emir Sanusi was notorious for his violent repression of NEPU, having been credited with the formation of the Yan

---

28. Cruise O'Brien, "Brotherhood Abroad," pp.16-17.

Mahaukita, the arm of the NPC that carried out the physical intimidation of opponents.[29] Similarly, some Tijaniyya leaders who were not among the Masu Sarauta (as was Sanusi) also actively supported the NPC. Malam Tijani, a Tijaniyya leader in Kano, for example, undertook tafsir in support of the NPC.[30]

Among NEPU leaders, there seemed to be few individuals who belonged to neither brotherhood. Indeed, Sa'ad Zungur, one of the founders of NEPU, maintained a somewhat anti-Sufi stance that may have helped to distance him and other NEPU leaders, such as Aminu Kano, from the turuq. To a certain extent, this tendency may be attributed to the fact that NEPU leaders advocated a more "pure" practice of Islam that drew on textual and intellectual sources rather than mystical ones.[31]

Both parties counted members of both brotherhoods among their rank and file supporters, as seen in the following statements from NPC and NEPU leaders, respectively.

> People joined the [Political] Parties irrespective of what sect or tariqa they followed. Whether Tijaniyya or Qadiriyya, there was no demarcation.[32]

and

> Both the NPC and NEPU have their own supporters from among both groups, so cannot say that Qadiriyya is supporting the NPC or the Tijaniyya is holding to the NEPU or the other way around. Both

---

29. Alhaji Tanko Yakasai, 21 January, 1993.

30. Alhaji Tanko Yakasai, 6 June, 1993.

31. Muhammad Sani Umar, "From Sufism to Anti-Sufism in Nigeria," in Brenner, ed. *Muslim Identity and Social Change in Sub-Saharan Africa*, (Indiana, 1993), p. 157.

32. Interview with Alhaji Inuwa Wada, 30 January, 1993.

groups supported both parties.[33]

The political expediency of maintaining support among both brotherhoods is clear. For the NPC, which sought to create the image of a "united North," it was essential to downplay the ties between the party's leadership and the Qadiriyya, while at the same time trying to draw in members of the Tijaniyya as a further base of support. Given the often antagonistic stance of the two brotherhoods, this situation created a serious political challenge for the NPC during the period in question. No doubt, the high-profile position in the NPC of prominent Tijaniyya like Emir Sanusi was critical to the NPC strategy. Indeed, the fact that the Sardauna's daughter was married to Sanusi's eldest son was considered to be an important symbol of the link between the Qadiriyya and the Tijaniyya in the NPC.[34]

For NEPU, siding with a particular Brotherhood was not a promising political move. Without cordial relations with the Qadiriyya, they had little hope of drawing the bulk of the Brotherhood's support away from the NPC and Masu Sarauta. Siding with the Tijaniyya as a "unified opposition" was of little appeal if the party hoped to have any base of support outside of the predominantly Tijaniyya areas of Kano and eastern Sokoto. Rather, it was in the interest of NEPU to maintain a sort of "brotherhood-neutral" stance while at the same time threatening the NPC's claim to religious neutrality. Indeed, these were the strategies of the NPC and NEPU from the 1950's to 1963, when the role of the brotherhoods in politics, and the parties' respective strategies, was to change radically.

Thus, during the 1950's, neither the leadership nor the membership of either party reflected a clear alliance with either the Qadiriyya or Tijaniyya. Further, the

---

33. Alhaji Tanko Yakasai, 21 January, 1993.

34. Alhaji Inuwa Wada, 30 January, 1993.

importance to the parties of drawing support from both turuq must be taken into account. These factors suggest that there are serious flaws in any attempt to ascribe clear party/brotherhood political boundaries during the period in question.

The fact that the party/brotherhood relationships were complex, though, does not mean that there was no such interaction at all. Several examples of the parties' relationships to the turuq are available from the period up to 1963. In late 1956/early 1957 there was yet another conflict between the Qadiriyya and the Tijaniyya in the Zamfara area of eastern Sokoto province -- the last major outbreak having been in 1949. Clashes between Qadiriyya and Tijaniyya followers led to dozens of casualties -- including the death of a Qadiriyya Imam.[35] The Native Authority of the region quickly brought in police to restore order. The Northern Region Government noted its "regret" over the clash, but stated that the government had brokered negotiations between the two groups and that the results were "encouraging."[36] NEPU, though, took a very different perspective on the issue. Numerous newspaper editorials published by NEPU members stated that only Tijaniyya members were being charged and imprisoned in association with the riots, and that this situation was evidence of the "religious bias" of the Northern Government.[37]

The timing of this clash between the Qadiriyya and Tijaniyya is also significant in that it coincided with the London Constitutional Debates. Paden reports that in "informal discussions with Aminu Kano," the NEPU leader admitted that NEPU had encouraged the conflict (by shipping young NEPU supporters from Kano to pose as Tijaniyya) as a means of making "a mockery of the idea of religious

---

35. Paden, *Religion and Political Culture*, p. 198.

36. *Nigerian Citizen*, 16 May, 1956. See also Paden, *Religion and Political Culture*, p.199.

37. See, for example, *Nigerian Citizen*, 6 February, 1957, 20 February, 1957, and 16 March, 1957.

tolerance" in the North.[38]

Such a strategy on the part of NEPU points up not an "alliance" with the Tijaniyya, but instead a rather overt manipulation of existing religious tensions to embarrass NEPU's opponents. Indeed, this strategy probably did more harm than good for the Tijaniyya in the Zamfara area. Not only did the violence lead to the arrest of many Tijaniyya, but NEPU's defense of the Tijaniyya led many NPC leaders to assume that there was indeed an alliance between the Brotherhood and NEPU. As Nasiru Kabara, head of the Qadiriyya and an NPC supporter stated:

> All people of Bakin Kasuwa villages like Zamfara, like Kaura na Mode, like Funtuwa, they accept Tijaniyya -- all of them. And, unfortunately, all those who accepted Tijaniyya there entered NEPU. They became NEPU members. It was as if they were challenging the Sultan and the Emirs.[39]

Evidence does not actually suggest such a move to membership in NEPU on the part of the Tijaniyya of eastern Sokoto. Indeed, many Tijaniyya seem to have resisted membership in NEPU, at least prior to 1963, for fear that it would simply provide yet another source of conflict with those who controlled the state.[40]

Another event that called into question the relationship of the political parties to the brotherhoods also occurred in early 1957. Beginning on 11 January, a NEPU member named Saidu Balla, himself a member of Tijaniyya, published a series of three articles entitled "Yaya Addinin Musulunci Yake?" ("What is the Religion of Islam?"). The first issue addressed by Balla was that of the basis for kabalu in the

---

38. Paden, *Religion and Political Culture*, p.198. See also *Ahmadu Bello*, p.307.

39. Shaik Nasiru Kabara, 27 June, 1993.

40. Malam Buhari, 23 May, 1993.

Qur'an and the Hadiths of the Prophet. Balla stated that kabalu-style prayer (typically practiced by the Tijaniyya) was indeed that which was proper, as opposed to the more common sabalu practiced by the Qadiriyya. Kabalu, though, was not the only issue addressed in the articles. Malam Balla voiced support for the radical stand taken by Isa Wali on the issue of "The Position of Women in Islam," and also took advantage of the issue of kabalu to attack the standard of education of the region's Islamic leaders.

> Here in Nigeria the majority of the Ulama are an ignorant lot. They are leading people astray. They preach to people to follow the path of Imam Malik ibn Annas who is said to have instructed his followers to perform sabalu.[41]

Given the politically sensitive nature of the issue of kabalu both historically and at the time of the writing, and the generally antagonistic tone of the articles, it is not surprising that Malam Balla was jailed within a few days and charged with "publishing sacrilegious matter."[42]

What is surprising is that Malam Balla was arrested by the Kano Native Authority, itself headed by the Emir of Kano -- who was the head of the Tijaniyya for Nigeria. Such was the complexity of the issue of the relationship of brotherhoods and politics during this period that a member of the Tijaniyya could be arrested by the head of that brotherhood on the grounds that he advocated kabalu.

Clearly, this situation placed Emir Sanusi (and the NPC) in a very delicate situation. There can be little doubt that NEPU leaders were trying to arouse religious tensions, a move that threatened to weaken the NPC's goal of creating a unified

---

41. *Gaskiya ta fi Kwobo*, 11 January, 1957.

42. *Nigerian Citizen*, "Statement by Kano N.A." 9 February, 1957.

Muslim North. The conviction of Balla in the Emir's court on the grounds of his advocation of kabalu would almost certainly weaken the position of the Emir as the regional head of the Tijaniyya and hence weaken one of the NPC's main links to the Brotherhood's support.

No doubt, NEPU was pleased with the situation and hoped to draw as much attention to the trial as possible. NEPU hired two lawyers to help with the preparation of the case.[43] The party's plans were thwarted, though, when Emir Sanusi brokered a deal with Balla and his family.

> The Emir himself he came to my family and asked them to please not go to court because I did not do anything bad. He said he detained me to protect me from people who might come to attack me. He promised to pay all my expenses for lawyers and everything and even to pay damages.[44]

Such a negotiated settlement between Malam Balla and Emir Sanusi was clearly the best hope for the NPC in not bringing the issue of kabalu to the forefront of Kano politics at this sensitive point in time.

Even before his installation as Emir in 1953, Sanusi had developed a close relationship with Shaykh Ibrahim Niasse of Koalak, Senegal. Perhaps more than any other single individual, Niasse was responsible for the remarkable expansion of the Tijaniyya in West Africa (particularly Northern Nigeria) during the twentieth century. Niasse had been influential in the region for some time, having renewed the silsila of Kano Emir Abbas in 1937. Over the course of the 1940's, Niasse made several low-profile visits to Kano to help organize and mobilize the Tijaniyya in the Northern

---

43. Interview with Saidu Balla, 17 January, 1993.

44. Saidu Balla, 17 January, 1993.

Nigerian region.[45]

In 1951, 1952, and 1953, Niasse made public visits to Kano while en route to Mecca. During these visits, he stayed with Sanusi, then <u>Chiroma</u> of Kano. After becoming Emir, Sanusi was to accompany Niasse on pilgrimage to Mecca on several occasions.[46] Throughout the 1950's, the close relationship between Sanusi and Niasse was a major means by which the NPC could hope to maintain the support of Tijaniyya members in the region -- despite such incidents as those in Zamfara. For example, Niasse made a visit to Kano just before the pre-independence elections of 1959, which helped consolidate Tijaniyya support for the NPC.[47]

While the relationship between Niasse and Sanusi seems to have been a very close one, as well as one of general benefit to the NPC, Niasse was still viewed with no small degree of suspicion by other leaders of the NPC -- particularly the Sardauna. One must keep in mind that tensions were still high between the Qadiriyya and Tijaniyya, and Niasse's efforts to expand the Tijaniyya presence in Nigeria had been a major factor in the escalation of these tensions.

It is also worth noting that Niasse was becoming a figure of increasing influence throughout West Africa. It is not unlikely that the Sardauna, himself a figure of growing regional and international influence during this same time, saw Niasse as a threat to his own power, both in Nigeria and in West Africa in general. A series of letters exchanged by Niasse and the Sardauna in 1961, along with intelligence reports regarding Niasse's activities, shed some light on this issue.

---

45. Paden, *Religion and Political Culture*, p.69.

46. Ibid, pp.110-111.

47. Alhaji Tanko Yakasai, 21 January, 1993.

I am on my way to Cairo on an official visit, after spending some days in Ghana where I was invited by Osagyefo Dr. Kwame Nkrumah, who has great love and respect for you. And I sincerely hope that real and cordial relations will be strengthened between your two countries. I should like to draw your attention to the Muslims and people of West Africa, to liberate themselves and to raise the Pan-African Banner, so that they may practice their beliefs and traditions freely. You are the only leader who can satisfy the African's desire and achieve their aims in your country.[48]

The Sardauna cordially replied as follows.

Thank you very much for your letter in which you congratulate me for the effort I am making to foster Moslem Unity. I am very much grateful for your prayers and for all that you have said about me. My intention to achieve Moslem Unity is a thing which cannot be expressed in words. I only hope that you will join me in praying for God's Guidance in achieving this very important task.[49]

Several points within this exchange are worth noting. First, it is significant that Niasse is both writing from Ghana and promoting Pan-Africanism. During the early 1960's, the state of relations between Nkrumah's Ghana and the NPC-led government of Nigeria were taking a decided turn for the worse, with the NPC chafing both at the increasingly socialist and Pan-Africanist ideology advocated by Nkrumah.[50] The NPC was staunchly conservative in its stand regarding alignment with the Capitalist West. Further, the NPC, as seen in the Sardauna's reply, was much more concerned with "Muslim Unity" than with Pan-Africanism. Indeed, it

---

48. Niasse to Sardauna, NAK, PRE 3, Acc., 21. 4 March, 1961.

49. Sardauna to Niasse, NAK, PRE 3, Acc. 21, 12 August, 1961.

50. Several newspaper articles from the period are indicative of growing tensions between the NPC and Nkrumah's government in Ghana. See "Nkrumah and West Africa, His Ambition is Pan-Africanism," *Nigerian Citizen*, 17 January, 1959 and "North Unlikely to Accept Nkrumah's Leadership," *Nigerian Citizen*, 24 January, 1959.

was NEPU and the NCNC in Nigeria that voiced calls for Pan-Africanism, and these parties were frequently suspected of receiving "assistance" from Ghana, particularly as Nigerian-Ghanaian relations deteriorated in the early 1960's.[51]

The Sardauna's reply is even more telling in light of a letter received by the Premier's office shortly after Niasse had arrived in Cairo. The letter, sent by a Hausa NPC supporter named Ibrahim Haruna who resided in Egypt, stated as follows:

> Many greetings to you. Greetings on drinking water. After Greetings, I am writing to tell you of the things that Ibrahim Kaulaha [Niasse] has come here and done to you. He has come to Cairo and al-Azhar [university]. They have given him much money with which to build mosques and schools. He said that more than 30,000 Nigerians have come to his place [in Senegal] seeking learning. This is because in Nigeria there are no schools, and this is because the leaders of Nigeria do not want the common people to learn. They have prevented this since the time of Usman dan Fodio. Adding to his lies he said Shehu Usman did not give life to religion but only killed the [Muslim] community and brought war.[52]

Such allegations were serious ones, and struck at the heart of many of the Sardauna's claims to international Islamic prominence, since when abroad he frequently lauded his role in providing religious services to Nigerian Muslims and stressed his blood relationship to Usman dan Fodio. Further, in the early 1960's, the UAR was a major source of funding for the Sardauna's Islamic projects in Nigeria. Aside from besmirching the Sardauna's name, Niasse's motives in making such statements are hard to identify precisely. It could be that Niasse saw the Sardauna as a rival Islamic leader on the regional level. It is also possible that Niasse was attempting to weaken

---

51. See for example, Robert Coughlan, "Black Africa Surges to Independence", Life, 26 January, 1959, p.106.

52. Ibrahim Haruna to Sardauna, NAK, PRE 3, Acc 21/450. March 20, 1961.

the Sardauna's international standing prior to a potential power play by Emir Sanusi of Kano. Whatever the case, the letter was given serious attention by the Premier's office, and Malam Haruna was encouraged to send any more information he had on Niasse's activities. One must wonder if the Sardauna's thanks to Niasse "for all that you have said about me" in his reply to the Shaykh represented a private joke.

To what degree the Sardauna's and the NPC's suspicions of Niasse colored their attitude towards Emir Sanusi of Kano is hard to judge. There can be no doubt, though, that the period from 1961-1963 saw expanding tensions between the Sardauna and the Emir of Kano. Sanusi was by many estimations the second most powerful leader in the NPC. As Emir of the most populous and economically productive region of the North and as head of the Tijaniyya in Nigeria, Sanusi commanded considerable political resources. Further, these political resources were expanding. In part thanks to his relationship with Niasse, the Tijaniyya was growing in influence despite the resistance of the Qadiriyya. Also, Sanusi had begun to move more firmly into the Tijaniyya camp in his own region of Kano. In 1962 he removed the influential Qadiriyya leader, Nasiru Kabara, from his circle of advisers, and replaced him with a Tijaniyya scholar. This step ended a long period of cooperation between the Tijaniyya Emirs of Kano and local Qadiriyya leaders.[53]

On yet another level, Kano's economic power, already potent, was growing even more quickly as the country sought to industrialize. This economic power increasingly became a threat to the religious and political influence of Sokoto, a case in point being Kano's choice as the site for the region's international airport. As long as he was Emir and head of the Kano Native Authority, Sanusi's power would only grow with that of the province.

---

53. Shaik Nasiru Kabara, 27 June, 1993.

By 1962, opposition and southern-region newspapers were speculating about the tensions between the Sardauna and the Emir.[54]   One article even suggested that

> The Emir of Kano is planning to break from Northern Nigeria and create a Kano State because he was not appointed the new Governor of Northern Nigeria and that the Premier of Northern Nigeria offered the post to a Kanuri to stop the Kanuris from asking for a Bornu state.[55]

While many articles were no doubt attempts to foment conflict within the NPC, they did indeed reflect growing tensions between the two important Northern leaders. Beginning in July of 1962, the Kano Resident, Mr. M. Cook, began sending a series of "Top Secret and Personal" letters to the Sardauna in which he enumerated various allegations regarding the Emir of Kano's lack of loyalty to the regional government. "The Emir has encouraged criticism and opposition to government policy, and has questioned government motives."[56]   Cook's letters also provided information regarding financial inequities in the Kano Native Authority's purchasing practices.[57]

The allegations in Cook's letters seemed to be the last straw, or perhaps simply a convenient opportunity, for the NPC Regional Government. In September of 1962, D.J.M. Muffett was named to head a special probe to investigate the "financial affairs of the Kano Native Authority." Muffett called upon the public of Kano Province to come forth with any evidence of any sort of wrongdoing on the part of the Kano Native Authority.[58]   Evidence against the Kano Native Authority did not

---

54. See, for example, *Sunday Express,* "The Bug in Sir A[hmadu Bello]'s Ear," 1 July, 1962.

55. *Citizen Post*, 20 July, 1962.

56. KSHCB, KanoPrOf, Security, 373.s.7/21-23.

57. KSHCB, KanoPrOf., Security, 373.2.7./31-34.

58. *Daily Mail*, "Kano Probe, Commissioner Sets Down to Work," 20 September, 1962.

seem to be hard to come by. Within the first two months of the probe, numerous officials within the Emirate were either fired or had resigned. In early 1963, Emir Sanusi resigned from the Emirship rather than face what appeared to be inevitable expulsion.

Interestingly, the issue of Sanusi's ties to Niasse and the Tijaniyya did not play a visible role in the Muffett inquiry. The focus of the inquest, on the official and public level, dealt only with the dubious financial dealings of the Kano Native Authority. Behind the scenes, though, the regional government was very much concerned with the potential that brotherhood-based tensions might flare-up during the enquiry. For example, rumors that Niasse might come to Kano to rally support for Sanusi were carefully monitored.[59]

Even though the issue of Tijaniyya influence did not play an overt role in the actual removal of Sanusi from the Emirship in Kano, his resignation was a crucial watershed for the role of the Tijaniyya in northern politics. Because Sanusi's resignation from the Emirship was also effectively a resignation from the NPC, the conservative party lost its key form of influence and contact with the Tijaniyya in Nigeria, which Sanusi still headed as Niasse's local representative.

Sanusi's replacement, Muhammad Inuwa, was himself a Tijaniyya, but did not recognize Niasse as his Shaykh, thus alienating the Kano Emirship from its ties to Senegal.[60] There can be little doubt that Inuwa was chosen in large part because of his lack of ties to Niasse. Emir Inuwa, though, died after only six months as Emir. He was replaced by Ado Bayero, who had no affiliation with either the Tijaniyya or the Qadiriyya at the time. Bayero did bring the influential Qadiriyya leader Nasiru

59. KSHCB, KanoPrOf., Security, 373.s.7/58.

60. Paden, *Religion and Political Culture*, p.117.

Kabara back into the Emir's inner circle of advisers, clearly showing that he was taking a decisive step away from associating the Kano Emirship with the Tijaniyya.[61]

Even though Sanusi was removed from the Emirship, he was not removed from his position of leadership among the Niasse Tijaniyya. Indeed, the conflict between Sanusi and the Sokoto-based NPC served to rally Tijaniyya support around him.[62] Sanusi was "exiled" to Azare, south of Kano, and many Tijaniyya leaders traveled to visit him there and pay their respects. Numerous poems, many in Arabic, were written by Tijaniyya malams protesting Sanusi's removal and treatment. The Northern Regional Security Service kept careful track of the movements and activities of all Tijaniyya malams and leaders who were associated with Sanusi.[63] In particular, there regional government was concerned with Sanusi's ongoing relationship with Niasse.

> As the Ex-Emir appears to have become a focal point for local Tijaniyya activity, it is necessary to insure that he is not used as a pawn in Pan-African political activity through the influence of Sheik Ibrahim Niasse of Koalack.[64]

Sanusi's removal from the NPC did indeed serve to focus the Tijaniyya politically. No longer was there a conflict between Qadiriyya and Tijaniyya interests that had existed in the NPC. It was the creation of the Kano Peoples Party (KPP) in early 1963, shortly after Sanusi's resignation, that was to serve as the focal point for Tijaniyya participation. A newspaper article described the new party as follows.

---

61. Paden, *Religion and Political Culture*, p.157.

62. Alhaji Tanko Yakasai, 21 January, 1993.

63. KSHCB, KanoPrOf, Security 373.s.7. KSHCB, KanoPrOf, 6410. NAK, PRE 2188/51-53.

64. NAK, PRE 2188/53.

> A new political party has been formed in Kano following the resignation of the former Emir of Kano, Alhaji Sir Mohammadu Sanusi. The party, the "Kano Peoples Party" criticized the decision of the Northern Nigerian Government in asking the former Emir to resign his appointment. In a statement in Kano, the General Secretary of the new party, Malam Ali Wazirchi, said that the way and manner the former Emir was made to resign was absurd. He called on the people of Kano Emirate to support the new party which he claimed was out to oust the NPC rule in the province.[65]

Indeed, the central platforms of the KPP were the reinstatement of Sanusi as Emir and the creation of a Kano State, which would be independent of the Northern Regional Government. These two platforms were tailor-made to draw upon Tijaniyya and "Kano Nationalist" sentiment over the treatment of Sanusi. Many disaffected members of the NPC who were Kano natives, such as Alhaji Baba Daradara (NPC Minister of Transport), went over to the KPP.[66] Other NPC members did not cross the carpet officially, but offered covert financial support for the KPP. Alhaji Inuwa Wada, who was not only NPC Minister of Works but also a Tijaniyya with close personal ties to Niasse and Sanusi, secretly donated £1000 to the new party.[67]

Essential to the founding of the KPP, though, was the aid, both financial and institutional, provided by NEPU. Clearly, the NEPU leaders were quick to recognize the political value of the rift between the Sardauna and Sanusi. During the Muffett probe, Aminu Kano ordered NEPU members not to offer evidence against Sanusi, despite the long record of extreme antagonism between NEPU and the Kano Emir.[68]

---

65. *Sunday Times*, 14 April, 1963.

66. Interview with Alhaji Baba Daradara, 7 June, 1993.

67. KSHCB, KanoPrOf., Security 373.s.7, 28 August, 1963.

68. Lawan Danbazau, 20 January, 1993. Dr. Akilu Aliyu, 1 May, 1993.

Such a step on the part of NEPU helped open the door for cooperation with Sanusi and his supporters once the Emir was forced to resign. At first, NEPU's support for the KPP was covert, consisting of funds and office space in a NEPU-owned building. Later on, in January of 1964, the KPP and NEPU were able to ally officially.

> In order to attract Sanusi supporters we engineered the creation of the Kano People's Party. The organization was made up mainly of people who followed Sanusi and eventually it was openly aligned with NEPU.[69]

Along with the assistance given to help form the KPP, NEPU took steps to help attract the support of the Tijaniyya. In September of 1964, shortly before the December elections, Aminu Kano traveled to Senegal to meet with Shaykh Niasse. NEPU campaign posters for the 1964 election featured a picture of Kano being "blessed" by Niasse -- clearly an appeal to the Tijaniyya vote.[70]

In many ways, the move to support the KPP and garner the Tijaniyya vote was a political retreat for NEPU. Such a move could not help but alienate many of the party's supporters who belonged to the Qadiriyya or who did not affiliate with a brotherhood at all. Such a strategy, born out of more than a decade of defeats by the NPC, represented NEPU's realization that it had no hope of competing with the larger, wealthier and increasingly well-entrenched NPC on the Regional level. By focusing on such elements as Tijaniyya and "Kano Nationalist" support, NEPU hoped to create a more local base of power in the form of a Kano State. While NEPU and the KPP were not to attain a separate state during the First Republic, the strategic political retreat did help keep the northern radical opposition alive in the face of ever-

---

69. Alhaji Tanko Yakasai, 21 January, 1993.

70. Saidu Balla, 17 January, 1993. Tanko Yakasai, 21 January, 1993. Inuwa Wada, 30 January, 1993.

expanding NPC power in the latter years of the period.

The period from 1963-1966 also saw the NPC change its strategy and relationship in regard to the Tijaniyya and the Qadiriyya brotherhoods. Central to the NPC's strategy during this period was the attempt to create a new brotherhood built around the person of Shehu Usman dan Fodio. Named the "Usmaniyya", this organization was not necessarily intended to perform all the roles of a Sufi brotherhood, but was rather an organization which sought to unify the region's malam class around the person and image of the Shehu. "Usmaniyya" awards were given to individuals (always NPC members) who had offered "outstanding service to the region."[71] As Paden states on the subject:

> The doctrines of Usmaniyya clearly relate to the themes of authority and community. In 1964 the Sardauna of Sokoto... published a bilingual (Arabic and Hausa) anthology of works purportedly by his great-great-grandfather, Usman dan Fodio. The central piece in the anthology was Wa lamma balagtu, in which Usman dan Fodio claims to be "head of all the saints" and proposes a specific wuridi that would guarantee entry into paradise. The work does no mention tariqa, nor is any mention made of Qadiriyya wuridi. Yet the work was widely interpreted in northern Nigeria as an attempt to attribute to Usman dan Fodio the creation of a new, simplified, all-encompassing tariqa.[72]

The potential utility of the Usmaniyya to the NPC is clear. If it were accepted by the region's populace, the Usmaniyya would help to reduce conflict between the Tijaniyya and Qadiriyya by giving them a single focus on the person of Usman dan Fodio. Further, because Usman dan Fodio was a local figure, the Usmaniyya could potentially reduce the influence of international sources of religious authority such

---

71. *Nigerian Citizen*, 16 June, 1965.

72. Paden, *Religion and Political Culture*, pp.180-181

as Ibrahim Niasse. Finally, the contemporary leadership of the Usmaniyya would, no doubt, fall to the person of the Sardauna. The NPC had spent years building the image that the Sardauna was the inheritor of the legacy of his great-grandfather Usman dan Fodio.[73] Viewed from a political angle, the creation of the Usmaniyya was an attempt to draw together political and religious authority in the Northern Region and to place the Sardauna at the pinnacle of this power structure..

The NPC support for the Usmaniyya, though, was not well received by the bulk of the region's Sufi leaders. Following the removal of Sanusi, the Tijaniyya were already at odds with the regional government. Important Qadiriyya leaders, too, saw the Usmaniyya as an attempt to sideline their authority. Nasiru Kabara of Kano was offended by the political agenda behind the move.

> [the Sardauna] meant that they would form a political party around the tariqa of his grandfather. It was not religion, it was something different.[74]

Despite the efforts of the Sardauna and the NPC to establish the Usmaniyya as a force to promote the religious and political unity of the North, the ongoing conflicts between the Qadiriyya and the Tijaniyya (riots broke out in Argungu in 1965) and the growing tensions between these brotherhoods and the NPC limited the effectiveness of the strategy. Indeed, when the Sardauna was assassinated in 1966, the Usmaniyya crumbled almost immediately -- clearly showing how closely linked the movement was to its leader and a certain set of political goals.

A final point to be considered regarding the relationship between the NPC

---

73. See Chapter One, "Party Politics and the Legacy of the Sokoto Caliphate" for more detail on this issue.

74. Shaik Nasiru Kabara, 27 June, 1993.

and the Qadiriyya is that of the possible impact of the Sardauna's growing relationship with the Saudi royal family. Since the late 18th century, the Saudi family have been ardent supporters of the conservative teachings of Muhammad ibn Abd al-Wahhab. A major component of al-Wahhab's teachings were his attacks on Sufism. To what degree the Sardauna was influenced by the strict anti-Sufism of the Wahhabist Saudis, or to what degree such an effect was feared by the region's Sufi leaders, is hard to judge. It is at least very likely that Shaykh Abubakar Gumi (Grand Qadi of the Shari'a Court of Appeals), who served as the Sardauna's interpreter on his trips to Saudi Arabia, was so influenced. Up to the time of his death in 1992, Gumi was a vociferous opponent of Sufism in Nigeria, and his Izala movement continues to be a growing force of Sunni orthodoxy in Nigerian Islam.[75]

CONCLUSIONS

The presence and of the turug in Northern Nigeria and their role in the politics of the region point up several important points regarding the period of the 1950's and early 1960's in West Africa. The interaction between multiple spheres of religious identity and political motivation highlight the complexity of the era. The interplay of local, regional and international political forces through the institutions of the brotherhoods, as in the case of Niasse's pan-Africanism and the Sardauna's pan-Islamism, point up the polyvalent nature of religious, political and regional identity in this period.

In the context of Nigeria's Northern Region, this chapter shows that the relationships between the parties and brotherhoods defy any attempt to oversimplify the various players' motivations and relationships. The fact that the NPC and the Qadiriyya were

---

75. For an excellent discussion of Gumi's anti-Sufism, see Umar, "From Sufism to Anti-Sufism" in Brenner, *Muslim Identity*, pp.154-178.

both groups which could be considered "insiders" to the state apparatus did not guarantee their cooperation. Indeed, the political maneuvering of the NPC leadership, particularly the attempt to centralize religious authority through the creation of the Usmaniyya, led to an increasing antagonism between the party and the Qadiriyya -- leading to a growing disjuncture between political leaders and the Qadiriyya. This incident points up that there were limits to how much the religion could be manipulated before meeting popular and intellectual resistance. Finally, the "outsider" status shared by NEPU and the Tijaniyya did not guarantee cooperation. In many respects the Tijaniyya may be considered to have been pro-NPC until the break between Sanusi and the Sardauna. Only in response to a particular set of political circumstances, particularly the removal of Emir Sanusi, did NEPU and the Tijaniyya cooperate -- certainly not because of some sort of shared ideological perspective.

CONCLUSION:

ISLAM, POLITICS AND HISTORY IN NORTHERN NIGERIA

From the preceding chapters, it is evident that the religion of Islam was a central factor in the politics of Nigeria's Northern Region for the period from 1950 to 1966. The NPC and NEPU's very different political agendas and relationship to the state, combined with their contrasting interpretations of Islamic ideology and of the region's religious history, were to surface in a number of different political settings. In particular, this work has focused on the conflicting constructions of the region's religious and political history in the debate over the future of the Native Authority system, the conflict within and regarding the nature of the region's Islamic legal system, the question of women's political rights, the parties' ability to offer religious services to the northern Muslim populace, and the relationship of the parties to the North's dominant Sufi brotherhoods. Each of these themes points up the instrumentality of religion in the politics of the period. Having examined each of these issues in some detail, it is now possible to draw a few central themes out of the preceding analysis. Finally, this conclusion will examine the significance of the parties' particular strategies in terms of their long-term impact in the period since the end of Nigeria's First Republic.

Throughout the 1950's, the debate between the two parties was largely over the question of what sort of political structure was best suited to the Northern Region as it moved towards independence as (the dominant) part of a Federal Nigeria. Neither party denied that change in the structure of government was necessary; they simply disagreed on the form and extent of that change. The NPC sought to maintain as large a role for the Masu Sarauta as possible, while NEPU fought to minimize the political role of these traditional leaders. The conflict over the continued administrative role of the Native Authorities and the traditional rulers around whom the system was built was central to this debate over what represented the proper form of governance for the region. The central strategy of the NPC was to draw upon an interpretation of Islam and the region's history which defended the political status quo -- the power of the traditional rulers who traced their origin back to the leaders of the Sokoto Jihad. Thus, the NPC both presented a positive picture of the Sokoto Caliphate and stressed the legitimacy of the inheritance of power. In no case was the example of "inherited legitimacy" made more strongly than in the person of the Sardauna, the great-great-grandson of Usman dan Fodio.

The NEPU leaders, on the other hand, attacked the position of the traditional rulers in the Region's government, and put forward a perspective of the region's history which maintained that the contemporary Masu Sarauta were only the most recent in a long line of rulers who had perverted the goals of Usman dan Fodio. Further, NEPU maintained that inheritance was not a legitimate form of succession in Islam, but that the only true qualification for Muslim leadership was greater piety and knowledge -- criteria to which the NEPU's leadership of radical scholars could lay claim.

The NPC's control of the Northern Region's institutions of state, both through their position as the party of government and through their close relationship with the Native Authorities created a situation in which the party wielded de-facto control over the region's Shari'a court system. The willingness of the NPC to use this institutional control to restrict the activities of the opposition (with covert encouragement from the British Colonial administration), led the <u>alkali</u> courts to become a central arena for the religious conflict between the NPC and NEPU. Despite the NPC's control of the courts, NEPU was able to make use of loopholes in the region's dual court system and to highlight the NPC's abuse of the system in a way that often blunted the value of the courts to the ruling party. Of particular importance in this conflict was the way the parties sought to interpret the Shari'a as it applied to the court cases which arose out of Western-style party politics. The extent and complexity of this conflict within the courts, exacerbated by the fact that neither party was able effectively to outmaneuver the other, eventually led to changes in the structure and position of the <u>alkali</u> courts and Shari'a law in the Northern Region. These institutional changes include the creation of the Moslem Court of Appeals in 1958 and the implementation of a (secular) Penal Code in 1960.

The debate between the NPC and NEPU over women's political rights and roles was another important issue pertaining to the interaction of religion and politics in influencing the nature and structure of Northern Region government (in this case, the pattern of representation) during the 1950's. While both the NPC and NEPU formed women's wings in the early 1950's, the NPC was stridently opposed to the right of suffrage being extended to women. The debate over women's right to franchise peaked in 1956 and 1957 as NEPU sought to draw attention to the issue in anticipation of the London Constitutional Conference (1957). The NPC was successful in keeping the vote from being extended to women, in part because they were able to limit the debate to the issue of whether or not Islam sanctioned a political role for women. This tactic helped draw attention away from the potential political impact of the extension of voting rights to the significant minority of non-Muslim women who lived in the North. While NEPU leaders, male and female, continued to agitate for women's suffrage throughout the period, the failure to pass the measure in the mid-1950's effectively meant that the cause was lost as long as the NPC remained in power.

The interaction of religion and politics during the 1950's was in no small way influenced by the presence of British administrators. During the period of colonial rule, the British had acted to restrict the extent to which religion and politics were mixed -- at least visibly. This is not to say that the British did not recognize in some ways the close relationship between religion and politics in Islam. Rather, they supported a particular brand of Islam, in this case the conservative, state-friendly Islam of the NPC and not the radical, socialist-tinged Islam of NEPU. As such, during the 1950's, the British colonial administrators supported the religious programs and strategies that benefitted the NPC -- such as subsidization of the Hajj and manipulation of the Shari'a courts. Public projects such as the NPC government support for the Hajj, though, were accepted by the British only as long as they conformed to the familiar Lockian prescription of providing a service which the citizens could not provide for themselves -- such as the arrangements for pilgrims' international travel. It is important that the nature of this British influence was, more often than not, covert. Thus, long-standing British policies often set the context for debate, and acting administrators frequently made their wishes known via confidential communications, but they rarely entered into the extensive public debates over the future of Northern Nigeria – especially when religious matters were at issue.

The low profile of the British administrators influenced the nature of decolonization. "Anti-colonial" and "Nationalist" sentiment were minor aspects of the politics in Nigeria's North, as compared to the degree to which they were found in other African regions. This was in no small part a result of the close relationship forged between the North's traditional rulers and the British during the latter years of

Indirect Rule. Indeed, as seen in Chapter One, the NPC stressed a perspective of the region's history that downplayed the impact of colonial rule and portrayed what impact there had been as positive. In general, the "Nationalism" of the NPC was more a nationalism of northern consciousness -- an identity built around the image and history of the Sokoto Caliphate, than it was of a newfound Nigerian identity.

The radical leaders of NEPU did ascribe to a certain degree of anti-colonialism, as would be expected of a party allied to the NCNC. Still, the focus of NEPU was not so much on overthrowing the British (whose impending departure was evident from early in the 1950's), but on unseating the power of the traditional rulers as defended by the NPC. The oppression of the Talakawa in the North, maintained the NEPU leadership, predated colonial rule, and would continue without the British unless radical steps were taken to restructure the system of authority in the region.

The coming of independence heralded a new era of Islamic politics in Nigeria's North. Religious services to the region's Muslim community became a major means by which the parties sought to secure the support of the populace -- a situation which greatly favored NPC as the party of government. Extensive mosque-building projects and conversion campaigns represented an extensive expansion and reinterpretation of the role of the Northern government in the provision of religious services to the region's Muslim community. NEPU, without access to the coffers and institutions of government, could only continue to offer education to the populace through the Islamiyya schools and tafsir.

Another change that came with independence was that both parties were able to expand their international Islamic contacts -- a tendency which the British had always sought to restrict for fear of both Pan-African and revolutionary (for example,

Mahdist) Islamic influence. This expansion of contacts allowed both parties to seek external Islamic alliances which could be used to enhance their influence and legitimacy with Nigeria's Muslim populace. Cases in point are the extensive contacts forged by the NPC with Saudi Arabia and NEPU's contacts with the Niasse Tijaniyya in Senegal.

During the 1960's, the NPC sought to centralize religious and political authority around the person of the Sardauna. A major component of this strategy was the attempt to elevate the person of Usman dan Fodio (the Sardauna's great-great-grandfather) to the likeness and role of a Sufi Shaykh. Such a tactic held the potential of expanding the religious authority of the Sardauna and the significance of Sokoto (the power base of the NPC) as a religious center. Further, this tactic promised to weaken the influence in Nigeria of international Sufi leaders. This move, though, threatened the long-standing ties between the Qadiriyya brotherhood and the region's political leaders. Many Qadiriyya leaders, such as Nasiru Kabara, chafed at this strategy, since it was clearly intended to enhance the religious authority of certain NPC leaders (particularly the Sardauna) at the expense of the Qadiriyya.

Similarly, the break between the NPC and Emir Sanusi of Kano in 1963 effectively severed the ties between the NPC and the Tijaniyya brotherhood, of which Sanusi served as the Nigerian head. NEPU's move to take advantage of this break, in part through the vehicle of the Kano Peoples Party, served to garner the radical party the support of the region's Tijaniyya. Thus, the period of the early 1960's saw a weakening of the ties between the NPC and the Region's Sufi populace and the creation of a close relationship between NEPU and the Tijaniyya.

In terms of the interaction between religion and politics, the situation in Nigeria's Northern Region at the end of the First Republic was a complex one. The

NPC was in firm control of the Northern Region and was also the party of government for the Nigerian Federation -- a situation strengthened by the breakdown of the Western Region government of the Action Group. NEPU, after years of defeats on the regional level, had staged a strategic retreat to the Kano area where the party drew upon Tijaniyya and Kano nationalist support to maintain its local influence. While still active on the regional level, NEPU had little hope of affecting government decisions and policy by this point.

In 1966 the NPC was in firm control of the northern government. The party had spent more than a decade constructing an image of the North that stressed the continuity of a religious and political tradition that traced its origin back to Usman dan Fodio, with the Sardauna (and, by extension, his fellow NPC leaders) being the inheritors of that long heritage. The religious status of the Sardauna was further enhanced by his extensive international Islamic contacts -- particularly with Saudi Arabia. These contacts also helped provide the NPC with an extensive "war chest" of funds to subsidize the provision of religious services to the Islamic community in the North. The combination of religion and politics had become so central to the NPC's strategy of government during the 1960's that the Sardauna and his fellow NPC leaders had been able to undertake massive campaigns to convert non-Muslims in the North to Islam without the issue of the propriety of such an action on the part of the region's political rulers being called into serious question. For political leaders to proselytize actively for mass conversion of the populace to Islam and to define such activities as a duty of the state was far removed even from the government assistance rendered to pilgrimage in the 1950's. By 1966 the line between religion and politics in the North had all but vanished.

The situation in 1966 would certainly suggest that, of the two strategies, the NPC's was the most successful. NEPU's war of ideas, often waged through the print media and presented in the form of complex discussions of Islamic ideology and analysis of the region's history, were often inaccessible to the large bulk of the region's populace.   Further, the NPC offered concrete services and a sense of continuity to those who cooperated -- and held the power to punish those who did not. NEPU called for radical changes in a setting that was already turbulent, offered little that was concrete to the bulk of the region's populace, and certainly had no real capacity to punish its opponents.

Of course, it is hardly a radical statement to draw the conclusion that the wealthy and powerful won out over the poor and progressive. What does need to be noted is the structural context of the NPC's "victory" over NEPU. The power of the NPC, from the party's creation, rested in no small way upon the continued power of the traditional rulers in the Native Authority system and on the semi-autonomy of the Northern Region within the Nigerian national government. The Native Authority system effectively guaranteed the NPC control over local government in the North even before elections were held, and this local control was very much responsible for the ease with which the NPC was able to establish control over the Northern Region. Further, given the organization of the Federal system of government in Nigeria, control of the North meant control over the National government. Hence, the NPC was able to become the national party of government without contesting a single seat outside of the Northern Region.

Thus, the power of the NPC was tied to a very particular form of governmental organization, and when the Federal government was brought down by military coups in 1966, the NPC suffered even more than it might have otherwise. Gowan's reorganization of Nigeria into twelve states, and the replacement of the Native Authorities with military administrations destroyed both the NPC's links to administrative power and its claim to legitimacy. Also of critical importance was the death of the Sardauna in the Ironsi coup.. The NPC had so closely tied its religious legitimacy to the person of the Sardauna that no other member of the Masu Sarauta was able to take his place. While traditional leaders continued to wield political influence in the North, their formal power was quickly lost when Nigeria moved to a unitary system of national government under the Gowan administration.

Indeed, in retrospect, the NPC's attempt to build its legitimacy around a construction of the region's history which placed the Masu Sarauta as the defenders of an inherited tradition of religious unity can be viewed as a failed attempt to combine religious and political authority in Nigeria's North. While Nigeria's federal system helped make this an effective strategy for the North, it was not acceptable to the national Nigerian polity. There can be little doubt that the coup which led to the Sardauna's death was in part a response to southern fears of domination by the Northern Region. The federal system had both supported the rise and helped lead to the downfall of the NPC.

Interestingly, during the years of military rule that followed the fall of the First Republic, it was the idea-driven philosophy of NEPU that was to triumph over the institutionally-powerful NPC. Under the military regimes of Gowan, Muhammad and Obasanjo, the leaders of NEPU were to hold a number of influential positions and were to see many of their key political aims realized. The Native Authorities were dismantled and traditional rulers were (at least formally) restricted to ceremonial rather than administrative duties. The Federation was replaced with a system of 12 states. With the return to civilian rule in the late 1970's, the right of suffrage was extended to women in the North. Further, the NEPU's key institutional endeavor, the Islamiyya schools, continued to grow in popularity. Ironically, although NEPU had sought to empower the North's populace, it was only with the end of democratic civilian rule that the key aims of NEPU were to be realized.

BIBLIOGRAPHY

ARTICLES, BOOKS AND THESES

Abun-Nasr Jamil M. *The Tijaniyya: A Sufi Order in the Modern World*. London: Oxford University Press, 1965.

Sir Ahmadu Bello. "Text of Speech Delivered at the Historic Ceremony of the Opening of the Rebuilt 100,000 Sultan Bello Mosque on Friday, July 5th 1963." Kaduna: Government Printer, 1963.

----------. *My Life*. Cambridge: Cambridge University Press, 1962.

Ahmed, Leila. *Women and Gender in Islam: Historical Roots of a Modern Debate*. New Haven: Yale University Press, 1992.

Ajayi, J.F.A., and Michael Crowder. *History of West Africa*. New York: Columbia University Press, 1973.

Anderson, Benedict. *Imagined Communities*. New York: Verso, 1991.

Anderson, J.N.D. *Islamic Law in Africa*. London: Frank Cass and Company, 1955. (First Published as Colonial Research Publication #16 1954 by H.M.S.O., January 1955.)

Andrew Ripjon and Van Kuappert. *Textual Sources for the Study of Islam*. Tobwa, New Jersey: Barnes and Noble, 1987.

Anwar, Auwalu. "Struggle for Influence and Identity: The Ulama in Kano, 1937-1987." MA, University of Maiduguri, 1989.

Atanda, J.A. Garba Ashiwaju and Yaya Abubaker. *Nigeria Since Independence, The First 25 Years*. Ibadan: Heinemann, 1989.

Bajojun, Ismail A.B. *The Life and Works of Uthman Dan Fodio: (The Muslim Reformer of West Africa)*. Lagos: Islamic Publications Bureau, 1975.

Barkindo, Bawuro M., ed. *Kano and Some of its Neighbors*. Kano: ABU press, 1983.

Bivar, A.D.H, and M. Hiskett. "The Arabic Literature of Nigeria to 1804: A Provision account." *Bulletin of the S.O.A.S.*, XXV, Pt.1, 1962.

Braji, Ibrahim. *Nigerian Intra-Party Conflicts, a Study of the PRP Crisis, 1980-1983*. Kano: DOK, 1983.

Brenner, Louis. *West African Sufi: The Religious Heritage and Spiritual Search of Cerno Bokar Saslif Taal*. Los Angeles: University of California Press, 1984.

----------, ed. *Muslim Identity and Social Change in Sub-Saharan Africa*. Bloomington: Indiana University Press, 1993.

Buchanan, Keith. "The Northern Region of Nigeria: the Geographical Background of its Political Polity." *Geographical Review*. (13), October, 1953.

Bull, Mary. "Indirect Rule in Northern Nigeria, 1906-1911," in K. Robinson and F. Madden, eds. *Essays in Imperial Government Presented to Margery Perham*, Oxford: Oxford University Press, 1963.

Callaway, Barbara, and Lucy Creevey. *The Heritage of Islam: Women, Religion and Politics in West Africa*. Boulder, Colorado: Lynne Rienner Publishers, 1994.

Cantori, J. "The Political Implications of Islam in the Middle Belt of Nigeria". MA, University of Chicago: 1962

Chamberlain, John W. "Kano Field Notes, May 11 - October 1971." Together with materials from Gidan Shatine. The collected field notes of his research into the history of Matlanst Islamic scholarship in 19th and 20th Century Kano" with help of Dr. Phil Shea.

Clarke, Peter B. *West Africa and Islam: A Study of Religious Development From the 8th to the 20th Century*. London: Edward Arnold, 1982.

Clarke, Peter and Ian Linden. *Islam in Modern Nigeria*. Munich: Kaiser-Grunwald, 1984.

Cohen, Abner. *Custom and Politics in Urban Africa: A Study of Hausa Migrants in Yoruba Towns*. Los Angeles: University of California Press, 1969.

Coles, Catherine and Beverly Mack, eds. *Hausa Women in the Twentieth Century*. Madison: University of Wisconsin Press, 1991.

Crowder, Michael. "Political Tension in North Nigeria II," *West Africa*, 11 January, 1958.

----------. *Pagans and Politicians*. London: Hutchinson, 1959.

----------. *A Short History of Nigeria*. New York: Praeger, 1962.

----------. *The Story of Nigeria*. London: Faber and Faber, 1962.

Cruise-O'Brien, Donald. "Brotherhood Abroad." *West Africa*, (11-17) January, 1993.

Danbazau, Lawan. *Siyasa da Addini a Nijeriya*. Kaduna: Vanguard Printers, 1991.

Dantatta, Abdulkadir. "Modern Hausa Poetry by Sa'ad Zungu." M.A. Thesis, University of Wisconsin, 1971.

Delancey, Mark. *Nigeria: A Bibliography of Politics, Government, Administration and Internal Relations*. Los Angeles: Crossroads Press, 1983

Doi, A. I. *Islam in Nigeria*. Zaria: Gaskiya Corp., 1984

Dudley, Billy. *Parties and Politics in North Nigeria*. London: Frank Cass, 1968.

Elaigwu, J. Isana. "The Shadow of Religion on Nigerian Federalism, 1986-1990" Paper presented at the annual meeting of the ASA, Baltimore, 1990.

Elayo, A.D. *Jama'tu Nasril Islam: Two Decades of Activities in Nigeria*. BA, University of Jos, 1984.

Emiko Atimomo. *Nindadiu Umar. An Authentic Ideology for Politics in Nigeria: Problems and Prospects for Nation Building*. Lagos: A. Atimomo, 1981

Enwere, J.C. *A Provisional Guide to Official Publications at the National Archives Kaduna*. Kaduna: 1962.

Enwerem, Iheanyi. A Dangerous Awakening: The Politicization of Religion in Nigeria.. Ibadan: IFRA, 1995.

Esposito, John L. *Islam and Politics*. Syracuse, New York: Syracuse University Press, 1984.

Falola, Toyin. *Islam and Christianity in W. A.* Ibadan: The University of Ife Press, 1983.

Feinstein, Alan. *African Revolutionary: The Life and Times of Nigeria's Aminu Kano*. Enugu, 1987.

Gledhill, Alan. *The Penal Codes of North Nigeria and The Sudan*. London: Sweet and Maxwell, 1963.

Gumi, Sheikh Abubakar. *Where I Stand*. Kaduna: Spectrum Books, 1992.

Hargreaves, John D. Decolonization in Africa. New York: Longman, 1988.

Haynes, Jeff. *Religion in Third World Politics*. Boulder, Colorado: Lynne Rienner, 1994.

Heussler, Robert. *The British in Northern Nigeria*. Oxford: Oxford University Press, 1968.

Hiskett, Mervyn. *A History of Hausa Islamic Verse*. London: School of Oriental and African Studies, 1975.

----------. *The Course of Islam in Africa*. Edinburgh: Edinburgh University Press, 1994.

----------. *The Development of Islam in West Africa*. New York: Longman, 1984.

---------- ed. *An Anthology of Hausa Political Verse: Hausa Texts*. London: School of Oriental and African Studies, 1977.

Hodgkin, Thomas. *Nigerian Perspectives, an Historical Anthology*. London: Oxford University Press, 1960.

Hogben, S.J. *Mohammedan Emirates of Nigeria*. London: Oxford University Press, 1930.

Hudson, R.S. Regional Commissioner. Report on *Provincial Authorities*. Kaduna, Ministry of Local Govt. "A Review of the State of Development of the Native Authority System in the Northern Region of Nigeria on the first of January. *Journal of African Administration*, VII, 2, April, 1955, pp.77-88

Hunwick, John. "An African Case Study of Political Islam: Nigeria." *Annals of the American Academy of Political and Social Sciences*. 524, November, 1992, pp.143-155.

Jalingo, A.U. "Islam and Political Legitimacy in Northern Nigeria." *Kano Studies*. Vol.II, #3, 1982-1985.

------------- "The Radical Tradition in Northern Nigeria"
PhD, University of Edinburough, 1981.

Kani, Ahmad Muhammad. *The Intellectual Origin of Sokoto Jihad*. Ibadan: Iman Publications, 1988.

Kani, Ahmad Mohammad and Kabir Ahmed Gandi, eds. *State and Society in the Sokoto Caliphate*. Sokoto: Usman dan Fodio University Press, 1990.

Last, Murray. *The Sokoto Caliphate*. London: Longman, 1977.

Lubeck, Paul M. *Islam and Urban Labor in Northern Nigeria: The Making of a Muslim Working Class*. London: Cambridge University Press, 1986.

Lugard, Lord Fredrick. *Dual Mandate in Tropical Africa*, London: William Blackwood and Sons, 1922.

----------. *Political Memoranda*. London: Frank Cass, 1970.

Lawan, Mohammed. "Wakokin Siyasa na Hausa." BA, University of Sokoto, 1983.

Merkl, Peter H. and Ninian Smart. *Religion and Politics in the Modern World*. New York: New York University Press, 1983.

Mernissi, Fatima. *Beyond the Veil*. Bloomington, Indiana: Indiana University Press, 1987.

Mews, Stuart. *Religion in Politics*. London: Longman, 1989.

Musa Barah Mash. *Wakokin Saka na Siyasa*. MA, Bayero University, Kano, 1986.
Naniya, Tijjani, Muhammad. "The Transformation of the Administration of Justice
in Kano Emirate 1903-1966." PhD, Bayero University, Kano, 1990.

Nicholson, I.F. *The Administration of Nigeria, 1900-1960: Men, Methods, Myths*.
New York: Clarendon Press, 1969.

Nimtz, August H. Jr. *Islam and Politics in East Africa: The Sufi Order in Tanzania*.
Minneapolis: University of Minnesota Press, 1980.

Nwabueze, B.O. *A Constitutional History of Nigeria*. London: C. Hurst and Co.,
1981.

Paden, John. "The Influence of Religious Elites on the Community, Culture and
Political Integration of Kano, Nigeria." PhD, Harvard, 1968.

----------. *Religion and Political Culture in Kano*. Los Angeles: University of
California Press, 1973.

----------. *Ahmadu Bello, Sardauna of Sokoto: Values and Leadership in Nigeria*.
Zaria: Hudahuda Publishing, 1986.

Perham, Margery. *Native Administration in Nigeria*. London: Oxford University
Press, 1937.

Perham, Margery and Mary Bull, eds. *The Diaries of Lord Lugard*. London: Faber
and Faber, 1963.

Pitten, Renee Ilene. "Marriage and Alternative Strategies: Career Patterns of Hausa
Women in Katsina City." PhD, SOAS, 1979/1980.

Post, K.W.J. *The Nigerian Federal Election of 1959: Politics & Administration in
a Developing Political System*. London: Oxford University Press, 1963.

----------. "The Northern Elements Progressive Union: A study in Northern Nigerian
Radicalism." Nigerian Institute of Social and Economic Research, Conference
Proceedings. Ibadan: 1964.

----------. *The Price of Liberty: Personality and Politics in Colonial Nigeria*.
Cambridge: Cambridge University Press, 1973.

Rowell-Jackson, Edward John. "The History of Islam in Hausaland." MA, University of Iowa, 1971.

Schnacht, Joseph. "Islam in Northern Nigeria." *Studia Islamica*, VIII, pp.122-146.

Shawalu, Rima. *The Story of Gambo Sawaba*. Jos: Echo Communications Ltd., 1990.

Sipikin, Alhaji Mudi. *Wakokin Ilimi da Tarbiyya Donyara* Lagos: Thomas Nelson, 1971.

Sklar, Richard and C. S. Whitaker. *Nigerian Political Parties*. New York: Columbia Univeristy Press, 1963.

Sklar, Richard. *Nigerian Political Parties: Power in an Emergent African Nation*. Princeton: Princeton University Press, 1963.

Smith, Sir Bryan Sharwood. *Recollections of British Administration in the Cameroons and Northern Nigeria 1921-1957: "But Always as Friends"*. Durham, North Carolina: Duke University Press, 1969.

Smith, Donald Eugene, ed. *Religion and Political Modernization*. New Haven: Yale University Press, 1974.

----------, ed. *Religion, Politics and Social Change in the Third World*. New York: The Free Press. 1971.

Smith, M.G. *The Affairs of Daura*. Los Angeles: The University of California Press, 1978.

----------. *Government in Zazzau*. London: Oxford University Press, 1960

Sulaiman, Ibraheem. *The Islamic State and the Challenge of History: Ideals, Politics and Operation of the Sokoto Caliphate*. London: Mansell Publishing Ltd., 1987.

----------. *A Revolution in History: The Jihad of Usman dan Fodio*. London: Mansell Publishing Ltd., 1986.

Tahir, Ibrahim A. "Scholars, Sufis, Saints and Capitalists in Kano 1904-1974: The pattern of Bourgeoisie Revolution in an Islamic Society." PhD, University of Cambridge, 1975.

Trimmingham, J. Spencer. *A History of Islam in West Africa.* New York: Oxford University Press, 1962.

Tukur, Muhammad. "Values and Public Affairs: The Relevance of the Sokoto Caliphal Experience to the Transformation of the Nigerian Polity." PhD, Ahmadu Bello University, 1977.

Turaki, Yusufu. "The Institutionalization of the Inferior Status and Social Political Role of the Non-Muslim groups in the Colonial Hierarchical Structure of the Northern Region of Nigeria; A Social-Ethical Analysis of the Colonial Legacy. PhD, B.U. 1982.

Umar, Muhammad Sani. "Islam in Nigeria: Its Concept, Manifestations and Role in Nation Building", in Atandah et al eds. *25 years of Nigerian History.* Ibadan: Heinemann, 1989.

Usman Abba, Ed. *Sir Ahmadu Bello, A Legacy.* Jos, Nigeria: ITF Printing Press, 1992.

Watos, William H. Jr. *Religious Politics in Global and Comparative Perspective.* New York: GreenWood Press, 1989.

Williams, Pat, and Falola, Toyin, *Religious Impact on the Nation State: The Nigerian Predicament.* Avebury: Ashgate, 1995.

Whitaker, C. S. *The Politics of Tradition: A study of Continuity and Change in Northern Nigeria, 1946-60.* Princeton: Princeton University Press, 1970.

Yahaya, A.D. "The Native Authority System in Northern Nigeria 1950-1970: A Study in Political Relations with Particular reference to the Zaria Native Authority: PhD, Ahmadu Bello University, 1974.

----------. *The Native Authority System in Northern Nigeria.* Zaria: Ahmadu Bello University Press, 1980.

Zungur, Sa'ad. *Wakokin M. Sa'adu Zungur.* Zaria: Gaskiya Corporation, 1968.

NEWSPAPERS

Bornu People

Daily Comet

Daily Mail

Daily Times

Gaskiya Ta Fi Kwabo

London Times

Nigerian Citizen

Northern Star

Sodongai

Sunday Times

West African Pilot

DOCUMENTS

Abbreviations:

AH = Arewa House
KanoPrOf = Kano Provincial Office
KSHCB = Kano State History and Culture Bureau
NAK = National Archives, Kaduna
NDMSIS = Northern Division Monthly Security Inteligence Survey
MaidugariPrOf = Maiduguri Provincial Office
MakPrOf=Makurdi Provincial Office
PRE = Premier's Office
SokPrOf = Sokoto Provincial Office
ZarPrOf = Zaria Provincial Office

"Administration of Justice in Kano State." KSHCB, Nigeria KR/1570 19256.

"Adult Literacy Campaign, Northern Region, 1955-1958." NAK, BauchiPrOf 5/1. ACC/126. Agency Mark 362 vol. II.

"Algiers to Cape Motor Rally, 1950-1951, 1952-1953." NAK, MaidugariPrOf ACC/1909-1910, Agency Mark 5373.

"Alhaji Muhammad Sanusi, Emir of Kano Personal File, 1954." NAK, PRE 2, ACC/77, Agency Mark E/4159.

"Applications for Registration of a Public Collection by N.E.P.U., 1947-1961." KSHCB, Kano State Archives Ministry for Local Government, ACC/832, Agency Mark LAW/30/01.

"Articles in the *Daily Times*, 1952-1953." KSHCB, KanoPrOf 5/1, ACC/3589, Agency Mark 7856. Vol. II.

"Child Prostitution. 2) Purdah, 3) Control of Prostitution under Moslem Law (1944-1951)." NAK, ZarPrOf 4/14, ACC/45, Agency Mark C.1/1944.

"Civil cases against Kano N.A. 1964." KSHCB, Ministry for Local Government, ACC/900, Agency Mark MAG/25 C.3.

"Complaints by NEPU, 1954-1955." KSHCB, KanoPrOf ACC/1936/D/203/5.

"Complaints by NEPU, 1953-1958." NAK, SokPrOf 3/22, Agency Mark PLT/1.

"Complaints in Sokoto." NAK, SokPrOf 3/2. ACC/337, Agency Mark 881/A Vol. VI.

"Confidential Reports: Emir of Kano, 1963-1966." KSHCB, Cabinet Office, R-Series, ACC/64, Agency Mark R/361.

"Confidential Reports and Instructions, 1931-1966." KSHCB, Cabinet Office, R-Series, ACC/65, Agency Mark R/362.

"Control of Juveniles Accompany Koranic Malams." KSHCB, Kano State Archives Ministry for Local Government, ACC/871, Agency Mark L6D/LE6/COW/56.

"Corporal Punishment, Correspondence, Policy and Instructions, 1939-1956." NAK, ZarPrOf, ACC/702, Agency Mark 865, Vol. II, Vol. IV/B.

"Correspondence with NPC Bauchi, 1961-1965." NAK, PRE 20, ACC/216, Agency Mark PRE/115.
"Correspondence with NPC Kano Province, 1961-1965." NAK, PRE 2, ACC/317, Agency Mark PRE/160.

"Correspondence Referred to the NPC Headquarters Kaduna for Action, 1962-1966." NAK, PRE 2, ACC/252-255, Agency Mark PRE/120/S/17 vol. I - IV.

"Courses on Islamic and African Customary Law, 1958-1960." NAK, PRE 3, ACC/54, Agency Mark AS/105.

"Court Cases 1959-1968." NAK, PRE 3, ACC/16, Agency Mark AS/II/81.
"Debates of the Northern House of Assembly, 1947-1960" The Northern Regional Legislature. NAK, NH2.

"Debates of the Northern House of Chiefs, 1947-1961."
The House of Representatives, NAK, NH3.

"Debates of the House of Representatives, 1953-1961." NAK, HR1.

"Debates of the Senate, 1960-1962." NAK, HR2.

"Disturbances-Kano Province, 1963-1967, List of Intelligence Reports for Nigeria
States." KSHCB, ACC/56, Agency Mark 147.

"Drinking of Beer by Muslims, 1953-1955." NAK, MaidugariPrOf. ACC/2305,
Agency Mark 6237.

"Education, 1959." AH. 3/E1.

"Elections Federal and Regional, Complaints, 1960-1961." KSHCB, Ministry for
Local Government, ACC/593, Agency Mark ELE/84.

"Election's Office Newspaper Clippings." NAK, SokPrOf 4/1, ACC/2202/ Agency
Mark 1.

"Electoral Commission, Report on the Nigeria Federal Elections, 1959." AH, 3/E2,

"Emblems, 1956." NAK, ZarPrOf 4/25, ACC/87, Agency Mark C.81/1956.
"Emir of Kano, 1959-1965." NAK, PRE 2, ACC/181. Agency Mark AGNN/1136P.

"Emir of Kano Personal File, 1963." KSHCB, Ministry for Local Government,
ACC/557, Agency Mark CMI/43.

"Emir's Court, Kano, 1964-1969." KSHCB, Ministry for Local Government,
ACC/1166, Agency Mark NCT/3/Vol.III.

"Emir's Court, Kano: Appeals from to High Court, 1943-1965." KSHCB, Ministry
for Local Government, ACC/1189, Agency Mark NCT/53.
"Federal Elections, 1959." NAK, SokPrOf 4/1. ACC/2203, Agency Mark 2.

"Federal Elections, Potiskum, 1954." NAK, MaidugariPrOf ACC/1776, Agency
Mark 5045/56.

"Federal Elections, Bedde, 1954." NAK, MaidugariPrOf ACC/1777, Agency Mark
5045/6/7.

"Female Education in Bornu Province, 1950-1953." NAK, MaidugariPrOf ACC/1968, Agency Mark 5448A.

"Female Education, 1946-1956." NAK, SokPrOf ACC/1893, Agency Mark C.145.

"Flags-Political Display of, 1945-1957." NAK, SokPrOf 61/1. ACC/1886, Agency Mark C.127.

"Forced and Communal Labor, 1937-1965." KSHCB, Kano State Archives, ACC/809, Agency Mark LAB/1.

"Forced Communal Labor." NAK, ZarPrOf 4/24, ACC/84, Agency Mark C. 3/1955.

"Genealogical Trees of North Ruling Families." KSHCB, KanoPrOf ACC/2634-2643, Agency Mark 5992/5.4.

"Government Officers' Relationship with Political Parties, 1961." KSHCB, KanoPrOf 2, ACC/PLT/173.

"Hejaz: The Situation in and the Reports on Soviet Activities in the." AH, K4797.

"High Court sessions, 1956-1968." KSHCB, Kano State Archives, ACC/893, Agency Marks MAG/8/Vol I.

"History of Islamic Political Propaganda in Nigeria - Memo written by Mr. Toulinson." AH, Book filc/281.

"Honourable Sir Ahmadu Bello, Sardauna of Sokoto, Personal File 1957-1965." NAK, PRE. Vol.2. ACC/174-176. Agency Mark PRE/97, Vols. I and III.

"House of Assembly question March 1955, Political Matters, 1955." NAK, PRE 1, ACC/10, Agency Mark R/7901/S.12.

"Immediate Policy Objectives Northern Region, 1952-1956." NAK, ZarPrOf 4/21, ACC/78, Agency Mark C.3/1952.

"International Moslem Organizations, 1963-1966." NAK, PRE 2, ACC/457, Agency Mark PRE/280.

"Interviews with the Premier, 1960-1963." NAK, PRE 2, Agency Mark Gen/69

"Islamic Law as Applied to Christians, 1938." NAK, ZarPrOf 5/1. ACC/190, Agency Mark C.4001. 1st vol.

"Islamic Propaganda-Secret and Confidential Volumes, Reports by Messrs. Tomlinson and Lethem, 1927-1956." AH, S.N.P. Files- Secretariats N. Provinces Box #5, ACC/37 File#4678.25

"Islamic Propaganda. External Intelligence, General Exchange of Intelligence with the French." AH, 4682 vol.II. .

"Jamatal Nusril Islam, 1965-1966." NAK, PRE/20, ACC/144, Agency Mark PRE 51.

"Jamiyyar Islamiya School Maiduguri, 1951-1955." NAK, MaidugariPrOf, ACC/2091, Agency Mark 5732.

"Kano Native Authority vs. Ibrahim Illa Husain Ringim and others, 1952." KSHCB, KanoPrOf 5/1, ACC/3542, Agency Mark 7746.

"Kano Native Authority Standing Rules, 1952-1963." KSHCB, Ministry For Local Government, ACC/1349, Agency Mark RUL/23.

"Kano Peoples Party, KPP, 1963." KSHCB, Ministry for Local Government, ACC/1307, Agency Mark PLT/38.

"Kano Province Reports of District Officer, Northern Division." KSHCB, ACC/52, Agency Mark 39.

"Kano Township Intelligence Reports, 1957-1967." KSHCB, ACC/51. Agency Mark 38.

"Labor Office Kano Reports, 1950-1965." KSHCB, Kano State Archives, ACC# 809, Agency Mark LAB/20.

"Laws of Nigeria, 1) Europeans, b) Americans, 1948-1959." KSHCB, Kano State Archives, ACC/844, Agency Mark LAW/34/vol. II.

"Liquor for Northern Province, General Correspondence, 1948-1956." NAK, SokPrOf ACC/256, Agency Mark 1502S.1.

"Magistrate Court Sessions, 1939-1968." KSHCB, Kano State Archives, ACC/895, Agency Mark MAG/23.

"Matters affecting Pilgrims, 1961-1965: Requests for Pilgrimage Assistance." NAK, PRE 20, ACC/415, Agency Mark PRE/240. Vol I and II.

"Mohammadan Festivals, 1961." NAK, PRE 2, ACC/206, Agency Mark PRE/107.

"Mohammadan Law in Northern Provinces, 1951-1955." NAK, ZarPrOf 4/20, ACC/74, Agency Mark C.5/1951.

"Mohammedan Propaganda, 1926." AH, S.N.P. files- Secretariats Northern Provinces, Box #2. ACC/12. File #2392.

"Morocco and Fez -- Connection of Nigeria and Merchants with." AH, 11513. .

"Moslem Affairs, 1956-1963." NAK, PRE 2, ACC/124. Agency Mark AGNN/1094.

"Moslim Associations, 1958-1962." NAK, PRE/20, ACC/20.

"Moslem Court of Appeal Judgments, 1957." KSHCB, ACC/1200, Agency Mark NCT/70.

"Moslem Court of Appeal Law-Routine Correspondence and Rules 1956-1958." KSHCB, Ministry for Local Government, ACC/846/847, Agency Mark LAW/37/38.

"Moslem Enquires, 1958." NAK, PRE 2, ACC/125, Agency Mark AGNN/1094A.

"Moslem Law - Handbook and Monographs on." KSHCB, KanoPrOf, 5/1. ACC/075, Agency Mark 175 S.

"Moslem Missionaries - General Correspondence: 1937-1947." NAK, KanoPrOf 5/1. ACC/780, Agency Mark 2131.

"Moslem Movements in Nigeria - Survey 1953-1955." NAK, ZarPrOf 5/1. ACC/129, Agency Mark C.68.

"Mosques for Schools, 1954-1955." NAK, KanoPrOf 5/1, ACC/3861 Agency Mark 8754.

"Nakedness in North Provinces, 1953." NAK, MaidugariPrOf. ACC/2312. Agency Mark 6252.

"Native Authority areas Map, 1958." NAK, PRE3, Co.1, ACC/52, Agency Mark, A.S.II/172.

"Native Authority Staff, Confidential Correspondence, 1942-1967." KSHCB, Cabinet Office, R-Series, ACC/78, Agency Mark, R/412.

"Native Courts in W. Region, 1959-1966." NAK, PRE 3, ACC/15. Agency Mark AS/II/78.

"Native Court Specific Cases and General Correspondence, 1948-1960." KSHCB. Kano State Archives, Cabinet Office Kano R-Series, ACC/45, Agency Mark R-256.

"Native Courts Commission, 1950-1956." NAK, SokPrOf 61/1, ACC/1931, Agency Mark C.245.

"Native Court of the Emir of Hadejia." KSHCB, Ministry for Local Government, ACC/1171, Agency Mark NCT/9.

"NCNC Deluges. 1) Tour of Nigeria, 2) Propaganda, 3) NEPU, 4)F.U.N.A.S. 1946-1956." NAK, ZarPrOf 4/16. ACC/55, Agency Mark C.11/1956.

"NEPU, 1957-1962." NAK, PRE 3, ACC/121, Agency Mark ASI/918.

"NEPU, 1947-1959." KSHCB, KanoPrOf 2, ACC/PLT/2/73.

"NEPU/AG, 1954." KSHCB, KanoPrOf 2, ACC/PLT/4.

"NEPU Court Cases, 1955." KSHCB, KanoPrOf 2, ACC/PLT/5.

"N.E.P.U. Complaints and Court Cases, 1961-1966." KSHCB, Kano State Archives, ACC/1299, Agency Mark PLT/5/Vol III.

"NEPU, 1958-1960." KSHCB, KanoPrOf 2, ACC/PLT/26.

"NEPU, Reports on Party Meetings" NAK, KanoPrOf, ACC/2921, Agency Mark 6410/S.I. Vol. II/1055.

"New Contact Correspondence between Political Bodies and Government, 1951-1954." KSHCB, KanoPrOf 5/1. ACC/3083, Agency Mark 6661/S.9. 1st Col., 2nd Vol.

"Northern Division Affairs, General Correspondence." KSHCB, Ministry for Local Government, ACC/1303, Agency Mark PLT/24.

"Northern Peoples Congress and other Politial Parties, 1952-1960." NAK, PRE 2, ACC/1, Agency Mark Gen/81 Vol II.

"Northern Peoples Congress, 1960." NAK, PRE 3, ACC/118, Agency Mark ASI/915.

"Northern Peoples Congress-*Jamiyar Mutanan Arena.*" KSHCB, Kano State Archives Ministry for Local Government, ACC/1300, Agency Mark PLT/8.

"Northern Region House of Assembly Minutes and Debates, 1956-1960." KSHCB, Ministry for Local Government, ACC/558, Agency Mark ELE/26.

"Northern Region of Nigeria Law report, 1958-1961." NAK, Legal and Judicial. LJ/3, ACC/573-2.

"Northern Women Organizations, 1963." NAK, PRE 2, ACC/471, Agency Mark PRE 291/Vol I.

"Official Engagement Speeches by the Premier, 1956-1965." NAK, PRE 2, ACC/35-40. Agency Mark PRE/7/Vol. II - V.

"The Penal Code Law, 1959-1961." KSHCB, Kano State Archives. ACC/850, Agency Mark LAW/56.

"Personal Complaints, Kano Province, 1956-1962." NAK, PRE 2, ACC/29, Agency Mark AS/1/142.

"Personal Letters to/from the Governor - Deputy Governor, 1953-1958." KSHCB, Cabinet Office, R-Series. ACC/114, Agency Mark R/526.

"Pilgrim Affairs, 1960-1962." NAK, PRE 20, ACC/1, Agency Mark PM 18 Vol II.

"Pilgrim Affairs Pilgrimage Agreement, 1958-1959." NAK, PRE3, Co.1. ACC/2-3. Agency Mark, PM 18 S.6/7 Vol. II.

"Pilgrimage to Mecca, 1965-1967: Arrangements." KSHCB, Kano State Archives, ACC/758, Agency Mark I/40.

"Political Activities of Government Servants, 1951-1952." NAK, SokPrOf, ACC/1532, Agency Mark 7780.

"Political Activities of Native Authority Staff." NAK, SokPrOf, 3/2, ACC/1737, Agency Mark 7780 s.1.

"Political Affairs, 1958-1965." NAK, PRE3, ACC/122, Agency Mark ASI/919.

"Political and Constitutional Future of Nigeria, 1951-1954." NAK, MakPrOf/1, ACC/1919, Agency Mark 3722/5/1.

"Political Flags, Badges and Emblems, Rules, 1965." KSHCB, ACC/1304, Agency Mark PLT/25.

"Political Bodies in Nigeria, 1948-1955." NAK, ZarPrOf 5/1, ACC/118, Agency Mark C.45.

"Political Officers, 1961." NAK, PRE 2, ACC/68, Agency Mark AS/1/432.

"Political Parties, 1959." NAK, SokPrOf 3/12, Acc/1938, Agency Mark F/ELE.C.2.

"Political Rights of Women, 1957." NAK, PRE 2, ACC/2, Agency Mark R/2219.

"Prayers for use in the Northern Regional Houses of Assembly and Chiefs, 1967." NAK, PRE 3, ACC# 20, Agency Mark AS/II/98.

"Premier's Speeches, 1962-1963." NAK, PRE3, Co.1. ACC/57
Agency Mark, A.S.

"Premiers Touring Notes, 1958-1965." NAK, PRE 2, ACC/178-191, Agency Mark PRE/99/5.1-5.13.

"Press Releases, 1962-1965." NAK, PRE 2, ACC/433, Agency Mark PRE/255/Vol. I.

"Public Enlightenment General Correspondence 1961-1968." KSHCB, Kano State Archives, ACC/775, Agency Mark IF/113.

"Publications and Extracts, re: Verification of Newspaper Reports." AH, 11309 A.

"Publicity Propaganda Advisory Committee." NAK, PRE 2, ACC/15. Agency Mark PM 344/Vol. II.

"Punishment of Officers in Native Court in So-Called Political Cases, 1957." KSHCB, Kano State Archives, ACC/1206, Agency Mark NCT/79.

"Religious Affairs of the Muslim Community 1960-1965." NAK, PRE 2, ACC/145, Agency Mark PRE/53.

"Religious and Moral Instruction in the Northern Provinces (1951-1952)." NAK, MaidugariPrOf, ACC/2062, Agency Mark 5676.

"Religious Disputes, 1959" KSHCB, KanoPrOf 2, ACC/PLT/36.

"Reorganization of Legal Judicial Systems of Northern Region, 1958-1962." KSHCB, Kano State Archives, ACC/1207, Agency Mark NCT/96.

"Report on the Kano Disturbances, May 16, 17, 18, 19 1953." AH, RP/A53.

"Report on 1954 Pilgrimage." NAK, KanoPrOf 5/1, ACC/1363, Agency Mark 3645/5.1

"Reports and Complaints against Native Authorities, Including Chiefs, Intelligence Reports for Nigerian States." KSHCB, ACC/61. Agency Marks 373/ S.7.

"Reports Relating to Parliamentary Elections 227. 1) Report on the Niger Federal Elections December 1959." NAK, RG7.

"Request for Religious Books 1961-1966." NAK, PRE 2, ACC/404, Agency Mark PRE/222.

"School for Arabic Studies-Policy, 1944-1955." NAK, MakPrOf/1. ACC/48. Agency Mark, 72 vol. II.

"Secret, 1964." NAK, PRE 2, ACC/19, Agency Mark ACC/19.

"The Sharia Today." NAK, Legal and Judicial, LJ5 ACC/582-4.

"Speech by Aminu Kano." NAK, ZarPrOf, Acc/4/16 C.11/1946. .

"Statement by the Government of the North region of Nigeria on the Re-organization of Legal and Judicial systems of the North Region 1958." NAK, Policy Papers. 334 PP1.

"Supreme Court and Appeal Cases, 1945-1956." NAK, MaidugariPrOf. Agency Mark 4598.

"Touring Reports from Administrative Officers - Sok. Prov 1957-1958." NAK, SokPrOf 3/30, ACC/2196, Agency Mark TOU/43.

"Victimization of members of the public in Kano Emirate, Ibrahim Wambai and 3 others 1963." KSHCB, Kano State Archives Ministry for Local Government, ACC/1310, Agency Mark PLT/41/c.1.

"Women Holding Posts in the Government Service, 1948-1954." NAK, ZarPrOf 7/1. ACC# 675. Agency Mark 781 Vol. I.

"World Moslem League, 1962-1965." NAK, PRE 2, ACC/458-459, Agency Mark PRE/280, Vol. I and II.

"Written Complaints, Kano Province, 1960-1963." NAK, PRE 2, ACC/28, Agency Mark AS/1/141.

INTERVIEWS

15 August, 1991, Dr. Ahmadu Jalingo. His house, Bayero University (old site). Dr. Jalingo was a member of the NEPU Youth Wing and was Personal Secretary to Malam Aminu Kano during the Second Republic.

15 August, 1991, Dr. M.T. Liman. His house, Bayero University (old site). Dr. Liman was a member of the NEPU Youth Wing and was a ranking official in the PRP during the Second Republic.

18 August, 1991, Dr. Ahmadu Jalingo. His house.

18 August, 1991, Dr. M.T. Liman. His house

12 November, 1992 Dr. M.T. Liman. His house.

17 January, 1993, Malam Saidu Bala. His house, Kano (old city).
Malam Bala was an early member of NEPU who came to prominence after writing a series of newspaper articles regarding the proper practice of prayer in Islam.

20 January, 1993, Malam Lawan Danbazau. His house, Kano (old city). Malam Danbazau was a founding member of NEPU and one of the creators of the Islamiyya schools. He was also NEPU's key adviser on Islamic Law.

21 January, 1993, Alhaji Inuwa Wada. His house, Kano (old city). Alhaji Wada was a ranking NPC member. He served both as Minister for Works and Minister for Defense during the First Republic.

21 January, 1993, Alhaji Sule Gaya. His house, Kano (old city). Alhaji Gaya was a ranking NPC member. He served as Minister for Local Government during the First Republic.

21 January, Alhaji Tanko Yakasai. His house, Kano (Hadeja Road). Alhaji Yakasai was one of the founding members of NEPU and a member of the Nigerian Communist Party. For several years he served as Editor-in-Chief of the *Daily Comet*.

22 January, 1993, Alhaji Mudi Sipikin. His office, Kano (old city). Alhaji Sipikin was a founding member of NEPU. He wrote a number of the party's political poems.

30 January, 1993, Alhaji Inuwa Wada. His house.

9 February, 1993, Dr. Isa Hashim. His office, Bayero University (new site). Dr. Hashim was a civil servant in Kano during the First Republic. He later advanced to the position of Permanent Secretary for Economics under the Gowan Administration.

16 February, 1993, Dr. Isa Hashim. His office, Kano, (Wudil Road).

4 April, 1993, Alhaji Baba dan Agundi (Sarkin Dawaki Mai Tuta). His house, Kano (old city). Alhaji Baba dan Agundi was a NEPU member and adviser on Islamic Law. A member of the Kano royal house, he was one of the few members of the Masu Sarauta to openly side with NEPU.

17 April, 1993, Alhaji Tanko Yakasai. His house.

19 April, 1993, Dr. Isa Hashim. His office, Kano, (Wudil Road).

24 April, 1993, Dr. Akilu Aliyu and Dr. Isa Hashim. Dr. Hashim's office, Kano, (Wudil Road). Dr. Aliyu was one of NEPU's foremost political poets.

1 May, 1993, Dr. Akilu Aliyu. Senior Conference Room, Federal Teachers College, Kano (old city).

3 May, 1993, Lawan Mai Turari. His house, Kano (Sokoto Road).
Malam Mai Turari was a trader in perfume (he now specializes in baked goods) who authored many political poems for NEPU.

17 May, 1993, Malam Lawan Danbazau. His House.

23 May, 1993, Malam Buhari. His house, Kano (old city). Malam Buhari is a prominent Tijaniyya leader in the Bariki ward of Kano city.

5 June, 1993, Hajia Jumai Wool. Senior Conference Room, Federal Teachers College, Kano (old city). Hajiya Wool was a member of the Kano Women's Wing of NEPU.

6 June, 1993, Alhaji Tanko Yakasai. His house.

7 June, 1993, Alhaji Baba Daradara. His house, Kano (old city). Alhaji Daradara
was a NPC member who served as Minister for Transport during the First Republic.

27 June, 1993, Shaykh Nasiru Kabara. His office, Kano (old city).
Shaykh Kabara was a prominent leader of the Qadiriyya and supporter of the NPC
during the First Republic. He is now the regional head of the tariqa.

15 May, 1994, Malam Lawan Danbazau. His house.

19 May, 1994, Alhaji Tanko Yakasai. His house.

INDEX